Praise for One Wheel—Many Spokes

"This is the next best thing to unicycling cross-country yourself.
Brace yourself for a wonderful adventure."

—KEITH CASH, CROSS-COUNTRY UNICYCLIST

"Guinness World Records has been recognizing outstanding achievement for
half a century, and this record is as impressive as any we've published."

—GUINNESS WORLD RECORDS: UPON AWARDING LARS CLAUSEN
HIS SECOND LONG DISTANCE UNICYCLING RECORD

"A tremendous ride, an engaging story, and an awesome family
await between the covers of this book. The Clausen's journey is
a great service for our Inupiat people."

—SARA OKLEASIK, DR. OF PHYSICAL THERAPY,
INUPIAT ESKIMO, NOME, ALASKA.

"This is the journey of a soul, of a man looking for himself, his true self beyond
the masks we wear to get through the day—and to live as that person on the
journey of a lifetime… He risks the road less traveled, that journey of graced
discovery amid the unknown and uncontrollable. He invites us to life."

—DAVID MILLER, EDITOR, THE LUTHERAN MAGAZINE

"A book of theology, politics, philosophy, sociology, history, literature,
anthropology, psychology, spirituality, and geography, all flowing from
the mind and heart of one man as he follows his dream. Amazing!"

—DANIEL ERLANDER, PASTOR, CARTOONIST, AUTHOR,
MANNA AND MERCY

One Wheel
—
Many Spokes

USA by Unicycle

By Lars Clausen

Illustrations by
Anne Jacobsen Clausen

Photos by
Anne Jacobsen Clausen
and Robert Martin

For you Michael,

One Wheel Wishes,

Lars Clausen

Soulscapers
P.O. Box. 152
Greenbank, WA 98253
www.onewheel.org

One Wheel — Many Spokes:
USA by Unicycle

Published by:

 Soulscapers
P.O. Box 152,
Greenbank, WA 98253
www.onewheel.org

Order Information:
Book Trade and IPG Accounts:
Independent Publishers Group; Order Department;
814 North Franklin Street; Chicago, IL 60610.
(800) 888-4741; Fax: (312) 337-5985; *www.ipgbook.com*

All Others:
Soulscapers; 800-281-5170; *www.onewheel.org*;

Cover by Karen Ross: karoons@yahoo.com
Interior layout by Michele DeFilippo: michele@1106design.com

Publisher's Cataloguing-in-Publication

Clausen, Lars, 1961–
    One wheel--many spokes : USA by unicycle / by Lars
Clausen.
    p. cm.
    LCCN 2003093814
    ISBN 0-9719415-9-9

    1. United States--Description and travel.
    2. Clausen, Lars, 1961---Travel--United States.
    3. Unicycles--United States.   I. Title.

E169.04.C53 2003   917.304'931
                        QBI03-200520

Dedicated to

Anne, and our children,

KariAnna and Kai

"Security is mostly a superstition.

It does not exist in nature…

Life is either a daring adventure

or nothing."

—Helen Keller

.

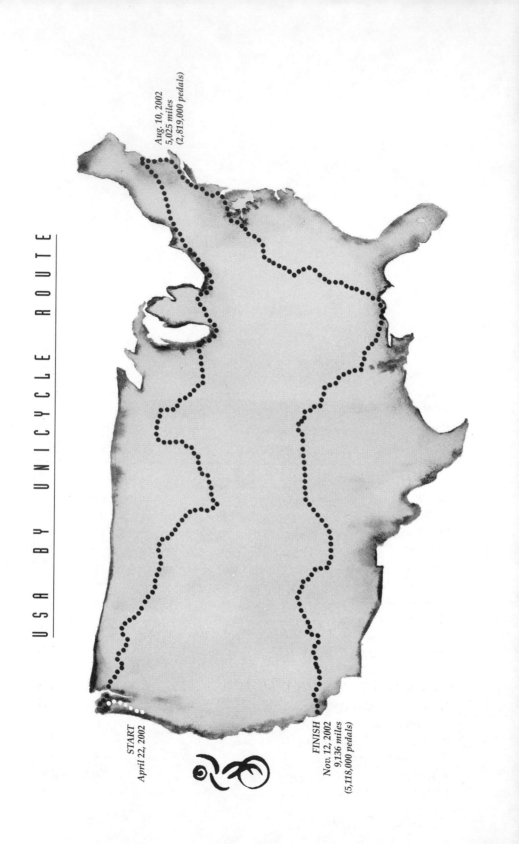

USA BY UNICYCLE ROUTE

Aug. 10, 2002
5,025 miles
(2,819,000 pedals)

START
April 22, 2002

FINISH
Nov. 12, 2002
9,136 miles
(5,118,000 pedals)

C O N T E N T S

F O R E W O R D

M ark Twain once defined a classic as a book that everyone would like to have read, but no one wants to read. Lars Clausen has done what many people would like to have done, but no one else has ever tried. He has uni-cycled through every state in the Union in one summer.

Anyone who has had an impulse to get off the interstate and onto the "roads less traveled" in our land, to ratchet down from seventy miles an hour to seventy miles a day, and to know our country from the shoulder of the road, will be captivated by *One Wheel – Many Spokes*.

5,118,000 turns of the unicycle wheel. 9,136 miles. All fifty of the United States. Supported by his wife and two children who accompanied him in an aged motor home, this is a determined and remarkable achievement.

Even more important than the pedaling is the vision which Clausen brings to his ride, making *One Wheel – Many Spokes* an important story of our country. He rode as a benefit for Inupiat Eskimos in Alaska, whom he had served as a pastor for four years. He explored Native American lands and people from coast to coast, discovering stories of destruction as well as resilience. He pedaled through Manhattan and to the World Trade Center ruins, starting his trip just months after the terrorist bombings, riding into a nation in the grip of deep fear.

It is hard to imagine a more vulnerable way to travel than by unicycle. In doing so, Clausen uncovers one of life's less obvious lessons: When we become vulnerable to our surroundings we open ourselves to hospitality and care. This is a story that confirms our wishes as human beings and as members of the global community. Hospitality is stronger than fear. Compassion is more effective than isolation.

Lars Clausen has done the work of a good citizen. He has looked deeply into the heart of our country and has accomplished an adventure that will inspire us for years to come. It was said of Albert Schweitzer, "He was a man of courage because he did what the rest of us would have done if we had had the courage." Bismark once said that the great challenge was to translate military courage into civilian courage. For readers of this book the challenge may be to translate unicycling courage into moral, political or personal courage.

—Bob Kerrey
President, New School University, Manhattan
Congressional Medal of Honor Recipient
Presidential Candidate, 1992
United States Senator, 1987–2001
Governor of Nebraska, 1981–1985

1
Flahs

When we remember we are all mad, the mysteries of life disappear and life stands explained.

MARK TWAIN

The Alabama afternoon pushes the limits of heat and humidity for unicycling. I drink three quarts of iced tea from the deli where I am resting. Outside, as I walk across the dusty gravel lot to the road, a police cruiser spots me and slows. Pulling over on the grass shoulder the car stops. Two officers peer from inside. The one riding shotgun motions me to his window.

"Are you riding that?" he asks.

"Yes," I answer, beginning my journey's third encounter with police. The driving officer takes over in the slow pattern that southern speech can so easily assume.

"You're riding *that* on *this* road?"

"Yes."

"On this road. You're riding *that?*"

"Well, yes, by the side of the road."

"By the side of this road?"

"On the white line."

"On the white line on *this* road?"

"Well, next to it. Alongside of it."

Shotgun finally breaks in and asks if I have my ID.

I hand him my card.

"You don't have ID?" he asks.

"Sorry," I answer, taking back my VISA card and handing him my Washington driver's license.

The driving officer starts an ID check on me.

"This your name?"

"Yes, Lars Clausen."

"What do you call that thing?"

"A unicycle."

He begins reporting my name over the radio, "Clowz'n. C, Charlie. L, Lima…"

"This is a dangerous road," Shotgun tells me over the backdrop of the alphabetic recitation.

"Logging trucks. Trucks from all over the country drive on this road. You shouldn't ride this road."

"I've been unicycling all the way across the country," I answer.

Are they going to ban me from this road? I am already racing dark. My wife Anne and the kids are camping near Eufaula, twenty-five miles ahead. Shotgun continues with his warning.

"Where are you going?"

"Florida."

"There's gonn'a be a lot of flahs."

"Flahs?"

"Yeah, you want to see the windshield of my truck? Lots of flahs as soon as you get south of Eufaula."

"Right. The flies. Another man just warned me about those."

"We're recording all your information," the driving officer tells me, "so if you get killed on this road we can tell people you were warned not to ride it."

A woman's voice comes back on radio while he's talking, "We've got everything except that first name. Can you repeat that please."

"Lohs," he repeats. "L, Lima…"

"Do you have a job?" he asks when he's done.

"I'm a pastor. A preacher."

"So is he," the driver points to Shotgun.

There are long pauses between all of these exchanges. My quick return to the road is gone, but after 6,300 miles this tour is paying off. I've learned patience.

"What denomination are you?" asks Shotgun, restarting the conversation.

"Lutheran. How about you?"

"AME. Church is just over that hill. See that corner up there?" He points a hundred yards ahead, "A man got killed there by a car."

"Maybe then you can escort me down this road?"

"We don't have those kinds of resources," the driving officer replies immediately. Death warnings free; protection unavailable. This seems like a bad time to ask about pedestrian and cyclist rights.

By the time we're done, the sun is noticeably lower in the sky. I get my ID back.

Shotgun Preacher gives me his benediction. "I prefer my preachers in the pulpit, not in the grave. You be careful."

Free. I jump on the unicycle, heading south on Alabama 165, racing darkness now, pedaling ever farther into this journey.

An hour farther on, I reach the forested hill leading down to Cottonton. A lone old gas station is the only building here. A dozen folks who passed me on the road are waiting to see me pedal in. I go inside for a twenty-ounce Pepsi and a Snickers bar. Then I walk back outside to stand and share their welcome kindness.

The attendant comes out of the store. "Were you laying down back there beside the road?"

"No."

"The police just called and said they had a report that you were hit and were down on the side of the road."

"Whatever," I reply. "I'm just trying to ride."

Shotgun must have been really worried about me dying. He has no way to know that spurring this whole venture is the mid-life recognition that I will not live forever, no matter what I do. Although the unicycle is an unusual vehicle, the journey is a common one. "We never really and genuinely become our entire and honest selves," said Mark Twain, "until we are dead—and not then until we have been dead years and years." He recommended that, "People ought to start dead and then they would be honest so much sooner."

What I'd like Shotgun to know is that this ride is reviving my life. Spoke by spoke, I am adding experiences to the wheel of my life.

2
Busting Loose

*There comes a time in every rightly constructed boy's life
when he has a raging desire to go somewhere
and dig for hidden treasure.*

MARK TWAIN

My day comes on April 22, 2002. I wake up in Tillamook, Oregon, step out of our newly purchased ancient motor home, and enter the dark, drizzling Pacific Coast dawn.

"Good luck," Dad calls to me. He has volunteered to be my support crew this first week and to drive the motor home.

I hope that over the winter I've put my forty-year-old body through enough unicycle training for the journey ahead. At six-foot one, with my red beard, some people call me a Viking; since growing my blonde hair long others have begun joking that I look like Jesus. I walk across the parking lot to get signatures verifying the start of this attempt for the Guinness long-distance-unicycling world record.

"You're doing what?" asks Trish, unsure if she's heard right after her all-night shift at the Shilo Inn.

"I'm unicycling across America," I repeat. "I hope to be at the Statue of Liberty on August 10."

Time, date, location, verification address: She provides the necessary information on the slip of paper I hand to her.

Oregon

At 6:22 a.m. I pedal past the Tillamook Cheese Factory and put into motion a dream that has required a full winter of preparation. I feel none of my customary new-beginnings apprehension this morning—just pure, total, utter amazement that I'm on the road and a full summer lies ahead.

It is eleven months since my family and I left Michigan and headed to Washington's Whidbey Island to explore the question, "How, now, shall we live?" I have watched too many friends settle for less than the life they dreamed. Mark Twain provided the necessary encouragement for our family to make a move:

> *Twenty years from now you will be more disappointed by the things you didn't do than by the ones you did do. So throw off the bowlines. Sail away from the safe harbor. Catch the trade winds in your sails. Explore. Dream. Discover.*

Back then in Michigan, at the middle of my life, three weeks before my fortieth birthday I busted loose from my moorings. My wife Anne and our children, seven-year-old KariAnna and four-year-old Kai, were willing accomplices. Other than a chance to explore our lives, we didn't know what was ahead. As we loaded our mini-van for the drive west, I asked Anne if I could put my unicycle in on top of the luggage.

"See if it fits," she offered.

It did. I had some vague intention that the unicycle could help me lose the twenty extra pounds I'd picked up in four years of campus ministry at Michigan State University: too many pizzas with students, too little exercise because of sore feet.

With the unicycle on board we headed for Washington state. Even on the interstate, blasting along at seventy miles an hour, refueling at nondescript gas stations, and eating fast food day after day, my sense of freedom was increasing with each accumulated mile. Other times of freedom also came to mind as we drove—bicycling solo across the United States, and tandem-bicycle touring through Europe for our honeymoon.

When we got to Washington and reached Whidbey Island, we began moving in to share our friends' home on Whidbey Island. Kai was ecstatic and KariAnna depressed. Kai, the most gregarious one of our family, gained an instant playmate, another boy his age. KariAnna, alone, cried to me, "There aren't any girls here."

I went over to the couch and pulled her into my lap, stroking her long blonde hair and tear-stained cheeks. Silently we sat together.

"Do you want to learn to unicycle?" I asked at last, trolling hope, seeing if she might bite.

"I guess so," came her quiet response.

And in the way that people spin dreams to make the present bearable, KariAnna and I cheered ourselves with possibilities.

"We could ride all over together," I offered. "We could ride to the store for ice cream. We could even unicycle across the country together," I expanded.

"Yes," KariAnna answered softly.

"When should we do it? In five years maybe?"

"How old will I be then?"

"Twelve."

"Okay."

A few minutes later we were down on the floor doing sit-ups and push-ups together, getting in shape for this vision that had brought joy to KariAnna.

KariAnna wasn't the only one struggling with this new change in our lives. A few days after the boxes were unpacked Anne turned to me, "Are you all right?" she asked. "Your eyes are glazed over and far away. What's the matter?"

Nothing was the matter—except that we were venturing into a new valley of uncertainty, a new unknown. This place can feel like the valley of the shadow of death, tempting us to turn from our dreams and return to familiar securities. I'd been there before. I poured another cup of coffee and waited for my eyes to return.

They refocused within a month. Out unicycling one day a vision opened to me as memories of bicycling across the country came flooding back: the sight of the white shoulder line, the asphalt road, the smell of the forest, the sound of the breeze and passing cars, the heat and the sweat that come with turning pedals. Why wait five years? I would ride across the country on a unicycle the next year. Doubtfully practical, undeniably powerful, the vision persisted despite the truth I had never pedaled more than a five-mile ride on a unicycle. In my mind's eye I saw the next summer stretch out before me, pedaling state by state from West Coast to East, living on the shoulder of the road.

Within a week Anne agreed that we would do this adventure as a family. "We started our marriage with a tandem-bicycle honeymoon. We can try this too."

*

Now, on this first morning I am pedaling north on the shoulder of Highway 101. Lagoons here are filled with birds. Every few miles the road swings close enough for me to hear waves breaking on the shore. Log trucks roar by and leave the scent of fresh Christmas trees. At an oyster packing plant in Bay City, shells are stacked like gravel piles. Two men out testing the morning shout greetings from their porch across the highway. A man and his son, waiting for the school bus and accompanied by their chocolate lab, wave and smile.

Ahead of me a man pulls a fish from the lagoon. The drizzle stops and the gray sky lightens. Farther on a bicycle is pedaling into Garibaldi. On my one wheel I actually gain on the cyclist. He turns off before I catch him. A fishing bucket is jostling around in his handlebar basket.

As planned, Dad is driving the motor home this morning as my support crew for this first week. Past Garibaldi he pulls off the road to check on me.

"Everything is going perfectly," I tell him.

Hans, my dad, is a Danish immigrant and retired engineer who grew up plowing fields with horses. His seventieth birthday comes this summer. He celebrated his fortieth by running his first marathon. I am thankful for his help with getting this ride started. He's the one who taught me to bicycle at the age of five. He's the one who taught me to unicycle when I was ten.

We plan to meet ten miles farther in the town of Manzanita. I am riding eleven or twelve miles an hour on these flat stretches of Highway 101. Just out of Nehalem the road turns a corner and suddenly a steep rise ends twenty-five miles of flat riding. I slow to a precarious wobble, shouting at myself, "Ride, ride, ride!"

I barely push over the top without falling.

Dad is waiting at the Edgewood Lounge parking lot when I catch up to him.

"The owner invited us in for a cup of coffee," he says on first seeing me. "His name is Phil. He's from Alaska and used to work in Nome."

It's dark inside, too early for the lounge to be open. Phil is the only one there.

"What can I pour you?" My dad is always ready for coffee. I get a cold Coke.

"Your dad says you used to live in Nome."

Phil turns out to be a clinical psychiatrist. His work took him to Nome and many other villages in Alaska before he moved to Oregon and bought the Edgewood.

"Yeah," I answer, "we were just visiting in Nome two weeks ago."

We had been in Nome to be part of the Seward Peninsula's Spring Conference, and to receive a blessing for the start of our adventure. Along with the unicycling, we are hoping to raise awareness of Lutheran Inupiat Eskimo ministry on Alaska's Seward Peninsula.

I ask Phil, "Do you remember the Lutheran church across the street from the hospital?

"Sure."

"I used to be the pastor there."

People's response to my profession ranges from admiration to disdain. Phil shows a glimmer of surprise but reveals no opinion.

"So how does this all work, your ride, I mean?"

"Well, the ride is "One Wheel – Many Spokes," I begin. "I pedal the wheel, but there are a lot of different spokes in this adventure."

I tell Phil about the $5,000,000 endowment, the five thousand miles on our route to the Statue of liberty, and how that translates to 3,300,000 turns of the wheel.

"That adds up to $1.49 per turn of the wheel." I say. "We're hopeful we can help get the endowment filled."

We are planning to speak in churches all across the country and tell the Seward Peninsula story—how there are fewer and fewer traditional societies left in our fast-paced modern world, and how this endowment will provide a stable resource to continue working out the intersections between ancient traditions and the pressures of the modern world.

"The Inupiat people will make all the decisions about how to use the money." I continue. "That's why Anne and I care so much about this project."

"Alaska's a special place. Why'd you leave?"

"I tired out after three years. You must know what it's like working where our modern ways clash with traditional culture."

"Yeah, I'd say so. I ended up working a lot with those problems. I tired out too. I hoped running this lounge would be a good change of pace."

"Is it?"

"It's mostly good. We have lots of tourists in the summer, but winter is long and gray and lonely. Too many people around here drink too much alcohol to get through winter. That's not fun to deal with. It's strange being the psychiatrist who sells alcohol now. But everyone feels better when the sun shines, and it doesn't get any better than today."

Phil is settling in here at the Edgewood, and I am turning to the open road—both of us are searching. I could easily spend the day here talking, exploring the oddity of this psychiatrist turned restaurateur. He might have as much fun with me, an engineer and a pastor heading cross-country by unicycle.

"There are lots of grades ahead," he says as he bids us farewell in the parking lot. "You'll find them longer but not as steep as that hill you climbed to get here."

"Thanks for the Coke."

"Pace yourself this summer."

I get back on the road and start up a two-mile-long grade. Phil's words are still in my head, "Pace yourself." When I trained on Whidbey Island I often saw bald eagles soaring over me. This always seemed a good sign. Now, halfway up this climb, three buzzards take off from a tree and start circling over me.

"Not yet," I yell up to them, "you're too early."

3
Shakedown

Custom is petrification; nothing but dynamite
can dislodge it for a century.

MARK TWAIN

The buzzards give up at the top of the grade. Highway 101 continues to climb over rocky capes and descend to follow sandy beaches. The coastal forest is dark and rich with hemlock and fir. Halfway to Seaside my right pedal crank starts clicking. The bolt holding it on is working loose. My dad is ten miles ahead in Seaside, getting lunch ready. He has the tools, so I pedal on, the click growing more pronounced.

The unicycle I'm riding is called "The Big One," a thirty-six-inch wheel the Coker Company has provided for this ride. The wheel is a foot larger than the Schwinn I've ridden for the past thirty years. Since this model was backordered for over two months, arriving five weeks before the ride, I am still getting used to its high perch and long stride.

Three of the past five training weeks were lost to a fractured elbow from a fall, the only broken bone I've ever sustained. A fellow unicyclist who is also a professional clown had told me of his success with using clipless cleats to lock his feet onto the pedals. After the broken arm, I decided I'm no clown and clipless pedals aren't for me. I was out of the sling only a week before my ride's start date.

Now, on this first day of touring, the arm feels fine, and we've managed to start on schedule. I still feel like a giant on this three-foot wheel, with the top of my head gliding almost eight feet above the ground. The euphoria of new beginnings makes up for every challenge. Clicking loudly, I make Seaside at noon. Forty-eight miles!

Dad has lunch waiting at the side of the road. After tuna sandwiches and fruit, we retighten the crank. We've got a spare Coker along and all the extra parts I anticipate needing. Another manufacturer, Semcycle, has provided me a twenty-eight-inch unicycle in case I need it for the Rockies: The smaller wheel diameter will make hill climbing easier.

When it's time to go, Dad watches my three blundering attempts to mount. The axle is eighteen inches above the ground. To mount, I jump a foot and a half into the air, get my feet positioned on the pedals and try to start moving forward before falling off in any of the four compass directions. Adding to the challenge are the short pedal cranks. Because a unicycle has no gears, the only way to get either higher speed or more torque is to change wheel sizes or crank lengths. I've switched the standard six-inch cranks to short four-and-a-half-inch cranks to get more speed, but they make getting started a real trick. At last I wobble into the right direction and begin riding the last miles of the day to Astoria. Anyone watching this process would wonder at my prospects.

The morning drizzle turns to bright sunshine, a rarity for the rain-laden Pacific Northwest coast. Traffic picks up in the afternoon. The highway flattens out and becomes four-lane. People are waving out their windows and honking their horns. A man stops ahead and gets out of his car to video my passing.

"New York," I shout back to him when he asks my destination. His face shows surprise.

The biggest challenge of this first day awaits just before Astoria. A half-mile bridge separates me from the city. The shoulder could be two feet wider for safety, especially with the strong side gusts that make me weave. I study the bridge and then, after four attempts I get mounted on the unicycle and head onto the bridge's tight shoulder. Thousands of miles of challenges lie ahead, but this is the one for right now. Traffic passes close, and on the other side of the guardrail the drop to the river is abrupt. I keep one eye glued to my rearview mirror, watching for semis and the windblast they carry with them— ready to jump off and walk if necessary. While I cross, I count eight trucks driving on the far side of the road. Amazingly, thankfully, none pass in my direction until I'm across the bridge.

I find Dad in town, parked outside a travel agency. The owner fills out my Guinness World Record attempt slip. The current distance record for unicycling is 3,876.1 miles, set in 1985, by Hans Peter Beck for his tour across Australia. The distance is farther than a straight-line crossing of the United States, but not by much. After I learned of this record the dreams of my young childhood came back, those from the days spent poring through Guinness Books. Although a record is not the central purpose of this ride, it's going to be fun to try for it.

After signing my slip the travel agent suggests we might get permission to park overnight at Hauke's Market, just up the street.

"Sure," agrees the manager when we find the grocery store. "And if you want to come inside, we've got a deli right here where you can make yourself at home."

We park with a view of the Columbia River. After setting up the motor home, we come back inside Hauke's, laptop computer and cell phone in hand. The phone is brand new to us, purchased for this trip. Anne and I are banking on it to keep us connected on our travels. There will be places where we're out of cell range, but here in Astoria I can call home to Anne.

"We're missing you," Anne tells me. "KariAnna made a calendar today to check off the days until we meet you at Neah Bay."

There are now just five days to Neah Bay, the most northwest corner of the continental United States. We are calling it the official start of this ride across the country. If there is confusion about where we're actually starting this ride—in Alaska, or Oregon, or Washington—it is because just once this past winter, Anne put her foot down.

"Forget riding through all fifty states," she said. "Just focus on getting across the country from Neah Bay to the Statue of Liberty."

Anne was right, of course, but I'd just shown her an exciting addendum to my vision. Looking at a map of the United States, I had suddenly seen a route back to the West Coast that could let us cycle all forty-eight of the continental states. From the Statue of Liberty we could head down the Appalachian Mountains to the Gulf of Mexico, and pick up the eastern and southern states. From there we could angle back up to the corner of Missouri and Oklahoma. At that point it would be a straight shot west to get the last states.

"No way," she repeated.

Our one compromise is that if everything goes perfectly on the way across, we can talk about maybe, perhaps, possibly, riding on past the Statue of Liberty. Just in case, we've mapped our route to pass through all the northern states on our trip east. To our original starting point of Neah Bay, Washington, I added this shakedown week so we could include Oregon and make it our second state. Alaska was our first state. Two weeks earlier, when we'd been there for the Spring Conference, I took my unicycle along and rode five miles around Nome; I even rode out on the Bering Sea, covered over by six feet of ice. Now if anyone asks I can answer, "Yes, I ride on water!"

We are using this first week of riding as a shakedown; everything is flexible. The only goal is to get used to living on the unicycle tour. This is also shakedown time for our old RV. We've already fixed a fuel line leak and diagnosed a failing bearing on the smog pump. From Neah Bay onwards, we have a set ride schedule with presentations at churches all across the country. We even have our date set for arriving at the Statue of Liberty— August 10—if everything works out.

When I lie down on this first night, the feelings come flooding in. We're on the road—this trip is really happening! Before us is a whole summer of family adventure. Tonight it feels as if it is too much even to have dreamed.

I have not always jumped so easily into new adventures. Rather, I grew up a good boy trying hard to stay in the center lane. I was an Eagle Scout, an honor student, an appointee to the U.S. Air Force Academy. If I started anything, I would stick with it until the end.

The first time that I ever quit anything meaningful was the Academy. I didn't mind them hazing me and yelling at me the whole first year, but when it came my turn to create hell for the newcomers, I was filled with questions. Why should we make life so miserable for new students? What's the point? Eventually I spiraled towards the existential question—*why do anything?* After I decided to leave and explore my questions, officers pressured me to stay. One captain appealed to honor and idealism.

"If you stay here," he said, "you have to be prepared to give your life for your country."

The other officers all focused on the comfortable life I could enjoy in the Air Force: job security, free travel, cheap commissary prices, and a great retirement in just twenty years. Those weren't the perks I was looking for.

In retrospect, learning to quit is one of my better achievements, though I received little support for developing the skill. Instead, my companions have often been predisposed towards eliminating unknowns rather than stepping into them. Quitting means change. Change brings uncertainty.

Parting with the Academy was the beginning of my slow drift towards the shoulder of the road. I expected quitting once would be enough, but it was only the beginning. There was the engineering Ph.D. I left for my six-thousand-mile bike ride across the United States.

Later there was the six months that Anne and I left seminary while we honeymooned by tandem from Stockholm, Sweden to Gibraltar. We told everyone that if we could survive six months together, bound by two wheels and the steel frame, we could make it through anything. We have survived, and thrived, and come to a most unexpected place. Tonight, after a final look out the window and across the Columbia River, I fall asleep at last.

4
On The Road

You can't reach old age by another man's road.

MARK TWAIN

Washington

C rossing the bridge from Astoria into Washington, I begin riding north into my third state. Only one bend north of the Columbia River stands the road sign that marks the westernmost point of the Lewis and Clark Expedition. So much has changed since they arrived here in 1805. Today I travel a wide highway. When they arrived here they were searching for a winter camp that would give them a chance of surviving winter in this wild, unexplored land.

In these first miles of Washington state, Highway 101 winds along bay after bay. I sail along on the unicycle through breathtaking landscapes. Whoever designed 101 liked banked curves, crowned roads, and sloping shoulders—all great for cars traveling at sixty miles per hour. Unfortunately, these features tip unicycles. Other unicyclists have warned me about road crowns and sidewinds. The curves are the trickiest here at the start of the ride, especially curves that climb and turn left at the same time. One of them throws me off balance; I lose momentum and then struggle to keep going. Already I'm thankful for the handlebars and brakes that I have built onto the unicycle, especially the handlebars. With them I have much better stability and control for riding on uneven surfaces, for climbing hills, and for riding against heavy winds.

At lunchtime on this second day I reach Southbend and hear shouting from across the street. The workers at Pacific Seafood are on break, hollering for me to come and visit. It's an oyster plant. The workers are of many nationalities. While we visit I learn about oysters and they ask about unicycles.

"Lots of oysters," says one man who has announced he is from Portugal. The conveyor out back creates a constant clatter as shells spill off its end into a gleaming white pyramid.

"No computer store here," they say, looking surprised when I ask.

"Try Raymond," they offer.

The laptop connection to our cell phone needs one more adapter, which has to be mailed to us. Already dwindling are my hopes of writing every day and e-mailing updates to our five hundred friends and supporters. Computers and unicycles share a kind of digital similarity. On a unicycle you are either balanced or you are not. With the computer you either have all the right connections or you don't. Riding the unicycle is starting out to be easier than reporting on it.

Even after visiting Radio Shack, I'm still stuck for what to do about the computer. I know the updates are probably as important as the unicycling if this trip is to be successful for the Seward Peninsula Lutheran Endowment. But, I reason, I am after all on a unicycle trip. I decide to get out and do some more riding.

I am soon sweating again on this bright afternoon. After a couple of miles I forget the computer frustration and settle into my place on the shoulder of the road, riding up and down through Weyerhaeuser's timberland. In each area signs report the dates of the last cutting, the last replanting and the next projected harvest. Huge stumps still have visible notches, chopped in a bygone day when lumberjacks stood on springboards to hand saw these giants.

Six miles from Aberdeen a short young man steps out on the road, pointing a huge contraption at me. It is intimidating, like being clocked in a speed trap, and as I pass he waves me down.

Holding his gargantuan camera, Kevin Hong introduces himself. "We've been getting calls at the paper all afternoon. One trucker told us he saw you in Seaside yesterday and then again up here today."

Kevin asks if he can drive ahead and get pictures as I ride past. We end up at the office of the *Aberdeen Daily Globe* for an interview, and then he offers me the opportunity to connect to e-mail.

It's almost dusk by the time I'm finished, but my mileage for the day is 83.5, my highest ever. We head over to the Wal-Mart parking lot to sleep for the night. After the long day today we plan a short ride for tomorrow. We will use the morning for errands; the spare tire on the RV isn't holding air, and we also need a new headlight.

We end up leaving Aberdeen just after noon. I have a slight soreness in my left heel. During the last hour of riding yesterday I felt it tightening up. I will take it easy, thankful that we're headed to Amanda Park today, only forty-four miles up the road. The weather is warm, and the sun is bright.

Three days into this journey I'm still thinking about the ride almost all the time, trying to get adjusted. Some things are becoming routine. I ride. I wave. People wave back. Cars honk.

Dad is also getting into a pattern. He leapfrogs ahead of me in the motor home and I catch him every hour and a half or so. Katie and Luther, our two Siberian huskies, are coming along on this trip, and Dad usually has them leashed outside in the sun when I catch up. At Humptulips he's gotten a copy of the *Daily Globe,* which he hands over. "One Wheel Across America: Pastor Rides for Eskimos," reads the front-page headline above the picture and article. No wonder so many people are honking and cheering today.

While I rest I call Janey McCauley from the Associated Press and tell her how the ride is going on this first week.

"What do you eat?" Janey asks.

"Everything," I answer. "I've got a mix of almonds and chocolate chips along on the unicycle. Usually when I stop at a store I get a quart of chocolate milk."

She quizzes me on my daily mileage, where I sleep, how tired I am, and how my rear end feels. "Can you call me again on Sunday?" she asks, when she's gathered the information.

"Sure, I'll call. We'll be at Neah Bay."

After another ten miles I ride into Olympic National Park. Immediately the trees tower higher above me. Everything I saw earlier this afternoon was managed timber, either second or third growth, much of it clearcut. In one section I had listened to the buzz of chainsaws, watching loggers clearing a hillside. A few miles into the park a sign announces the Quinault Natural Area. Here the trees are old growth, weathered giants, their tops seem to reach the sky. The road is but a tiny corridor through this forest where even motor homes are dwarfed. I feel like a miniature of myself. At the same time, just being in an old growth forest like this brings a sense of fulfillment. It lasts only a few miles, but it's a picture of what all these woods were like a hundred years ago.

Just before Amanda Park I see two kids playing in their yard. The sister is lying on the grass under the trampoline, the brother jumping on top.

"Yuck," hollers the girl.

The boy bounces back to his feet, at the same time pulling his trousers up over his rear end. They don't notice as I pedal by. I think of KariAnna and Kai—three more days until I see them.

The motor home is parked in front of the local store when I approach. My heel has been hurting when I ride uphill, and I'm thankful to finish the day. Kathy, who is working the register, has read the newspaper earlier and invites us to make ourselves at home. She fills out the Guinness Record form and has me sign a business card for her. She also lets me try their phone line, but once again I can't get the computer to work.

When I come back outside, a fit-looking man is looking at our motor home. "Just wanted a little inspiration," he says.

Dave turns out to be a teacher at the high school and a bicyclist. We talk traveling for awhile and then he invites me to the school in the morning.

"We have a computer support person who can probably get you straightened out."

"That would be great."

"He comes in around eight o'clock. The school's just a hundred yards up the road from here." It will be worth another late start to get e-mail out again.

We are in the Quinault Rain Forest tonight on the Quinault Indian Reservation. Jim, the owner of Camp Seven Pizza, is serving us French fries, talking to us about the ride, and keeping my dad's coffee cup full. I'm typing the day's events into the laptop. Another twenty minutes and the restaurant will close. Jim comes over and sits down with us.

"I've got a little motel up the road," he offers. "You can stay there complimentary tonight if you'd like." With strangers extending aid each day, I feel surrounded by a web of support and encouragement. My dad and I drive up to the motel and get a much-needed shower. I fall asleep content.

"I know what you do," a young boy says the next morning. Children are gathering around me before the start of classes here at Quinault Lake School.

"You show off and then people give you money," he finishes.

Waiting for the computer technician, I end up posing with the kindergarten and second grade classes and answering questions. One of the second graders blurts out of turn, "Can I come with you?"

I call on him when he raises his hand a bit later. He hesitates with his question, forming it carefully in his mind and then asks the exact same words again. A few minutes later he sneaks over to me with a piece of paper and pen, looking for a consolation autograph. Greg is his name, a boy with the traveling instinct. One day he'll undoubtedly head off to dig for hidden treasure of his own.

A minor miracle happens this morning—thanks to Dave I get our e-mail sent and our "onewheel.org" web page updated. I pedal away from school and Amanda Park this morning, wondering if every town ahead will offer similar hospitality. A dozen of the kids say they saw me riding on the road yesterday. Half a dozen of them know we parked the motor home at Jim's motel.

I ride past two more rainforests today, proof of how rare these bright skies are. The first forest is named Queets, and soon after I come to Kalaloch where Dad has lunch ready. Thirty-three miles on the odometer.

"Clay-Lock," the woman corrects, after I try to pronounce the name at the Kalaloch Resort. She is filling out my Guinness form.

"People told me all morning to keep my eye out for you. I'm glad you stopped. Whatever possessed you to try something like this?" she asks.

"I've been riding a unicycle since I was ten. I want to see if I can get this wheel across the country."

Farther north I pass by the turn-off into the Hoh Rainforest. Our road map shows the locations of the world's largest Western Hemlock, Yellow Cedar, Subalpine Fir, and Douglas Fir, all in this area. As I ride I see old growth stumps big enough on which to pitch a large tent. It is so wet here that new trees grow out of the old nurse stumps. Some of them are forty feet high. Our destination today is Forks, a logging center for the last hundred years. The logging museum is here, but we're too early in the season, so it's closed.

I finish riding just after five o'clock in the afternoon, tired, sunburned, and ready to be finished after sixty-four miles. My knees are fine, my legs are fine, my rear is fine. My thighs are a bit chafed from rubbing against the seat all day, but the worrisome part today is my left Achilles tendon. It's been growing tighter, stiffer, and more swollen these last two days. During the last fifteen miles today it hurt to push up the grades. I hope the pain is temporary.

Anne is home tonight when I call. I tell her about my heel.

"You should take it easy. Eighty-three miles was too much in one day," she tells me.

I reply defensively that this is what the week is for, to see what I can do. But I know she's right; we have a long way ahead of us. I can't afford an injury right at the beginning.

Anne says she received a shipment of art from Alaska today: Inupiat Eskimo carvings and fur dolls that can be sold for the endowment fund.

"People will love seeing these," Anne says as she describes them. "I can't wait to get to Neah Bay."

"Me too. And don't worry, I'll take it easy riding tomorrow. I'll have the whole weekend to rest." We talk a few more minutes together, anticipating being together again.

It is drizzling when I wake up, and it drizzles until the last hour of the ride to Neah Bay. The final fifteen miles of road wind up and down steeply. Highway 112 hugs the shoreline, and the shoulders are small or non-existent. Every mile feels long today. I'm soggy. My heel hurts. In Clallam Bay, after stopping at the store, it takes nine frustrating attempts to get balanced atop the unicycle.

Relieved to finally reach the Makah Tribal lands and Neah Bay, I see four high school girls standing by a beach as I ride past.

"Awesome," one of them yells, "that is so totally awesome."

I am beginning to dry out as I hear these words, at the same time seeing the first patch of blue sky. Yes, this does feel awesome to be riding into Neah Bay, the most northwest corner of the continental United States. Five days, three hundred five miles—I'm tired, but I've made my goal for this first week.

I pull in at Washburn's store. Early in the century it was famous for selling Makah baskets. This afternoon there's a table out front run by the high school class of 2002.

"My mom made the chili," says the student who is serving. I order their biggest bowl, full of spice and warmth.

The tribal center is three miles outside of town, and we drive over to see where we'll meet on Sunday. The facility was once an Air Force base GATOR station. High security radar monitored Cold War activities. Three hundred people were stationed here during those years. A dozen years ago, when the base was no longer needed, it was turned over to the tribe. Randy, the caretaker, shares this history while he shows us the old cafeteria we'll be able to use.

"Pretty much everything works. Stove. Refrigerator. Sinks. Around the corner is where you can park your motor home. It's going to get real quiet out here as soon as work time is over."

The generous hospitality makes us feel at home. Backed by mountains and facing onto a small valley, we can see coastal rocks a couple of miles in the distance.

"The weather is supposed to be sunny this weekend," Randy continues. "We get 144 inches of rain a year here. But when the sun shines, it's unbeatable." He leaves us with a key and well wishes, entrusting the tribal center to us for the weekend.

Except for computer problems, everything has gone well on this shakedown ride along the Pacific Coast. During this past week I could have been anyone, experiencing the hospitality of the road: a plumber, broker, logger, teacher—single, married, sane, or not—following the white line north. Tomorrow I will be a pastor again. The bishop from Alaska and other church officials are coming to help celebrate the start of this ride for Seward Peninsula Lutheran Ministry.

If Mark Twain were here to watch my ride, he might like the unicycle but he would mistrust my profession. In *The Adventures of Huckleberry Finn*, an orphan boy and a runaway slave show how our established communities so regularly get in the way of real care. Some of the worst of Twain's perpetrators of stifling propriety are preachers. Having been in the trade for almost ten years, I sympathize with his critique. Already the unicycle is carrying me past cultural expectations into a more direct experience of life's rich diversity.

Huckleberry Finn got outside the conventions of his time by rafting down the Mississippi. Fifteen years ago, I first escaped by bicycling across the United States. Once, at a roadside campfire in New Brunswick, Canada, I spent the night with Monique and Christian, two cyclists from Quebec. Except for a single photo album, they had sold everything they owned and set off on their ride to learn about life. Christian could speak little English, but his words carried power.

> *There is a voice inside each of us. It suggests a way of living that is right. When we sold everything, it made it easier to listen to this voice. It tells us about truth and about love. It's hard to listen. So often we want to make our own plans because we have read something or because of some advice or warning from other people. Now I am trying to learn to listen—not to warnings—but to the voice that teaches love.*

By the time I finished all the pedals of my trek across the country, the cumulative unfolding of land and people was so powerful that I committed myself to pattern my life in light of this experience. In the fall of 1988 I enrolled at Pacific Lutheran Theological Seminary in Berkeley to explore how organized religion might give shape and direction to my experiences. Maybe I should have stuck with Mark Twain. At seminary I found myself back in the midst of convention. What a contradiction this seemed considering that the Christian faith was founded by one who died resisting social pressure to conform. I even got pressured into marriage.

Having fallen in love on my bicycle ride across the country, and then having developed our relationship by letter and phone, Anne and I decided to move together to seminary and explore our prospects for marriage. She came from Minnesota; I moved up from Los Angeles. In my second year I got kicked out of seminary for our living together. After much arguing it was agreed I could re-enter provided Anne and I got married "very quickly."

"Good," I replied, "We're already engaged to be married on June 23, eight months from now."

"Not good enough," the committee answered, "if you want to stay you need to get married within two weeks."

Against my natural inclination to get back on the road, Anne and I chose one week later to walk to the Alameda County Courthouse to sign a marriage certificate so that I could stay in seminary and become a pastor. With the stroke of that pen I returned from banishment to being accepted as an insider, but I had also come to know more deeply than ever what it is to stand outside assumed conventions. As Twain quipped, "Civilization is a limitless multiplication of unnecessary necessities."

After a long run of anger I came to regard my new perspective from the outside as a gift. The experience changed me forever. I take fewer things for granted, and I try to view a situation from as many angles as I can. Being an outsider is not always an easy gift to bear—witness the outcast Huck, the runaway slave Jim, the crucified Jesus—almost any outsider will do.

Sometimes, after preaching a sermon, a person will come up and thank me; "You were telling my story this morning." Now, at the northwest corner of our continental United States, I am turning again to search out the pieces of my own story.

On this single wheel my eyes turn backwards and forwards. I face to the past, hoping to recapture the transforming power of my cross-country bicycle ride and the life commitments I made then. I face to the future, wondering if the story from this coming journey will have power to hold life and death with new vision, new purpose, and new commitments.

5
Corners

Experience teaches us only one thing at a time—
and hardly that, in my case.

Mark Twain

Before folks start arriving at Neah Bay, Dad and I have some time to explore the Makah Nation. The finest tribal museum in the country is right here, the beneficiary of a mudslide five hundred years ago that simultaneously destroyed and preserved the seaside village of Ozette. Severe storms exposed the village in 1970 and threatened to wash it to sea. An archeological recovery was quickly organized. Over sixty thousand items from the effort are now under the care of the museum. Whaling, sealing and fishing artifacts, basketry and other tools, canoes, and even a replica longhouse are all on display at the museum, testimony to the strength of the traditional lifestyle here.

The Makah are a whaling people, and in this they share common heritage with the Inupiat people of the Seward Peninsula. Muktuk is still a treat served for special occasions. It consists of the skin and attached blubber of the whale, cut into fine pieces and eaten after dipping in seal oil. The remembrance of it takes my spirit right back to Nome. Whale hunting is infrequent on the Seward Peninsula, usually just a single whale every year or two. When one does give itself to a village, people come from far and wide to help with the preparation and distribution of the whale.

Perhaps the closest non-native people get to food being a spiritual experience is Thanksgiving turkey. Magnify that a hundred times and one can begin to imagine the importance of subsistence food gathering. Food, more than just calories and taste, is about the spirit. In the traditional way of understanding things, animals offer themselves to the hunter. I remember how many times Anne and I walked along the beach in Nome, seeing hunters dressed and ready to set out in their loaded boats.

"Going hunting?" I asked

"Maybee..." they answered, for the goal is not conquest of prey but submitting to the harmony of land and sea and its provision. What a different outlook this is from the one I received growing up in a Los Angeles suburb where everything we needed came from grocery and department stores.

The right to hunt whale is written directly into the Makah's treaty with the United States government, but for over seventy years, while the gray whale was on the endangered species list, the Makah did no hunting. In 1993 the International Whaling Commission determined that gray whale numbers actually were greater than the population existing before commercial whaling almost killed off the species. So far, one whale has been killed since the Makah resumed hunting. In 1999, a migrating gray whale "offered itself" to the people.

"The harvest of the whale and the celebration of the Makah people revived a critical cultural tradition," stated Billy Frank Jr., the Chairman of the Northwest Indian Fisheries Commission. "It's important to understand that the tribes kept these rights when they signed the treaties. They never gave them up. They never will."

The whale hunt sparked a huge protest by well-meaning advocates of whale conservation. It is not easy, no matter how noble the intentions, for one group of people to allow another the freedom to be true to their traditions.

As for the Seward Peninsula Lutheran Endowment that we will celebrate tomorrow as we officially inaugurate this ride, people often ask what place Christianity or the Lutheran Church have in Inupiat Eskimo culture. I ask the same questions myself, and fall back on events from our time in Alaska, a time when the experiences were far deeper than any explanations I had.

One time I was invited along on a seal-hunt with my friend Frank and his grandson John. Ten miles from shore, they wove their small Lund boat from the open water into the spring ice-pack of the Bering Sea. The motor pushed us through the ice-crowded water at what seemed perilous speed while we searched for "oogruk," the enormous bearded seal so prevalent in the springtime.

"There!" cried Frank suddenly as he cut the motor.

John's shot reached its target. Frank gunned the boat, and John harpooned the oogruk before it could sink into the icy water.

We tied up at a nearby iceberg, large enough to haul the seal out. Frank stroked his big knife to razor sharpness, then began to cut into the blubber to butcher the seal. All the while he chanted,

"Quyanna, Jesus."

Quyanna ("Kwee-yah-nah") is the Inupiat word for thank you. "Jesus" is the word for a "savior" from the deserts of the Middle-East. What does Jesus mean on an iceberg?

The bang of the gun. The roar of the two-stroke outboard. The chant of Jesus combined with twelve thousand years of arctic quyanna.

"We wanted to show our pastor what the hunt is like," Frank told me.

He handed me a small slice of warm steaming intestine. Frank ate a large piece. I ate my small one.

"Quyanna Jesus."

※

"Quyanna Jesus," I say again today at Neah Bay, still wondering how faith, culture, and history all weave together. By early afternoon, our company begins arriving and the celebration begins.

Uncle Tom and my cousins from Canada are the first to show up.

"Wow," exclaims my uncle. "What a place you picked to start!"

He's right. We're looking out over the bay, which is dotted with rock islands. Rain forest surrounds us, but overhead the sky is cloudless blue. This is everything I had hoped for, only better.

Then I see Anne coming. KariAnna and Kai jump out of the car almost before it stops. Hugs and kisses go all around. Anne and I are fifteen years down the road from when we first fell in love. We both look a little older, but in this moment of grand adventure we feel like kids once again.

Karl and Deb and Kaj are following. We've lived the past year in their basement on Whidbey Island. Their Kaj is our godson. Our Kai is their godson. The line between friend and family is a blur with us.

Next, putt-putting up in their 1982 Volkswagen Westphalia are our travel partners for the summer, Robert and Amy with their five-year-old Nathaniel and three-year-old Caroline. Robert's a six-foot tall ex-high school football team captain. At thirty years old his hair has already given up on him, making it easy to wear his biking helmet. He is an image of the strong, intimidating biker, but his head is filled with stories lived and the knowledge of constant reading. Amy is dwarfed by Robert's size but has a giant's measure of competence and confidence. Almost always she offers a smile that is framed by her short black hair. She is the most spiritual person of our group and hopes to find time to read and meditate along with taking care of our band of travelers. Robert and Amy were high school sweethearts when they were growing up in Colstrip, Montana. In truth, though, we know very little about them. We met at a New Year's party a few months earlier. After talking together for just half an hour Robert shocked us by turning to Amy and telling her, "On Monday I'm going to work and tell my boss I need four months off to bicycle across the country." Robert and Amy both work as physical therapists at Whidbey General Hospital.

Amy's response had been equally surprising. She answered with an immediate single word, "Okay."

It was that quick and simple. Really. Robert's boss agreed and now here they are. I used to think that Anne and I were impulsive until we met Robert and Amy.

As soon as we say hello, they ask me about my Achille's tendon.

"It hurts," I admit.

"Take off your shoes. We can get a look right now," Amy offers.

"You just need to ride some more," Robert concludes after checking my heel. "See how it's high on your heel where it's sore? That's where your muscles and tendon join. It will get stronger the more you ride. Take Aleve for the inflammation. You'll be fine."

Plenty of journeys have been stopped dead in their tracks by a bad ankle, a failed knee, or some other injury. What a relief to hear that I will heal as I ride.

Friends and family keep arriving, including my mom and my brother. The parking lot turns into a big reunion that eventually shifts three miles over to the Tribal Center.

"This is like being at our wedding all over again, "Anne says to me later in the evening. "People are here from so many parts of our lives."

Drama occurs during the night with the rushed departure of Karl and Deb and Kaj. At 4:30 a.m. they get a phone call that Karl's mom is failing quickly. Hurriedly, they throw their things into the van and speed away from the Tribal Center, trying to make the four-hour drive to Seattle in time to be with Nora, Karl's mom. She has been struggling all year, and last week it became clear that her remaining days are few. Karl and Deb agonized over whether to come all the way out to Neah Bay. Finally Nora said to them, "I'm fine, you just go."

We keep them in our prayers, getting up again a few hours later when the sky turns bright blue, another cloudless day. After breakfast our group of two dozen drives the five-mile gravel road from the Tribal Center to Cape Flattery. We bail out of cars and motor homes then hike the last half-mile to the cape with unicycles and guitars in tow. The cape is recognized as the most northwesterly point of the lower forty-eight states. The trail has hundreds of cedar steps. After the first few we are engulfed by forest. Three platforms give views out over wave-sculptured cliffs and onto a sea that is tranquil blue and green this morning. People remark what a perfect place and a perfect day it is for starting the ride. We share a feeling of holy space without a word needing to be said.

Of course, we gather and say some words anyway. Chris Savage sings "You're a family of God on a Journey," a song he wrote for us back when we left Michigan.

Bishop Ron Martinson has brought a banner made by folks at Alaska Native Lutheran Congregation. A bald eagle has been circling above us as we mark the beginning of this journey. I am reminded of seal hunting with Frank.

"Quyanna Jesus." I silently repeat his ancient words of thanks.

We linger; then we track back up the cedar board trail to start pedaling. Robert has been itching to start this ride from the moment he got the four-month leave. Even the five miles back to the tribal center have his eyes lit up with cross-country anticipation. Anne has her new recumbent bicycle ready. She can recline on this bike, a bit like a lawn chair on wheels. Kai has his bike. KariAnna has her unicycle. My brother Karl borrows one of my unicycles. Those not riding line up for more pictures.

"Look!" someone yells and points.

As we turn another bald eagle swoops close and circles around us. One time. Twice. Then again, close enough to see individual feathers. Weather, words, and now eagle's wings are marking this beginning. We all mount up and ride onto the road.

KariAnna pumps right along on her unicycle. Uphill and down, she makes a full two miles, her longest ride ever. Kai does the same on his bike, even though the hills are steep for him. My mom has been following in the car, ready to load the kids and drive them back to the Tribal Center.

When day's end comes, I'm overwhelmed with gratitude. We have been surrounded by love and care and well wishes; for the moment we are full of confidence to ride into all the unknown challenges awaiting. Time now to turn the corner and begin heading east across America.

6
By The Strait of Juan de Fuca

The most permanent lessons in morals are those
which come, not of booky teaching, but of experience.

MARK TWAIN

Another Bald Eagle has flown in to circle our departure from the Makah Reservation. We are back at Washburn's store, ready to ride in weather that continues clear and glorious. Well-wishes and photographs delay our start. My heel still hurts, but in the excitement I barely notice. Chris Savage and Gene Tenold are riding along with us. I say 'us' now because Robert is pedaling at my side from here on. A big cheer rises as we leave the parking lot. People driving by add honks and waves; most folks at Neah Bay have heard about our plans by now. Highway 112 between Neah Bay and Clallam Bay winds along the Juan de Fuca Strait, coast on one side, rainforest on the other.

When we meet everyone for lunch at Clallam Bay, they tell us about yet another eagle which soared after us as we began. While we are carbo-loading on leftover lasagna, KariAnna pulls me off to the side and asks to play by the little creek. Barefoot, she squishes onto the muddy edge of the water. Within minutes she is jumping, dancing, and skating all over this delicious mud, together with Nathaniel and Caroline.

"Come see this, Anne." I want her to get a view before the inevitable fall comes. A few minutes later, the slide happens and KariAnna is mud-coated from head to toe. Our kids already look as happy with this adventure as Tom Sawyer and Huckleberry Finn were with theirs.

"I suppose," Anne now says, "it's time for you to start riding again? " She looks at me as she contemplates kid clean up.

"I suppose it is," I respond, grateful for the opportunity she's just given me. Robert and Chris join me on the road with their bicycles, then ride ahead. Gene has turned back earlier.

Burnt Mountain is ahead. I have switched to five-inch pedal cranks today; they give a lot more torque than the short four-and-a-half-inch cranks I used all last week. Slowly and steadily I make it up the eleven miles to the crest of the mountain. The final three miles are the most challenging. My Achilles tendon still hurts, and I stop for a rest, sitting on the guardrail to catch my breath and scarf down two candy bars. There is so little traffic that, except for the pavement, I feel like I'm on a hike in the woods. My unicycle is propped against a signpost.

With its three-foot wheel and handlebars this unicycle will probably gather looks for as long as I am fit to ride it. Its ancestor, though, is not a one- but a two-wheeler. Unicycles evolved from bicycles—penny-far-things—the ones with the huge front wheel and the tiny back wheel. Penny-farthings were invented in the 1870s and became popular despite the challenge of riding them. Mark Twain himself learned to ride one, recording his adventures under the title, "Taming the Bicycle." The invention of the unicycle was prompted by the tendency for the tiny back wheel to lift off the ground whenever the brake was applied to the big front wheel. Eventually someone solved the problem. They cut the back wheel off for good.

Unicycle wheels as large as fifty-six inches and smaller than one inch followed. Strange inventions with wheels stacked three and more high were devised. Unicycles over one hundred feet tall really exist. Even more unbelievably, they have been successfully ridden. Back in 1934 Walter Nillson was already doing long-distance unicycling. And Steve McPeak pedaled from Chicago to Los Angeles atop a thirty-two-foot high unicycle. Before I started this ride I had no idea of what strange company I was joining. I just wanted to get out on the road.

My rest finished, I climb back on my one-wheel machine and soon reach the top. An hour later, at mile forty-two, I catch the others at the Hungry Bear Café. The yellow electric billboard outside announces our arrival. Woody and Kim and their parents, owners of the Hungry Bear, make us feel at home. Kim even bakes a birthday cake for my brother Karl's thirty-ninth birthday today. Woody downloads some of our pictures and prints out a birthday poster for the evening celebration. I watch all this from a table, my leg propped on a chair and my ankle draped with a bag of ice. When dinnertime comes I order the one-pound Hungry Bear hamburger. I'm full afterwards, but it disappeared faster than I expected.

Before we go to sleep Robert helps me change my pedals back to four-and-a-half-inch cranks to get a little more speed tomorrow. It takes ten minutes to make the switch using the pedal wrench, socket wrench, and crank puller; for this effort we get one gear change. On Robert's Cannondale touring bicycle he flicks his shift lever and has twenty-one instant gear choices. No one claims that unicycling is the most efficient way to travel!

We leave the Hungry Bear in a dense fog that lifts after our first hour of riding. The shoulder is ten feet wide in many places, so Chris and I ride side by side after the visibility improves. This is his first bike tour and he'll have more than a hundred miles in by the time he finishes at Whidbey Island. He stops at every espresso shop along the road, often riding one-handed on Anne's bicycle as he balances his coffee. Also, recent freedom from his smoking habit has him in high spirits.

While we ride, Chris and I remember our times together and find ourselves lamenting the increase in fear and global violence after 9-11 and the Afghanistan War. Our perspective has been shaped by working together during the aftermath of a five-thousand-person riot at Michigan State University. In the face of the clamor for retribution, we pushed for our church, campus, and community to consider the value of reconciliation and forgiveness. Soon after the riot, Desmond Tutu published his book about South Africa's experience with apartheid. We used it as the basis for a conference, borrowing the title and the theme of his book, *No Future Without Forgiveness*. Tutu argues for forgiveness in the most practical of terms. "We are bound up in a delicate network of interdependence," he writes,

> *to forgive is indeed the best form of self-interest since anger, resentment, and revenge are corrosive of that summon bonum, that greatest good, communal harmony that enhances the humanity and personhood of all in the community.*

"Maybe we need another conference," Chris offers, reflecting on these months since the terrorist attack. Fear seems to be making violence easy and peace a distant dream. Talking with Chris about these things, we find it is easier to be benevolent from the shoulder of the road. Beauty is always in sight and some new kindness always lies just around the next corner.

Just after passing Crescent Lake, I get a flat. Not on my tire, but on my seat. Before I catch up to the motor home and get a new tube, I end up riding seven miles without my air cushion. With every pedal I thank unicyclist Tim Ferry for his idea. We met last summer in Iowa after seeing a *Cedar Rapids Gazette* article announcing his breaking of the one-hundred-meter unicycle time for the Guinness World Record.

Tim had counseled, "Just duct tape a twelve-inch inner-tube on top of your seat. You'll be riding on air…"

"We can do better than that," my mom offered when I told her how comfortable this seat was. "Let me sew you a seatcover to hold the tube."

What gifts.

In the afternoon we meet our first stretch of busy four-lane traffic. Here in Sequim the weather is completely different from the rainforests on the west side of the Olympics where I rode all last week. By the time the clouds reach Sequim they have already dumped most of their precipitation in the mountains, leaving Sequim dry in the rain shadow of the Olympics. Here in the rainy Pacific Northwest, people move to Sequim for the sunshine. With all the buzzing traffic, I tuck myself over to the far right of the shoulder; the congestion takes my attention away from the land.

Our start-of-the-ride entourage is continuing to peel off one by one to head for home. As they depart, the road offers up new folks who join us for moments or hours. Lynette and Caroline from the *Bremerton Sun* drive an hour to find us. On this spring day, with the temperature at a season-high seventy degrees, they are in no hurry to get back to their newsroom. We do an interview on the shoulder of the road, and then they start leapfrogging ahead, jumping out of their car to take picture after picture as Robert and I pedal the day's last miles.

We finish our day of riding twenty miles farther than we had planned. The extra distance will get us to Whidbey Island sooner tomorrow, and Robert and I are looking forward to one last night at home. The advertisement for a $4.95 steak dinner at the Seven Cedars Casino clinches today's destination. When we arrive I roll the unicycle into the Totem Lounge, and we order our steaks.

First the security guard comes and removes my unicycle. "Post 9-11 security," he announces. "Don't worry, we'll have it right by our station and we'll have cameras on it too."

Then the manager comes over, talks to us about our ride and then signals our waitress that he is picking up the tab for our meals.

"I'll be checking your website," he tells us, shaking his head at the sight of us and what we are hoping to do. "Have a wonderful summer."

With dinner finished we drive back to Port Angeles for our first official on-the-ride presentation. Holy Trinity Lutheran Church, it turns out, was established in 1894, the same year as Seward Peninsula Lutheran Ministry began.

"No one here thinks of this congregation as a mission anymore, do you?" I ask them when I find out their founding date.

They answer no.

"A lot of people continue to think that I was a missionary in Alaska just because we lived and worked with native people. But their ministry has been there as long as you've been here. And their culture has been there in the same place for twelve thousand years, six times longer than the time since Jesus lived."

I go on to recount the story of how Lutherans came to be on the Seward Peninsula. It begins in 1894 because of reindeer. An early missionary recommended that reindeer herding begin on the peninsula to increase the food supply. Sami (Laplander) herders from Norway agreed to come to the Seward Peninsula and instruct the Inupiat people, provided they could have a Lutheran pastor in Alaska as they were used to in Norway. Arrangements were made, and soon the Sami herders arrived by train in Wisconsin to meet Tollef Brevig, their new pastor and his family. Together, they continued across the country by train. After a forty-four day steamer trip they landed at last in Teller, Alaska. Today, thanks to these hardy souls, reindeer and Lutherans both exist on the Seward Peninsula.

Near the end of the presentation Robert asks me, "Are you going to talk about your hair?"

People look surprised by the question. I am, too, but I get a good feeling right away for this Robert that I barely know. It's looking like a summer full of surprises and good humor with him around.

"Okay then, I will," I answer my new riding partner with the bald top.

"I'm growing my hair for Locks of Love," I begin. "They collect hair and make wigs for children who suffer from cancer or alopecia. This is my first time with long hair, and I've been surprised to have a number of people tell me, 'You've got to cut your hair.'"

"A friend from Ohio wrote to warn me, 'People are asking why they should give money to a longhaired hippie on a unicycle.'"

I ask people here their opinion of my long hair. A man my age with hair longer than mine recommends, "Cut it. I used to work in the investment business. Looks matter. I had the best suits and the best haircut I could afford."

An older white-haired woman raises her hand. "Keep it," is all she says, and smiles.

I share how I finally decided to leave it long when I realized that I fit every other culturally acceptable stereotype: I'm white, straight, married, have kids and a college education. The one piece of me that doesn't fit routinely gets singled out for attention and comment. There are many who can't just cut their hair or change some single feature to fit in: women facing the glass ceilings of business or seeking to become priests in many churches, people who aren't heterosexual, people of color, some immigrants, some Inupiat friends. I'm riding with long hair as a small personal reminder to value our diversity and differences.

Robert grins as I finish. Folks give generously to the endowment fund. For many this is the first they've heard of Seward Peninsula Lutheran Ministry.

As we re-box our display I look over to Robert, "This is our summer: ride, set up, pack up, ride."

"Sounds good to me," Robert replies. "I just want to ride, and ride, and ride.

On Wednesday morning, we're out the door of the motor home at 6:15, headed for home. The ferry dock at Port Townsend has *Bremerton Sun* newspapers on sale, and I see myself pictured on the front page.

"You were on the *CNN* ticker tape yesterday!" Vern Olsen tells me as we walk onto the ferry. He has his accordion along and sings songs as we make the crossing to Whidbey Island.

The ferry crosses to Keystone Landing in half an hour, and then we're back on Whidbey, back to all the busyness we have lived with the past winter. It was a challenge even to fit in the riding practice I needed. I made some fifty-mile training rides and a lot of twenty-five milers, but with all the preparations I usually had to settle for a daily seven- or ten-mile stint. Today will be the same kind of busy. Anne is exhausted from all the last minute preparations that she's been accomplishing this past week. Life feels easier on the road.

Chris, Robert, and I ride off the ferry for our last fifteen miles together. I stay with them until we reach the crest of the first hill on North Bluff Road. They take off coasting. I keep pedaling every stroke, uphill and downhill, too.

On the way home we pass close to Darrel Berg's home, and I remember how much he encouraged Anne and me as we were preparing for this ride. We were on the Keystone Ferry with Darrel, returning from a get-together with the retired Methodist pastors of northwest Washington. It was one month before the start of the ride.

"I'm eighty-one years old, and I live with some big regrets," said this pastor who started preaching at the age of nineteen.

"Today you made me think back to when I ran for Congress in 1972. That year Nixon was promising to get us out of Vietnam and instead, we were getting more and more involved in the war. I was going to get elected and get my hands on the levers and put a stop to it.

"My friends all thought I was crazy, and that I would settle down and forget about the race. That's what reminded me about this, Lars, when you were telling about setting out to ride all these miles and raise all this money with just a dream to get it all started.

"Do you know that I had a map of the eastern third of Nebraska and on it I had marked out a bicycle tour campaign of my whole district? I figured out how to get to every town during the race.

"I ended up not doing it. I was so busy with speeches and meetings no one thought I had time to be bicycling. My advisors talked me out of it.

"To this day I still wish I'd made that campaign tour by bicycle. I wouldn't care if I'd lost by a landslide."

When I told Darrel about Mark Twain's words that inspired us through a winter of preparation, he replied, "I'm living proof of those words."

> *Twenty years from now you will be*
> *more disappointed by the things*
> *you didn't do than by the ones you*
> *did do. So throw off the bowlines.*
> *Sail away from the safe harbor.*
> *Catch the trade winds in your sails.*
> *Explore. Dream. Discover.*

When I catch up to the bicyclists at home, Chris is exclaiming, "No wonder you guys are in good shape. Those are the hardest hills we've had on the whole trip. I hit forty-five miles an hour coasting down that biggest hill."

Something has indeed worked right with the training. It's day ten of my riding since Tillamook, and I'm feeling great. I grab a fast shower, and Anne drives us up to school for KariAnna's presentation. She is sharing the book she authored and illustrated this year at school. It is titled "Jessica the Lost Hummingbird," and the dedication is to her Michigan friend Roan Ma. KariAnna has gone from deathly fear of standing in front of the class to uncontained excitement about sharing this story. The illustrations astound me. Art is her passion, and she's never far from a marker and a scrap of paper to draw on. I sit in her classroom, looking around at all the students that I've come to know from volunteering during the year. The familiarity of this classroom makes "One Wheel – Many Spokes" seem momentarily strange.

Home by three we scramble to pack. I get a twenty-minute nap. The riding is tiring, but what really wears is staying up late and trying to keep abreast of writing, record-keeping, and the logistics of getting on the road each morning.

All of us are re-energized when we show up at Trinity Lutheran Church for the evening. Karl Olsen has put together a potluck and concert for us. It is made doubly special by his insistence to hold the concert even though his mother Nora died last Sunday, not long after they raced back from visiting with us at Neah Bay.

Before the concert we line up for the first potluck of the journey. Robert fills his plate to proportions that only practice and a lot of bicycling could allow for. The evening before, after we presented at Port Angeles, I'd been thinking we'd settle into a routine. Tonight's "One Wheel – Many Spokes" Trinity concert is assurance that whatever lies ahead will be filled with unique experiences.

The concert is a royal send-off for our time on Whidbey Island. Karl and Deb treated us exceptionally well this past year as we shared their home. We're hoping to see them again once more this weekend. Nora's funeral is at 11 a.m. on Saturday and, if possible, we'll drive back to Seattle for the service and get back on the route and schedule right afterwards.

"I'll pick you up at five in the morning," I tell Robert as he and his family get ready to leave the concert. He looks tired but content. With Nathaniel sleeping in his arms he and Amy and Caroline head home to bed.

We get home quickly and put our kids to bed. Their bed is next to ours and soon they're breathing in deep sleep. Anne and I turn to each other. This is the last night here for the rest of the summer, perhaps for the rest of the year. The moonlit firs outside the window and the worn dusty books along the windowsill highlight our familiar here on the brink of this new unknown. How will the kids do; will the motor home, the equipment, the money, and my body hold out? Can we keep the schedule; how will the relationship of Anne and me be impacted? We could have used another year to nail down all the details. We'll have to hope that we can live with all the incompleteness and imperfections that remain. Making love on this last night home, moonlight shining in on us, the two of us bridge the gap together, between all that has brought us here and all that lies ahead of us.

We lie awake afterwards, holding one another. Among all the things she could choose to say, all the reservations she has a right to express, Anne tells me only, "I'm lucky I found you."

She is more generous than I deserve. We're lucky all right. Thankful for each other. In a few moments we join our children in needed sleep.

Morning comes too early. Our friend Kristie shows up just as Robert and I start pedaling.

"Ben is going to remember this ride," she explains, "and I want to tell him about your starting out."

Ben is Kai's kindergarten classmate. He is the one who decided their family coin jar would go to the Seward Peninsula Endowment when it got full. His sister Marissa had picked rhododendron petals for us the evening before for a May Day blessing.

My dad passes us in the motor home soon after we start. When I get to the ferry landing, the others have already crossed.

As I walk onto the ferry, the ticket taker calls out to me across the line of cars that separate us. "Good Luck."

"Thank you," I yell back, and for a moment here on the dock, all the emotions well up inside and my eyes go watery. Those two little words of well wishing somehow sum up all the blessings and encouragement that have been showered on this ride these first ten days. I am heading off the island, heading away from home, heading into this whole summer of riding. The beginning has been not one single event but an unfolding. Boarding the ferry is another step deeper into the journey.

A man commuting by bicycle walks his bike onto the ferry with me. We recognize each other from a get-together earlier in the year. At that party he told me about a bike tour he made from Canada to Mexico. Sitting together as we cross to Mukilteo, he tells me he wishes he were coming along.

"The best things I've ever done are the hardest ones to explain to anyone else. A lot of friends didn't understand why I did my bike tour. It's still the highlight of my life."

7
Parade

It is the epitome of life.
The first half of it consists of the capacity to enjoy without the chance;
the last half consists of the chance without the capacity.

Mark Twain

A unicycle parade is our destination as we leave Whidbey Island. Of the six hundred students at Sultan Elementary School, over one hundred of them unicycle. They have offered to host us as we ride east on Highway 2 across the Cascades. On the way to the little town of Sultan, we are stopped in Everett by a man taking our picture.

"That's a thirty-six-inch wheel isn't it? I've been looking at those Cokers on the Internet and wanting to get one."

Kevin is somewhere in his thirties. As a kid, his doctor, for some reason I don't understand, told him he couldn't ride a bike.

"My uncle got me a twenty-inch unicycle instead, and he taught me to ride."

An hour later a car stops on the shoulder ahead of me. It looks like Kevin again with another person. A unicycle is pulled out of the car and I assume Kevin is going to ride with me for a stretch. Instead the unicycle is for his uncle. Roy hops on as I approach, and we ride up the road together for a few hundred yards. On my big Coker, I'm two feet higher than he is. He's pedaling furiously on his twenty-inch wheel to keep up while I go as slowly as possible.

"I always wanted to do what you're doing," he tells me, delight shining in his eyes. "I've been unicycling for forty-five years."

"You've got fifteen years on me. Come along on the trip."

He stays with me a few hundred yards more. "Good luck. I'm glad I got to do these pedals with you." Slowing down he turns back to Kevin.

Around the next bend Robert gets a flat. I take a rest while he fixes it.

"You know," he says as he waits for the rubber cement to dry, "I was kind of worried about riding across the country with a pastor."

"Still worried?"

"No, I think this is going to be all right. You don't seem much like a pastor."

He finishes putting his tire back on and we start riding again. "I'm not much on holy language and all that."

"Then you'll like this one. I've been told Martin Luther, the leader of the Protestant Reformation, once said, 'Pastors are like manure. When they all get together they smell bad. To do any good they have to be spread thinly on the field.'"

After Monroe we have ten miles to Sultan and the unicycle parade at one o'clock. Whidbey weather is continuing. Gray and drippy, a mist hangs in the air, raining on us at intervals. Thankfully the weather begins to lighten as we get closer. Dee Clarke calls on the cell phone, and I unclip it from my riding vest.

Dee gives us instructions. "Wait at the ARCO station and the police will meet you there." After we arrive at the gas station and down a cup of hot chocolate, Colleen shows up in her police car.

"Don't ride over the bridge yet. The kids want to see you coming across. They'll be waiting on the other side."

"Shall we ride down the sidewalk?" I ask.

"No. Straight down the middle."

When Colleen turns on the flashers, Robert and I head onto Highway 2 riding straight down the centerline as we cross the South Fork of the Skykomish River. Cars stop, and the police hold up a long line of traffic on this busy highway. All four of Sultan's police cars are flashing for us by the time we get across the bridge. We turn onto Fourth Street and suddenly sixty-two unicyclists and Robert and I are all cheering together. They are a sight to behold; I am as loud as any of them. We wait for Channel Four news to set up and then together all of us unicycle the four blocks to school. I ride as slowly as I can, and they spin their pedals to keep up, their legs going like sewing machines. Two kids are riding along holding the bricks that have balloons tied to them. The kids are ecstatic to be out on parade; I am every bit as jazzed as they are.

The line of riders stretches out as we ride. At school we gather up for a picture at the school sign, then we all pedal into the auditorium for a school assembly. All the kids from school are clapping and cheering. A huge wall map has our route across the country laid out on it in blue tape. Gus, one of the students, comes forward to give me a present. Speaking clearly into the microphone, he says, "Here, take this all the way to New York," and hands me an official Sultan Elementary School Unicycling Club tee-shirt.

When the ceremony is over a student walks up to show me a picture of her mom and dad's wedding—in the church at Nome—with me standing behind them as their pastor. Raven was only one year old when we left Nome.

"My family is coming tonight," Raven tells me, our small world getting another notch tighter.

Before the evening celebration, Robert and I get back on the road and spend the afternoon pedaling east on Highway 2, putting in more miles before tomorrow's climb over Stevens Pass.

"That was the best," Robert says of the parade. We ride along on its energy all afternoon, making it to Baring easily. In the morning we will have fifteen miles to the pass, and three thousand feet of elevation to climb.

Anne telephones while we ride, "I'm picking up the kids at school. We'll be there soon."

"WCCO in Minneapolis called us today," she adds, "The Al Malmberg show wants to do a weekly radio update with you all the way across the country." With such early publicity as the ride is receiving, we are beginning to imagine a quick filling of the $5,000,000 endowment.

Dad meets us in Baring for his last official duty as support crew. He drives us back to school for the dessert potluck with students and parents. There we talk about the ride, answer questions and sell tee-shirts, which Robert and I sign. The students put on a unicycle show.

Murray Reid approaches me. "I'm just starting to get into long distance unicycling. I have a hundred questions I'd like to talk with you about. I've been looking at getting a Coker soon."

Raven is back with her sister and aunt Robin. "Destiny had to work tonight. She's sorry she can't be here."

We visit and bring back memories of time spent in Nome with Daisy Jack, Destiny and Robin's grandmother. Daisy was still alive when we lived there, an elder who told us stories about the old ways and how she used to live: hunting, fishing, dog-mushing, raising her family.

Daisy would have liked this ride. She used to tell of mushing her dogs, many years before, along the old railroad line to her camp at Salmon Lake.

"We had little carts that fit on the tracks. The dogs pulled us all the way to the lake. I was always the fastest one. Even faster than my husband," she would laugh.

Remembering Daisy Jack, I also remember the church's camp on Salmon Lake. On Sunday afternoons in the summer, we loaded up the church

Suburban and made the drive to the country. Daisy and Alice Stein never missed a chance to go and pick willow leaves or blueberries or just enjoy hot tea with friends.

It's a full evening of unicycles and remembrances. When the crowd in the gymnasium thins out at last, the coaches invite KariAnna to ride the four-foot high "giraffe." I watch them help her and see their gentle skill in action.

"Put your foot here, grab here, climb on up."

KariAnna is sitting four feet in the air, so high that a chain connects the pedals to the wheel axle. Her head is higher than ours. She's a focused and beaming child. Dee and Bob put out a hand on each side of KariAnna, and she uses them to balance on her way back and forth across the gym. Another night of practicing and she could be riding it by herself.

Kai watches an extreme unicycling video while we pack up. I glance at it between packing runs to the motor home—rock-hopping, mountain trails, and more. My journey seems comparatively simple: point east, pedal.

Tonight we make up beds for all of us to sleep in our summer home. The Westphalia top pops up, and it has two beds for Robert and Amy, and Nathaniel and Caroline. They've recently acquired the 1984 camper and put a new engine in it for this trip. Anne and I decided last fall that we needed more than a tent for the journey. I found our old Sportcoach one day when I was out unicycling. It's a 1978 model, twenty-five feet long, beige on the outside, with seventies-fashion orange upholstery and dark cabinets on the inside. We bought it for five thousand dollars.

"We just need to get over and back across the country," I had reasoned to Anne. "It only has 73,000 miles on it. Surely it has more than 10,000 left in it."

Now this evening our vehicles are our homes. Rain patters gently on the roof. We've folded the big bed out across the rear of our motor home. The kids soon climb out of their bunks and crawl in next to Anne and me. In a moment they are breathing heavy in a deep sleep. I spoon into Anne.

"This is it," she says softly, happily.

We're together now. The road is home for the rest of the summer.

On Thursday morning, halfway up the pass, the rain turns to snow. On the shoulder of the road, discarded pop bottles are frozen solid. I have the five-inch cranks back on for this climb. Still, my legs burn as the climb begins to seem endless. The grade is about two hundred feet per mile; the elevation markers come slowly. I blow steam with each breath but a tee-shirt is enough to keep me warm as I crank toward the crest. Riding this slowly doesn't allow any room for error. I concentrate to push the pedals hard enough, to keep leaning into the hill for the right balance, and to avoid the small rock or bump that would mean a fall. Robert is far ahead of me on his bike, and I am all alone. Stevens Pass is the biggest riding challenge of the trip so far. I decide to try and reach the summit without stopping.

For a moment the pass becomes something to conquer. I am reminded of the ferry worker who wished me "good luck" the day before. Was he wishing me luck that I might overcome the challenges ahead? I think better luck would be for me to become absorbed into the experience of the ride. I've had enough days of conquering things in my life. I'd rather end up immersed in the experience.

The climb to Stevens Pass, the border between eastern and western Washington, is amazing to behold. On this side, the rainfall and snowfall are massive. The firs are deep green and cover the mountains. By three thousand feet the trees are all frosted with snow from the night before. Old snow has been on the roadside since fifteen hundred feet. Higher up, the snow banks are still four feet high and fresh snow is falling on them. I huff steam and pass through this snowscape in slow motion.

My bladder's request for relief has become more urgent. Cresting the summit without stopping won't make or break my life. But as I ride up Stevens Pass I have in mind all the other passes ahead: the Rockies of Montana, the Appalachians of New York, and the Green Mountains of New England. I decide to try for a non-stop ride to the top. It will be a confidence-building story to bring to the challenges ahead. I make a deal with myself. As soon as I get to the pass sign, I'll stop and relieve this growing pressure. An old antacid commercial comes to mind with changed words.

"Crank, Crank, Squeeze, Squeeze, oh what a relief it is."

I reach the ski area the same time my legs are starting to fatigue. When I reach down for my drink bottle I'm going so slowly that I lose balance and fall off. After peeing by the snow bank, I face downhill in order to remount the unicycle and then turn back into the climb. Around the next corner I can see I'm just a minute from the Stevens Pass sign—4061 feet in elevation. I'll count it as a straight-through climb.

Amy and Nathaniel are standing at the roadside, cheering my last few feet. Snowflakes are falling. Anne snaps a picture. Spaghetti is soon ready for lunch in the motor home, and I've got a story from Stevens Pass to bring to every challenge ahead.

Robert is freezing as we start down the east side of the pass. "Go ahead," I offer, "fly down this mountain. It has to be warmer down below." I'm warm because I can't coast and have to pedal every turn of the wheel, uphill or down.

A moment later he's off, a tiny flying dot, far ahead of me after just a few seconds. Two miles farther on an old Nissan pickup with Kansas plates pulls onto the shoulder ahead of me. A single traveler has stepped out by the time I arrive. Usually I ride by with a wave and a greeting; this time I jump off the unicycle. The tall lean man is driving alone, but sticking up over the passenger seat I see the ears of a small perky dog.

"Are you the person I heard about on the radio? Are you riding that unicycle to New York?"

When I confirm this, he stands in pure and utter amazement. We talk for a few minutes. Mike is returning to Kansas after an unsuccessful attempt at crossing the border to visit Canada, something about a missing permit to bring his firearm along. Instead of dwelling on his problems, he asks, "Is there anything I can do for you?"

Mike has obviously been sleeping in his truck for some days in a row. Low on resources, he is big on generosity. He offers help two more times.

"I'm fine, " I tell him. "Thank you. Two support vehicles are ahead of me, and I'm having the time of my life."

"This makes my trip," he says. In my rear-view mirror I see Mike watching until I pedal around the bend. He passes me and then toots a farewell as he continues back to Kansas.

After Mike drives off I ride for a few miles, remembering how we tried unsuccessfully to get the ELCA to create a link so people can give on-line. If Mike has already heard about this ride, there must be a lot of other people who have too, maybe even people who would click on-line to help out the endowment.

Oh, well. Early on in our planning we decided not to expect anything but rather to be grateful for whatever help the national church had to offer. We want to be able to enjoy this ride like Huck Finn enjoyed the Mississippi. This ride may be as close as I ever get to Huck's raft ride—my loss if I waste it on protocols, arrangements, and frustration. After a few miles I settle my thoughts back to the shoulder of the road.

The east side of Stevens Pass is a long and steady drop back to a thousand feet in elevation. We are now on the rain shadow side of the mountain; Ponderosa pines replace fir, growing more and more common with each passing mile. The sun comes out acting as though it belongs in this drier environment.

Thirty-four miles from the pass to Leavenworth—halfway there I am sleepy and tired. Too little sleep the last few nights makes the last miles stretch longer. At The Alps, a small gift and candy shop, I stop for a snack and come out with half a pound of chocolate-covered cashews. I eat them all within the next mile, a reminder of the challenges of this kind of travel: getting food, getting water, getting rest. And then there's the changing temperature, the wind, the climb and descent, adjusting my balance for every bump in the road, and watching out for traffic. Turning, turning, turning these pedals—never once coasting. I am surprised I have not been more tired. Instead, the physical exertion is making me more present and aware of each place that I pedal through.

Now these miles of Highway 2 follow the Wenatchee River as it roils through gorges. At places the shoulder of the winding road is a precipice, twenty feet above rushing emerald rapids.

Almost six hundred miles into this trip I realize that each stretch of road has held something beautiful to see. What a beginning. With the entrance into eastern Washington I feel we are finally entering into the heart of the ride. I roll into Leavenworth at 5 p.m. The ten-hour day, the pass, the tiredness combine to make me eager to stop.

A ten-year-old neighbor girl has been waiting for our arrival at our hosts' home. She learned to unicycle two years ago, and soon she and KariAnna are pedaling around together.

Dad has packed to head home to Los Angeles by the time I arrive. The motor home is crowded now compared to the time that he and I were all alone on the first week of riding. I give him a hug and my thanks for getting us started on this journey. Time now for him to get home and water the garden and check the mail.

"Come and see us later on the trip," we invite him.

"I might just do that," he says. "We'll see how the summer goes." He's had an easy time settling into the freedom and possibilities of retirement.

In the evening we head to the high school for the celebration of Cinco de Mayo. Much of the community is Hispanic, so it's a big community event. The food is free, and it's good. Tomorrow is Saturday. Anne and I will be waking early to drive back to Seattle for Nora Olsen's funeral.

✳

Funerals honor the one who has died, and they often make us think of our own lives and the passing of time. On the Sunday before I started this journey from Tillamook, Oregon, a bunch of us had lunch together in Forest Grove. Tyler Bechtel, who unicycled from Oregon to Florida in 1997, was there. We were talking about the Guinness World Record and Tyler's attempt to break it. While we were talking someone asked how old I am.

"Forty," I answered.

"Well, if you don't get the distance record," Tyler joked, "you'll surely get the record for the oldest person to ever unicycle across the country."

We all laughed at the time, but Tyler's comment kept coming back to me for the next couple of days. It is true that Anne and I started this sabbatical here at middle age to explore how we can best try to live out our second half, but I hadn't put this together with being an aged unicyclist. However, others are quick to make the connection. The AP article that Janey McCaulley wrote last Monday even started out: "Lars Clausen estimates he will celebrate his 41st birthday this summer around Lidgerwood, N.D., on day 45 of his cross-country unicycle trek."

Chris Savage wrote us after he got back with the news of a *USA Today* article: "Well, it's under the heading 'Offbeat' and it focuses on your age more than anything, but it is *USA Today!*"

When I bicycled across the United States at the age of twenty-five, no one asked my age. Now it's news.

So it is, as a newly old man, that Anne and I drive back to Seattle for Nora Olsen's funeral service, driving in two hours all the pedaling of the last two days. On the way over Stevens Pass we see the sign: "Warning, six percent grade next seven miles." That explains the tightness in my legs this morning.

Nora's service is just beginning as we step into St. John's Church. Her five children, their spouses, and most of her grandchildren are up front on the left side. The Olsens are the most musical family I know. As one who feels lucky to hit an occasional harmony part, I am always in awe of their easy way with music. Having led many funeral services, I watch them do with words and song what we all hope to do in times like these: honor life and make connections strong enough to hold together the past, the present and forever. The closing song is in Danish, one that I sang on many a Sunday evening as I was growing up. There at Nora's service I slip back into childhood with the words:

> *Altid frejdig, nar du gar*
> *Veje, Gud tor kende*
> *Selv om du til malet nar*
> *Forst ved verdens ende!*

In English the verses go…

> *Unafraid where e'er you go*
> *Choosing God to guide you*
> *Let your course run high or low*
> *He will strength provide you.*
>
> *In the darkness undismayed*
> *Like the stars made steady*

When sincerely you have prayed
Heart and soul are ready.

Give your life for what you love
Until death be loyal
God will bless you from above
Living will be royal.

Good words to have grown up with, to live with now, and to die with someday.

"Gud bevaerre dig. God bless you," says the pastor in Danish for the closing blessing of Nora's funeral service.

Driving back I once more remember Tyler's words about my age. So, "how old am I?" I reflect at the end of this long day. On my first ride across the country I didn't give a thought to old age and death. This time across I know that a day like Nora's is coming for all of us. This time across I see death as well as life. Death is the given. Living is the question. "In what manner shall I live? What is my purpose here?"

"How old am I?" Old enough to know that days are gifts, and every one an invitation to be lived fully; old enough to recognize this summer for what it is—a great time for unicycling and to be alive.

8
Mother Earth

*...the citizen who thinks he sees that the commonwealth's
political clothes are worn out, and yet holds his peace and does not
agitate for a new suit, is disloyal; he is a traitor.*

MARK TWAIN

Without any guarantee that we can keep a schedule, we plotted every day of this trip to the Statue of Liberty before we turned a single pedal.

"That's foolhardy," we were told by an experienced unicyclist. "I'll be amazed if you make it. Long-distance unicycling is much more difficult than touring by bicycle."

Scheduling allowed us to arrange presentations in advance; it also put huge constraints on our ride. Sundays are off-days, sabbath days, our ace in the hole, reserves for catching up if our schedule wears us down, if weather holds us up, or if other circumstances arise.

This Sunday morning we are on the road at a quarter to five to catch up our miles after Nora's funeral. Robert is driving the Honda back to Leavenworth, I'm working a new tube into my seat cover, and Anne is leaning against a pillow in the back seat, sleeping before she drives the car back.

"See you back in Chelan," Anne says when she unloads us.

Towns are spaced so that Robert and I don't need vehicle support today. We are in Wenatchee after eighteen miles. Entiat is another twenty miles up the road and then a final fifteen to Chelan. Today, being out on the road feels like old times, like when I bicycled across the country.

The Food Pavilion Supermarket in Wenatchee is our breakfast place. Robert makes the first score, huge cherry turnovers from the bakery section. I head for bananas, but at seventy-seven cents a pound I put them back when I find avocados are only sixty-six cents. We each take two. In the deli section are salt and pepper packets, spoons and a knife. With a quart of chocolate milk, I'm set. We sit down outside on a curb in the parking lot;

the plastic bag is our tablecloth. The sun is warm. Sunday brunch is spread and we savor each bite. I would not trade it for a hotel smorgasbord.

"Go ahead, Robert," I joke to him after we get back on the road. "We'll run out of things to talk about if we spend all our time together."

Robert zooms towards Chelan, arriving three hours before I do. Next to trains, bicycles are supposed to be the most energy efficient way to travel. Unicycles are not.

From Highway 2, I pedal north along alternate 97, which follows the Columbia River. Pine trees give way to sage and desert. A few miles farther I pass the Rocky Reach Dam where the Columbia River becomes Entiat Lake for the next twenty-five miles. This picturesque day makes it hard to believe the Columbia River is the center of a painful conflict between electrical power, salmon, agriculture, and recreation interests. Agreements to remove some smaller dams have already been reached, although in these parts dam removal proposals have become focal points for huge controversies about the fate of the Columbia, the Snake, and other tributary rivers.

Riding with a tailwind I breeze into Entiat and do another sidewalk lunch outside the Entiat Food Mart. A woman comes out, "I hear you're riding all the way across the country."

When I've answered her questions, she pulls money out of her pocket and gives me six dollars, "Here's the change I just got back. Use it for your ride. Good luck."

Sleepy after lunch, I ride a half hour and then lie down to nap in a roadside apple orchard. This is the apple capital of the world, folks here claim. Wenatchee just this weekend is celebrating the annual Apple Blossom Festival, but the apple industry has come on hard times. Whether apples have become less popular or the supply has increased in other parts of the world, I do not know, but prices are so low that many farmers are pulling out their orchards. Some are changing to grapes. Others are just selling their land. Many farmworker families have moved away for lack of work; there are two hundred fewer students in the Chelan School District this year.

Knapp's Hill is the one last climb ahead. I'm wondering about making it with the four-and-a-half-inch cranks, but it turns out to be easy. Each day I'm getting in better shape. Once over the top I expect an easy descent to Lake Chelan. Surprise. Fifty yards after the crest, a tailwind whips up, then turns around 180 degrees and slaps me in the face. I almost fall. The turbulent winds are typical of springtime; they grow severe on their journey down the fifty-mile glacial valley of the lake. Over 1400 feet deep, Lake Chelan is the third deepest lake in the country following Lake Tahoe and Crater Lake. Today it's the wind above the surface that impresses me. Dust gusts across the road like snow drifting in winter. Apple orchards are in full bloom, and as I pass them, their petals blow like snowflakes. Side winds, head winds, tailwinds, all whip me on this steep descent. I yank on my handlebars and try to use the brake to keep upright, just barely succeeding.

Down around the next corner the wind becomes less severe, and soon I ride across the Chelan River bridge and enter town. John from the local bike shop has come out to ride the last few miles with me. Robert is putt-putting his way toward us in the Volkswagen, and we stop in front of B.C. McDonalds. The owner comes out, "Let me buy you a beer," he offers. Robert and I order milkshakes, too, while we sit and talk.

We had planned to visit Holden Village on our trip past Lake Chelan, but it is filled to capacity hosting hundreds of high school students this weekend. In the summer, this retreat center hosts up to 450 guests at a time. In the winter a volunteer staff of sixty keeps the village functioning through the heavy snows of the North Cascades. Holden is special to Anne and me because it is where we met, back when we were volunteering in 1983. We've been there many times since with college students from Michigan State. The only access is a two-hour ferry ride on The Lady of the Lake up Lake Chelan and then a twelve-mile bus ride up the old mining road to the village.

We'll save our visit to Holden until after the ride. Instead we get an extra day of rest by staying with Dane and Jeannie in their cabin-like home which overlooks Lake Chelan and the town below. When their friends come for dinner our talk turns to apples.

"Some people lost a lot of money last night," Fletcher tells us, describing the crop damage.

As a kid I saw propeller turbines out in the orchards of the southern California orange fields. Here in Chelan there are turbines, too. Last night they had been working at full speed, buzzing like helicopters. When the temperatures get near freezing, these turbines keep the air moving as a last-ditch attempt to prevent freezing. The buzzing sound is desperate this time, futile in the face of the cold, killing frost. To farmers already suffering, this freeze may be more than some of them can survive. As we ride out of town the next morning the snow-white apple blossoms are already wilting and turning brown.

This morning we finally get the start that I've been hoping for. Up at 4:30, Robert and I pack our gear, eat some cereal and start on the road at 5 a.m. Everyone else is sound asleep. The dawn barely holds light. Visual details are indistinct; I hit a dip in the road and immediately fall off the unicycle. When I get back on, we head down Dane and Jeannie's hill. Their view is spectacular because their road climbs so high and steep. I fumble my way down it, yanking on the handlebars for balance.

"An ugly piece of riding," Robert says when we reach level again, "but you look all warmed up now. My hands are freezing."

By eight o'clock we have ridden twenty-five miles up Highway 97, almost halfway to our goal of Omak. At mile forty a headwind begins to build, but with the early start we don't care.

The cell phone goes off a little after ten in the morning. The caller is Mike Rogers from a radio station in Texas. "Are you really riding your unicycle while we're talking?"

He puts me on the air, and suddenly I'm telling people in Texas about unicycling through sagebrush, riding along the Okanogan River, and pedaling for Inupiat Eskimo people in Alaska. As a friend of mine likes to quote from the movie, *Dances with Wolves*, "The strangeness of life cannot be measured."

"I can hear the wind out there," Mike comments.

Trucks roll by, adding their noise to our conversation.

"What do you anticipate will be the biggest challenge?"

I answer too quickly that everything will probably go fine. When we finish our conversation I ask myself that question over again. What will be the biggest challenges? Maybe our schedule. Maybe getting through Manhattan. Or maybe heat and humidity. Or perhaps it will be our little band of eight. We are four adults, a three-year-old, two five-year-olds and an eight-year-old. Keeping this group together and happy for the adventure is the most important part of the whole trip. So far the teamwork is fantastic, and we are all having the time of our lives.

Anne and Amy pass us in the motor homes just before Okanogan, and we decide to ride the last eight miles to Omak for lunch. Amy has ravioli and ramen noodles waiting for us. If there's a secret to long-distance cycling, it seems to be getting up early. Three hours of good riding in the morning and the rest of the day seems downhill, even with a headwind.

"Should we ride some more this afternoon?" I ask Robert after lunch.

We have no presentation to make in Omak tonight. Tomorrow we are scheduled to pedal to Coulee Dam and then drive twenty miles to Wilbur Lutheran Church for an evening presentation.

"If we ride more now, we can pedal all the way to Wilbur tomorrow."

"Sure, let's go."

With sixty miles already finished, we ride east on Highway 155, into the 1.4 million acres of the Colville Indian Reservation. Our route intentionally includes as many reservations as possible because of our connection with the Seward Peninsula of Alaska.

Highway 155 follows Omak Creek for the first eighteen miles, so we expect a gradual climb. Instead the road starts up steeply as soon as we leave town. For the next twenty-two miles the road laces its way from hill to hill and ridge to ridge. Each ascent has a level stretch after the climb. As we gain elevation, we ride from the dry sagebrush and barren hills of Omak up through the first scattered pines and then a thickening forest as we gain elevation. No logging is visible from the road, and most of the houses are neat and well cared for. We ride in sun, but ahead the clouds look like rain. They blow away for a while. When we finally do come under them, they are dropping snow. The wind whips trash across the road as the snow starts. After the front passes the wind stops, and the temperature drops. We ride in the silence of straight falling snow.

"This is some kind of a great birthday ride," Robert says.

Neither of us has ever been on Highway 155 before, so every corner is a surprise. Twice we guess we're at the summit of 3258-foot Disautel Pass; finally, we hit a four-mile climb that gets us to the actual top. Anne has agreed to drive up and bring us back to the campsite at Omak. She passes us fifteen minutes before we make the summit. The drive back seems long. Whenever we drive, the road feels longer than what we've cycled. 82.33 miles today. Not our longest ride ever, but almost. Don't worry about numbers, I tell myself. Be thankful for the ride. Be thankful for another day.

Amy and Anne have found a campsite next to the Omak Rodeo and Stampede grounds. Our two old rigs are sandwiched in between huge luxury motor homes of the type that often pass by us. As we drive up, the younger kids are bicycling, and KariAnna is riding her unicycle.

"Let's go find a restaurant for Robert's birthday," Amy suggests.

We drive into town and celebrate with a birthday dinner for Robert at the Bread-line Café. Old bicycles hang from the ceilings, antiques cover the walls, and a surfboard, with WASHROOM in large letters, hangs above the restrooms.

"Just what I imagined for my thirty-first birthday," Robert jokes when we've gotten our seats.

We gather around the table like a single large family, starting dinner with old-fashioned milkshakes.

"To the ride," we toast with the big tin cups. "Happy birthday Robert."

All the bread on the table disappears quickly. I'm trying hard to keep calories coming in as fast as I burn them. My plate of smoked salmon pesto fettucine is large; I also get Kai's salad with all the dressing. Robert has ordered two servings of onion rings, but everyone is so full that I eat most of them myself. Amy has advice when I ask her about my worries of losing too much weight over the long summer ahead.

"Lots of complex carbohydrates," she suggests. "After that, eat anything and everything you want. You did well tonight."

Robert and I are up at five the next morning, both of us tired from yesterday's ride and wishing for more rest. Sleeping late is not one of Robert's birthday gifts, but the others sleep as we get ready. We drive the motor homes back to Disautel Pass, park, and start riding again.

It's cold at this elevation, and Robert freezes on the long downhill. I warm up quickly enough with my pedaling, but I feel out of balance for the first half hour of riding.

Nespelem is one of the few towns on the Colville Reservation. We pass a cemetery on the right, remarkable for the plastic flowers and adornments that cover every grave. One of them has a large "DAD" sign on top of it. A child's grave a couple of plots away is carefully decorated with toy trucks and cars, and what must have been a favorite stuffed puppy.

I catch up with Robert in town. He is warming himself on a bench in the sunshine talking with two Indian men on their way to work. Inside the gas-mart, Quick introduces himself and starts asking questions. Arches comes over to get something off the nearby shelf.

"Everyone here has a nickname," Quick tells me. "That's Old School on the phone there."

Old School finishes his conversation, and when Quick tells him we're riding across the country, Old School counters that we should get a plane in Spokane. Robert is alone when I get outside.

"This is nice," he says quietly, "really nice. No one was ever this friendly on the reservations I lived near in Montana."

"Really?" I ask.

"It was probably just me and my prejudices when I was growing up, but I don't ever remember people talking like this to me."

A few miles farther on is another cemetery, the one in which Chief Joseph is buried. He died here in 1905; he was the leader of his people when they were free and through their long struggle that ended up here on the Colville Reservation. On his visit to Washington D.C., after the many years of strife, Chief Joseph spoke:

> *Good words do not last long unless they amount to something. Words do not pay for my dead people. They do not pay for my country, now overrun by white men. They do not protect my father's grave. They do not pay for all my horses and cattle. Good words will not give me back my children. Good words will not make good the promise of your War Chief General Miles. Good words will not give my people good health and stop them from dying. Good words will not get my people a home*

*where they can live in peace and take care of themselves. I am tired of
talk that comes to nothing. It makes my heart sick when I remember all
the good words and all the broken promises.*

Twenty cars are parked outside the cemetery, and at least three-dozen
people are raking, tending, and decorating the graves.

Outside of town, caterpillars, hundreds of them, start crossing the road,
humping along hurriedly. Inspecting the road carefully, I see caterpillar
road-kill. The live ones scoot as if they know the danger of car tires and
the blasting wind of trucks. A single one is heading west across the road;
every other one is heading east. I can identify with the lone traveler. I'm
reminded of all the people who ask me *why* I am on this ride, even as I
wonder why these caterpillars are so determined to be crossing this morning. I could enjoy stopping to study them. Sometimes even traveling by
unicycle is too fast a passage.

I ride on. We have nothing planned for presentations or visits here on the
Colville Reservation. We called before the ride and tried without success to
make connections. It is enough just pedaling across this land.

Fifteen miles later we're nearing Coulee Dam, a huge sight, even from
miles away. When I finally arrive, Anne and Amy are playing with the kids
in a park. Robert arrived long before to explore the dam. We've done thirty
miles and its only 10:30. I suggest to Anne that I try to write on the computer for a couple of hours. The bakery and espresso shop looks a likely
place for a seat and an electrical outlet, but they have neither. Up the street
Anne asks at the Colville Indian Reservation Museum and Gift Shop.

"You can write in here," Anne comes out and tells me.

A short Native man named Tim welcomes me to the center and sets me
up at the artisan table. On my left side are beads in a basket. A mitre saw
is in front of me, and deerskin sewing scraps are stacked by the wall. A
poster with pictures and an explanation reads, "Who are the Colville
Indians?"

> *We are the Confederated Tribes of the Colville Reservation. We are
> the biggest and most advanced tribe in the Northwest. We have
> eleven different bands and ten bands originate from eastern
> Washington state and one band of the Nez Perce is originally from
> northeast Oregon. The eleven bands are Wenatchi, Entiat, Chelan,
> Methow, Okanogan, Nespelem, San Poil, Lakes, Moses, Palouse
> and the Nez Perce.*

I knew none of this history before our arrival here. I didn't know that the Reservation is named after an Army officer. I didn't know that Chief Joseph is buried here.

Tim comes over after I get started writing. Two tight braids of black hair fall over the front of his shoulders. He is quiet, but his words surprise me.

"All yesterday I was expecting someone to come here. When my boss came and told me to go home, I told her I was going to stay a little longer. This morning at four I woke up with the same feeling. I told myself, 'Whatever will be will be.' When your wife came in with her shirt (he pointed on his own chest to the place where we have our *One Wheel – Many Spokes* emblem), I knew that I was waiting for you."

Now that is an extraordinary welcome. Since we're on this journey, he shares a lesson he learned from his grandmother: "Take life day by day, minute by minute. You never know what's coming next. A day can be long enough. And when someone asks you for something, share with them."

Tim asks us for some posters and business cards. "We have lots of people come through here. I will tell them what you are doing."

I write for over two hours, and then it is time to pack up the computer, thank Tim for hosting us, and get back on the road to Wilbur.

"Here," he says, taking a small piece of root out from a packet of folded red felt. "This is the soul of Mother Earth."

"Once a year we go out and collect this. It's not a rare tree, but it's from the center of the tree." He takes a deerskin pouch on a beaded necklace, places the root inside, then places the necklace around my neck.

"This is the soul of Mother Earth," Tim says again. "And you are riding over Mother Earth this summer. When you get to the other water's edge, kneel down and say the prayers you have been praying all during your ride."

I leave saying more words of thanks, all of them inadequate. Back on the unicycle, I want only to pedal quietly and let this unexpected blessing settle in.

The climb out of Coulee Dam on Highway 174 is ten miles long and steep. The temperature this afternoon is in the fifties. The sky is clear. While riding across the Colville Reservation, I've learned a whole new piece of history.

Things I Didn't Know
- March 2, 1853: Washington Territory is established. Governor Stevens recommends "reservations" for the Indians.
- 1854: Stevens orders treaties negotiated to "extinguish Indian claims to the lands," and create reservations "so as not to interfere with the settlement of the country."

- April 9, 1872: Colville Reservation is established.
- July 2, 1872: Without consulting any tribes, Presidential Executive Order moves Colville Reservation to its present location, shrinking its size to 2.8 million acres.
- 1892: Northern half of reservation ceded to the United State for payment of one dollar per acre
- October 10, 1900: Presidential Proclamation opens reservation to homesteading, beginning in 1916
- December 1, 1905: McLaughlin Agreement cedes remaining 1.4 million acre Colville Reservation in exchange for eighty acre allotments to each Indian.
- 1956: 800,000 acres returned by Federal Government to tribal ownership.
- Colville tribal goal is repurchase of all reservation lands. 200,000 acres are still owned by non-tribal members.

As I pedal, the beads that Tim has placed around my neck clank against the cell phone clipped to my vest. Soon the beads are tangling in the antenna. There's a parallel in this tangle between ancient and modern ways. Whenever we speak, Anne and I explain that the endowment will help Inupiat Eskimo people to make their own decisions on how they want to mix their twelve-thousand-year-old tradition, the outside world, and their faith roots. This mixing is a complicated task. As the forced relocation of eleven tribes onto the Colville Indian reservation shows, native people have time and again been stripped of their independence and decision making power.

Now pieces from both these worlds are on my chest, clanking and tangling together. Tim has been working these issues out in his own life. Earlier he had told me: "Four years ago I went through a hard place in my life. That was the time I began returning to the old ways. I follow them as much as I am able to. They work for me."

On the climb out of Coulee Dam, Robert and I pedal from sagebrush and into pine country again, up and up and up. Around the final curve is a large red barn. When we reach it, we come to huge fields, rolled out like carpet to the very edge of the wild. The transition is abrupt. The line between wild and tilled is absolute. We cross into a treeless tapestry of fields where winter wheat is green and lush, and spring wheat is just barely sprouting. Fields that are planted without tilling still bear the swaths of last summer's harvest combines. Other fields have been furrowed for planting and are solid earth brown. The grade shallows out as the fields begin, but the crest is another two miles. From the top these fields form an endless mosaic.

After talking with Tim, I find this geographic demarcation even more striking. When agriculture first began in the Middle East, some 10-12,000 years ago, it set in motion the greatest human changes our world has experienced. Prior to that, for hundreds of thousands of years, cultures had been hunter-gatherers, attached to the particular land and place where they collected food. Migrations were slow. With the beginning of agriculture came the first food surpluses, encouraging everything from the development of written language to the specialization of skills, rapid innovations, the ability to support troops, quick migrations, and the development of complex cities.

One of the cultural distinctions between Native Americans and the immigrants to the United States is whether hunting and gathering or agriculture was the basic means of survival. Since agriculture began, it has been spreading throughout every corner of the globe. The wave rushed across North America in the 1800s. It was the settler's unrelenting pressure for farmland and minerals that forced the treaties and the reservations. Ironically, we are often taught that indigenous people are nomadic. In fact they are typically attached to a certain geography for thousands of years at a time. It's the agriculturalists who are nomadic, producing surpluses of children and goods, constantly searching for new land to till and new opportunities to develop. I'm a living example, a child of Danish immigrant farmers who ended up in Los Angeles.

Wilbur, eight miles dead ahead, is a tiny dot of eight hundred people in the distance. Rolling hills and headwinds mark the last of today's sixty-three miles. I arrive last, as usual. Anne and Amy and the kids have been at the school playground. Robert has an uncle who lives in Wilbur, and they are visiting together.

These fields are strange to us after two weeks of wild country that held everything from rain forests to oceans to deserts. In Wilbur our hosts help us make the adjustment. Bonnie and her husband Roger have opened their home to our crowd of eight.

Steaks and gravy, whipped potatoes and candied carrots, salad, strawberries, and cake are all on the table for our dinner. While we eat we learn about life in Wilbur. Roger grew up here, but...

"It's different now, that's for sure," he tells us.

"There are a lot less people here than a generation ago. When kids grow up they leave for college or the university. They never return, except to visit."

Bonnie continues, "There used to be a sawmill here, but when that closed we lost a lot of people. The school doesn't have nearly as many students. Someday we'll lose our railroad spur too, but it's still a great place to live. I wouldn't want to be anywhere else."

At the Wilbur Lutheran Church, Debbie has everything set up for our talk. We meet a woman who is going to teach this coming year in Gambell, Alaska, an island near the Seward Peninsula. Her questions remind us of when we first went to Nome and everything was new to us.

"Yes, it really can get to forty below with gale force winds. And, yes, the Bering Sea does freeze six feet thick in the winter.

"Yes, the only way in and out of the villages is by small plane. And then the only way out of Nome is with Alaska Airlines to Anchorage.

"Yes, the sun is only above the horizon for an hour and a half in December and January. But the long sunrises and sunsets keep it light for three or four hours each day. And yes, the days lengthen by eight minutes a day when spring returns.

"Yes, when you're off the road system in bush Alaska, costs are even higher, and yes, you'll be lucky to get fresh milk. In Nome it cost five dollars a gallon when we lived there. The small villages only had dried or canned milk. "

On Thursday morning we head for Spokane. The ride stretches on and on through farmland without us ever catching our groove. Everything feels long. We are fortunate, though, for just two days earlier Reardan had a nineteen-inch dump of snow. Today only traces remain as we ride through.

Spokane is a sort of last outpost on our trip. Ahead is some of the most rural land in our country. We won't see a bigger city until we reach Minneapolis, more than a thousand miles east. We take Friday off for errands and shopping. At Verizon, we finally solve a month-old problem and get a modem connection set up between our laptop and cell phone. From now on, whenever we're in range of a cell tower, we can be online.

The kids like the break at Riverside State Park. In the morning I carry toothbrushes outside where they are riding bikes.

"Stop for flossing!" I call out to them.

The sun is already warming the day. Lining up next to KariAnna and Kai, three-year-old Caroline says, "Fwoss me too."

Our little band is growing closer and closer. The kids have been taking turns doing sleepovers between our two vehicles.

After the day of stocking up, we load bikes and unicycles while the dusk deepens to darkness. This time of day I always feel like Barnum and Bailey, packing and unpacking after every performance. We have lots of cycles. Everyone except me has a two-wheel bike. KariAnna, Kai and Nathaniel have unicycles along. I've brought my twenty-four-inch unicycle for Anne and Robert to learn on. My twenty-eight-inch and spare thirty-six-inch also need loading. There are bikes on back of the Volkswagen Camper, bikes on top of the Honda, and a rack of unicycles on the Honda's back.

In the morning we'll head north for Sandpoint, Idaho. Anne and Amy will wake up later to get four kids and all our vehicles and gear headed up the road so that our ride can continue.

Mother's Day is on Sunday. Robert and I ride each day marveling that we've found partners and family who revel as much as we do in this unfolding adventure.

9
Mother's Day

Get a bicycle. You will not regret it. If you live.

MARK TWAIN

"We have got to find a card shop," Robert reminds me. Tomorrow is Mother's Day. Even the conservation center north of Spokane has a billboard out advertising a promotion.

Today our route begins a giant detour north to avoid rushing, roaring Interstate 90, the only route that goes due east from Spokane. All day long we ride along the foothill border of the Rockies, heading north to Sandpoint, Idaho.

Idaho

The Idaho border, state number four, comes up just at noon, and we lunch at Abilene Dam. The kids run up and hug us when we ride into the parking lot.

"I want to ride with you now," KariAnna announces as we prepare lunch.

"And you promised to ride with the dogs for exercise," Anne reminds me.

I switch to my smaller, slower Semcycle so that KariAnna can keep up and Katie and Luther can trot alongside for a few miles. KariAnna leads our way towards Priest River. With my yellow riding vest on her little shoulders, she beams a broad, proud smile as she pedals up the road. KariAnna is still planning for us to make a cross-country unicycle ride together in five years.

"I'll do a mile today," she says. At the mile mark she takes a break to rest her rear and then keeps going.

When Anne catches up in the motor home KariAnna exclaims, "Mommy, I rode three-and-a-half miles!"

While we rode we figured out that we can speed her up with four-inch cranks on her unicycle. We can also make an air seat on her unicycle.

"Can you do it tonight; please, please, please?"

Maybe she really will be ready for that cross-country ride in five years.

We ride along the Pend Oreille River in the afternoon. Osprey nests are built on top of the power poles, which parallel the road. I see eight of the big eagles flying as we ride. One holds a fish in its talons. Another is calling out and swoops from its nest just as I ride under it.

Jack and Alex's home is our destination. Jack is the dad of a friend of ours from seminary. He was a pastor for years before he turned to the practice of psychology, a streak of rebel in him that I find encouraging. They live ten miles east of Sandpoint, so our odometers hit ninety miles by the time we reach their home, my longest ride ever. The Rockies look down on this valley of the Lower Pack River.

The kids are bouncing and happy. They have been collecting pinecones with Alex for an evening campfire. Robert and I have been talking about riding another ten miles after dinner. Who knows if we'll ever get this close to a hundred miles again.

"Sure, go for it," Anne says, "Just don't hurt yourself. Remember you're preaching tomorrow."

Jack brings the food outside for dinner. Sitting by the riverbank we share a wonderful roast beef dinner.

"This should be enough energy for the last ten miles," I say, heading for thirds. Homemade cake with two kinds of ice cream is for dessert.

"The road just gets prettier from here," Alex tells us.

True enough, we're soon riding along the shore of Lake Pend Oreille. A roadside sign describes how ice dammed this lake in the last ice age. Back then the lake was eight hundred to a thousand feet deep and extended more than a hundred miles, all the way to Missoula. Even now it's huge, surrounded by peaks that still hold snow. The sun is fading and the sky has begun to turn colors. Robert gets a picture at mile ninety-eight by a lakeside pull-out. We ride through a town named Hope and click one hundred miles in the gathering dusk along the lake. Half a mile later we find a pullout and wait for Anne to pick us up.

Last spring a five-mile unicycle ride and memories of bicycling across the USA started the planning for this ride. My first fifty-mile ride in December had been a confidence builder. Getting over Stevens Pass was another important milestone. Now I have today's hundred-miler to add to the list of reasons for a growing faith in this journey.

A day like this could happen only with good care and good help. I finish tired, feeling the gift of family and friends that make up our team. Just one major oversight: Robert and I forgot Mother's Day cards!

On the morning of Mother's Day, May 12, I head into Sandpoint early to pick up those cards before going to preach at Faith Lutheran Church. At a Safeway Supermarket I step right back to the previous year and a ritual I hadn't known existed.

Last year, in Michigan, I had been busy before Mother's Day, so I stopped at a market for a card as I drove to church at 6 a.m. And there they were, the line-up of men at the card aisle. Another gaggle was assembled around the flowers.

This morning in Sandpoint, I realize I may have discovered a national ritual. There are few cards left and we, the gathered men, are sorting through remnants in hope of making the grade this day. I also shop for Robert, getting cards and tulip bouquets. An hour later I'm in the pulpit at Faith Lutheran Church.

Two holidays make me particularly nervous. Thanksgiving is one. Mother's Day is the other. In both of them our culture holds up images of perfect family and perfect motherhood, and makes a celebration of our "successes." All is fine when all's gone well, but this approach to these celebrations can make us feel like losers when our year has held unexpected tragedies or disappointments.

If there's anything that keeps me hanging onto my Lutheran faith, it is the insistence of our tradition that life is not first about performance but instead about the gift and the grace of living. I'm getting to be a better and better "performer" on my unicycle, but whenever I let a hundred-mile distance be the measure of my self, I become less. When faith turns into cheerleading for high achievers, we lose its power to describe life in all its complexities the way most of us really experience it. Faith's understanding is first and foremost not achievement, but sympathy, empathy, care, concern, kindness—in a word, compassion.

Thinking about Mother's Day, I remember the one that Anne and I lived through in Nome after our miscarriage. I'm glad I got to preach that sermon myself rather than hear one of the "everything's fine, keep your chin up, you're the greatest," messages that come across in too many advertisements and too many pulpits. I need to keep hearing that faith and life include everything—the good and the bad, the hard and the easy, the delight and the despair—and the promise that life both encompasses all our triumphs and struggles, and transcends them.

After church, back at the farm, Jack is working on a big pork tenderloin roast.

"Slow cooking, that's the secret," he tells me.

Since we started riding over the Cascades two weeks ago, our route has been following rivers: first the Skagit, and then the Skykomish to get over Stevens Pass; from there we followed the Wenatchee River to the Columbia River on our way to Chelan. The Okanagan River got us to Omak, and Omak Creek took us to Disautel Pass. Our route was overland to Spokane and up to the town and the water of Priest River, Idaho. Since then we've been following rivers again, like most people have always done before the advent of Interstate highways.

Today we're on Highway 200, following the Clark Fork. A half dozen osprey treat us to a show this Monday morning as they circle and fish breakfast at Denton Slough. One that we stop to watch is circling hopefully above where a small duck just dived. The duck surfaces for air and then dives quickly to safety. I want to see the outcome, but we've distracted the osprey and she flies off. Strange that most animals won't turn a head for a roaring log truck, but our bike and unicycle often set deer to running or other animals to fleeing. We are surprised when one osprey does fly our way, landing in the pine tree nearest us. We can see every feather while it perches.

Clark Fork comes up quickly, population two hundred. The gas station is closed, so we head over to the restaurant to get my form filled out for the Guinness record-keeping.

"First time I've seen a unicycle like that around here," remarks the stubble-bearded man standing outside.

I walk inside to ask the waitress for her signature. She's holding a carafe of coffee. After a look at my reflective yellow riding vest, elbow and knee pads, silver helmet and Spandex riding pants, she turns and heads wordlessly to the kitchen. Her look is a clear question: "What has this world come to?"

The stubble-bearded man has a seat by now, and he willingly signs my form before we head back out on the road.

From here we will follow the Clark Fork River for over a hundred miles. It's wide and full of water. A headwind comes up early, and my legs still feel the century ride from Saturday. It's slow going for a ways, but the pine forest and mountain views help me keep pedaling. *A River Runs Through It* could have been filmed here from Highway 200. After some miles we pass the Cabinet Gorge Dam then follow the reservoir until we come to the running river again. On this trip we have passed a lot of dams, which are storing precious water and generating needed electricity. More and more, though, I appreciate the wild places where swift water still flows.

A few more miles and we're at the state line in Robert's home state of Montana. "I love Washington," he says, "but everything is just bigger here in Montana." We'll spend most of the rest of May riding across this state. Two hundred yards after the Montana sign, we stop again for a picture at the "Mountain Time Zone" sign. Up the road another twenty miles or so I'll hit one thousand miles of riding.

Soon the country begins to open up; the vegetation shows that the land is drier. We stop seeing cedars and start seeing trees with small bright green leaves budding out on tall straight trunks covered with dark hanging moss: tamaracks, the only conifer that loses its leaves in the winter. As we ride on, we see more ranches. I'm looking at my odometer now, 985 miles since Tillamook.

Approaching the thousand-mile mark, Robert rides ahead and readies the camera. Anne and Amy happen to pass us on the last 100 yards. Click, click, and its done: a thousand miles.

Focusing on the odometer and the camera, neither of us notice the sign across the road until we start again. A big yellow billboard with black hand lettering announces: "ETCETERA JUST AHEAD." Etcetera turns out to be an antique store just a mile ahead. Maybe it is also description for our next thousand miles.

Twenty minutes later we catch up to Anne and Amy. Lunch is ready. Tacos and a huge plate of pasta fill us up. The kids have made a big find of pinecones and start collecting them. It feels good to rest awhile; today is the hottest of the trip so far, 84 degrees. We play with the kids and their forest findings before we get back on the road, heading for Thompson Falls.

"Let's meet at the ice cream shop," we all agree.

The ice cream is wonderful, reason enough to be in Thompson Falls. We are in town, though, because this is where our friend, Jim, died last year. It's a freaky thing when someone your age dies, especially a close friend. Tonight we are visiting the congregation he served. When he died here last January, it was sudden; he suffered a heart attack while driving his old pickup back to his house. People here are still grieving. When we lived in Nome, Jim was the pastor in neighboring Wales.

Six congregations make up Seward Peninsula Lutheran Ministry. Four of them (Brevig, Teller, Shishmaref, and Wales) are small villages of 150 to 600 people where everyone belongs to the church. Nome has a congregation in its community of 4500 people. The most recent congregation was established in Anchorage to serve people who have moved there from the Seward Peninsula.

While every one of the Seward Peninsula communities has harsh weather, Wales' is the most severe. Located at the most western point of the United States, Wales sits on the tip of the Bering Strait where the land bridge once was. On clear days Russia is visible across the strait. The wind is so unrelenting that in the winter, houses drift completely over, making villagers have to dig steps from roof level down into the snow banks to reach their doors. One time a visiting pastor was snowmobiling and unknowingly parked on top of the house where he was planning to visit!

When Jim lived in Wales, volunteers were in the slow and unpredictable process of building new housing for the pastor. During those two years, Jim ended up living in a seagoing storage container. When we asked Jim how he was doing, he replied, "I'm surviving."

In his case it was literally true. Whenever a storm came, it buried his container. To get out he had to open his door and shovel enough snow inside to carve a passage outside, and then shovel that same snow back outside. People in Wales nicknamed him "sheek-sheek" (squirrel) because of all the snow they saw flying out of his tunnel. As tough as it was for Jim, some people live in these container homes permanently.

Jim always kept both his humor and his realism. People in Thompson Falls have many stories to share, like how Jim was often found by the side of the road fixing his broken-down truck. He named it Flattery because, "Flattery will get you nowhere."

On the Seward Peninsula Jim kept asking the hard question,

"What does it mean to live in a community that is beyond despair?"

Many people on the Seward Peninsula suffer the same symptoms of alcoholism, drug addiction, and suicidal thoughts that are common wherever traditional cultures are impacted by an encroaching modern worldview. Jim was a sensitive mentor and friend for me through the difficult times. Mostly he listened. The only concrete advice he ever pressed on me was, "Lars, you don't have to hit a home run every time you're up to bat."

I check e-mail after the presentation. One is from Brian Crockett, who serves as pastor for both the Brevig Mission and Teller congregations. He was there when Jim lived in Wales and we lived in Nome.

Dear Lars & Company:

You and your company are being lifted up in our prayers. The people in Brevig Mission are still trying to understand what you are doing. The stories really help people to begin to see what is happening and what you are experiencing…

Brevig is sitting in the fog and the south wind. We have not had a mail plane for several days. The temperatures are hovering in the 30s. I have been unable to travel to Wales for a funeral, but Pastor Tim is traveling by snow machine to go to Wales and perform the funeral service.

The young people of Brevig Mission are hoping the weather will break so that they may travel to Wales and join in the annual Eskimo Dance Festival being held in Wales this weekend. They have been practicing their dances after school everyday this week.

The ducks are beginning to fly and the birds are returning from their travels to their winter vacation places. Many men in the village are beginning to travel to traditional hunting grounds for ducks. The next big activity will be boating for bearded seals and walrus.

There has been one question that came up for you. What happens if you lose the trail or end up traveling in white out? We need an answer. Thanks!

Brian

10
Uniglory

I am persuaded that the world has been tricked into adopting some false and most pernicious notions about consistency—and to such a degree that the average man has turned the rights and wrongs of things entirely around and is proud to be "consistent," unchanging, immovable, fossilized, where it should be his humiliation.

Mark Twain

Snacks from convenience stores and the traveling café of our motor home are usually enough to keep us stoked for the road.

"I'm real hungry this morning," Robert comments as we arrive in the two block town of Plains. With the wind at our back we've had a quick ride here from Thompson Falls. We stop at the Hilltop Café.

A large older man is hobbling into the café at the same time. He holds his car for support and then the wall of the building, concentrating on each tiny halting step. Inside, he talks to us; his speech is halting too, as if he passes his time alone.

"One time we had a bicyclist come through here who had only one leg."

He starts this story and ends by sharing his own bicycle ride, long long ago, from Missoula to here in Plains. The telling of it lights his eyes and sharpens his voice.

After breakfast, folks come out to watch us ride away from the restaurant. It is one of those times that balance can't be bought for any price. I try seven times before I finally get my perch right and pedal on down the road. Robert is laughing out loud at me. Folks in Plains will probably be wondering if we'll ever make it to New York.

Just east of town a train full of ocean cargo containers clanks and screeches its way past us. Most of the containers are lettered "Evergreen" on their sides.

"Look!" Robert says.

A long string of containers rolls by with the perfect name: "Uniglory."

Tomorrow we'll be in Missoula. Today we twist along the Clark Fork River, the wind at our back all day long. By evening we arrive at Arlee, on the Flathead Indian Reservation.

A visitor wouldn't recognize the reservation except for the signs. The Flathead people don't even have their traditional names. Explorers dubbed them the Flatheads before talking with them. Their traditional name, Salesh, means, "the people." (This is a common theme among traditional tribal names. Inupiat means "the *real* people.") Nor is this the traditional land of the Salesh. They were forced here from the Bitterroot Valley, now home to the retreats of movie stars and the very wealthy. The rightful chief of the Salesh never agreed to the move: A different chief, Arlee, cut the deal with the United States government and he's the one who got a town named after him. In 1904, further injustice divided the reservation into private family allotments of 40, 80, or 160 acres. Under the authority of the Flathead Allotment Act, the remaining land was opened to homesteading. Soon, even much of the native allotment land was sold to outsiders in exchange for cash. The privatization of the communal culture ended in destitution.

When Anne and I lived in Nome, I wondered if it would keep its native character or be overrun by non-native ways. In the small villages on the Seward Peninsula, residents are still almost entirely native. In Nome itself, the population is split almost exactly between native and non-native. As for the bigger cities, Anchorage is much less native. Seattle, named after the great chief, carries no visible native influence in its legal, educational, transportation, economic, or governing systems. Considered in these terms, the future for indigenous culture seems grim.

We read some of the Flathead history on a sign as we ride off the reservation the next morning towards Missoula. Thankfully, a few turns up the road I find a sign to lighten the day. So far it's the best one of the trip. I hadn't realized that Arlee is also the site of the famous Mule-Marathon. Mules are big in these parts. Robert takes out the camera again and gets a picture of me riding under a big sign by the roadside corral: "Busted Ass Ranch."

Perfect for mules and unicyclists. Words for my headstone: "Old unicyclists never die, they just go to the Busted Ass Corral."

On the road again, Robert warns, "Evaro Hill is just ahead." Robert bicycled all during his college years in Missoula, and this was a popular route. Since Plains, people have been warning us about Evaro Hill. Channel Thirteen is even there, filming at the top of the grade. It turns out far easier than Robert remembers; 1100 miles of riding are paying off.

Our presentation tonight is with campus ministry students, gathered together for the last time before summer; some of them are graduating. Afterward students come up to talk. One of them is Heidi Black; this is a surprise, as we knew her when she was a kid in Alaska. Small world. Another student waited for space to speak, "I'm really glad you came to visit us," the young man said.

"I'm glad too," I answer, and then I wait.

"I did really lousy when I started here at the university. In fact, I didn't make it. But I'm a real hard worker. I even bought a house after I left school," he tells me. "But I hate that house. I'm stuck now that I've got it." He continues, "The best time I had in my whole life was driving to Spokane with a friend one Friday night. We got there at midnight, and when we couldn't find a motel, we drove the rest of the night to visit a friend in Seattle.

"That was the best time of my life. Is that weird or what? I think I want to do Peace Corps or something. But I'm stuck with this house."

Twenty years old, he seems just a bit quicker to find the road that so many of us end up on in middle age, stuck by the things we own or have committed to. I listen to his medley of dreams and constraints. "You could sell your house," I venture.

He tells me some more stories, interesting stories, the pieces that make him who he is. Then he backs up, "I never considered I could sell my house. Maybe I really could."

"Maybe you can," I encourage, thinking of Mark Twain's blessing to "throw off the bowlines and set sail from safe harbor. Explore. Dream. Discover."

When the evening is done, we drive over to sleep at Tim and Mary's home, friends of Robert and Amy's. I fall asleep, remembering how much I loved being on a campus and spending my time with students.

Robert's cyclist friend, Tom, meets us on Thursday morning as we prepare to ride out of Missoula. The two of them are planning a fast 130-mile daytrip across the Continental Divide. I'll be poking along behind at a two-day pace. They guide me out of Missoula then shoot ahead and leave me cranking my pedals alone. Highway 200 follows the Blackfoot River east of town, another breathtaking ride. Today there is too much view for a single gaze. The farther I ride, the bigger the views get as the land opens more and more. All day long I spin my head back and forth, trying to drink in this land. I find myself breathing deeply, not from exertion but from trying to absorb the ranchland valleys and the snowcapped mountains that rim the horizon in all directions.

The only town on the map for today is Ovando. Fortunately, every fifteen or twenty miles I come to a gas station for refreshments. Around noon I pass the Paws Up Angus Ranch and get an uneasy feeling. Huge signs mark the ranch. Timbered arches cover the entrance roads. Grizzly bear prints are cut from steel and tacked to the signs, a proud-looking announcement of the conquest of this land—of domination. Sensitized by our reservation experiences and this past year of senseless terrorism and questionable war in Afghanistan, I ride these couple of miles with images of our violent America churning in my head.

I reach Ovando at one o'clock, and try a ten-minute nap by the stop sign as I wait for Anne and Amy. Ants end the rest after only six minutes. Trixie's Restaurant and Bar is a quarter mile ahead. Not very hungry after an earlier milk shake, I walk in for some fries and a place to wait for Anne and Amy.

"Are you the one heading up the road on a unicycle?"

Four men occupy the table: one young, three older. They push aside wrapping paper and invite me to join them. A "Women in Waders" calendar pictures a bikinied woman in hip boots, fly-fishing on a Montana river. Of the four men, two are named John, and two Paul. John and Paul are celebrating their birthdays. The other John and Paul at the table are treating them. I wouldn't be surprised if Pope John Paul were here too.

When they ask what I do, I answer that I'm a pastor; I wonder if they'll scurry the calendar away and make themselves "respectable." After the Paws Up Ranch, I'm unsure of this territory. But no, April in her waders keeps staring up at us, and John says, "With Lars for a name, you're Lutheran?"

I answer yes and he starts asking me about Baptists, telling me, "There are a lot of Baptists here." In a minute he's talking about a book by Diana Eck, *In Search of God, From Bozeman to Benares*. One of the leading scholars for inter-faith studies, Eck's book is on my shelf at home, waiting to be read. Finding kindred spirits here in Ovando is an unexpected surprise. In the hour we eat together, they confirm the futility of my stereotypes. The backgrounds of these two ranchers and two outfitters are, retired professor, New York City transplant, third generation miner, and retired math teacher.

"Eighth grade was my favorite," Paul says, "I loved those kids." His voice makes me wish he'd been my teacher.

We trade stories and I ask questions.

"So," I ask, "is that Paws Up place about dead grizzlies?"

John, the retired professor, laughs, "Paws Up is about money and making a big show. I call it Bras Up. It's owned by the folks from Frederick's of Hollywood, the lingerie company. They've got maybe ten- to twelve-thousand acres."

Later I ask if the movie *A River Runs Through It* has had an impact on places like this.

"Our business now is probably ten times what it was before the movie," Paul answers.

"The sequel to the movie was *A Realtor Runs Through It*," John adds. "Montana has changed a lot this last decade."

Paul buys my hamburger and fries, and I get ready to ride, wishing I could spend lunch often with these men. Back on the unicycle, my frame of mind is renewed and refreshed.

Anne and Amy still haven't shown up. Just after I turn from Highway 200 to 141, a construction pickup pulls off and waits for me.

"Do you have a motor home following you with a unicycle logo on it?"

"Yeah, I do," I answer, thinking they're just interested in our story.

"Just a minute ago it went straight on by back at the turn. We'll go catch them," the driver offers.

Our phones don't work out here, so there's no calling Anne.

"Thank you." I accept their offer of assistance. They turn around and accelerate fast to find Anne and Amy, a huge kindness in this vast country.

Half-an-hour later I see the Volkswagen and motor home in my mirror. By now the kids have christened it: HARVEY THE RV is penciled into the aluminum doorframe.

"Let's look for a campground around here," Anne says after she stops to make our plans. "I'm worn out."

An hour later I find them at a pullout on Nevada Lake Reservoir, the finish to eighty spectacular miles of unicycling.

At times we feel like the Beverly Hillbillies as we travel along in our old 1978 motor home, but Harvey has been working well so far with only 76,000 miles on the odometer. But now a brief inspection reveals a broken alternator belt. The kids are throwing pebbles in the lake. Anne and Amy are off on a bike ride. When they return we decide to all drive the fifty miles to Helena together in case Harvey has more troubles. We make the trip without problem, arriving just after Robert and Tom and their long ride.

"Lots of headwinds," they tell us, "especially at McDonald Pass."

Robert drives me back to Nevada Lake in the morning, "The Avon Café has a two-third pound burger," he informs me as I start off. When I get there I order the burger and a milkshake. It turns out to be a lot of ballast for the last thirteen miles to the crest of McDonald Pass. The headwind is strong as I approach the summit, making the final three-mile climb of the Rockies a balancing act and real workout.

"Pedal!" I tell myself. "Live this challenge."

Pedal, pedal, pedal. I don't fall off, and at last I top out at the pass, 6325 feet. My family is waiting for me. Surprise! They've brought along a one-pound hamburger. I should have skipped the Avon Café. A television reporter from Helena is also at the pass. "How is the ride going?" she asks.

"Better, far better than any of us ever dreamed."

The evening television report is titled, "One Wheel Wonder Makes It To Helena."

"It's all downhill from here," Robert assures. "Should be easy for 'The One Wheel Wonder.'"

11
Maybee

We can secure other people's approval if we do right and try hard;
but our own is worth a hundred of it, and no way has been
found out of securing that.

MARK TWAIN

From McDonald Pass and eastwards, water flows to the Missouri, the Mississippi, and finally the Atlantic. Twelve hundred miles into the trip we're headed into eastern Montana and the plains and prairies of the Midwest.

With expectations of flat land ahead, I switch for the first time to my four-inch short cranks. I've never tried them before, and it takes some practice learning to get started. On Sunday morning I test them out on the ride to Townsend. The route is mostly flat, and with a slight tailwind I ride twelve and thirteen miles per hour much of the time, even getting up to fifteen on one stretch. Riding with Tom and Robert pushes my pace.

Anne and KariAnna are waiting in Townsend when we arrive. We load the cycles and drive back to Helena for morning church with Tom and Jenny's family.

Helena, the state capital, is also home to the Roman Catholic Cathedral. Worship starts at 11 a.m., and it feels like the meeting of high Church and the high West. Everywhere you look in the Cathedral you see gold. Outside is Last Chance Gulch Street, named when Helena was a gold rush town. I spend the hour in church thinking of our trip so far; a rich and multi-colored tapestry is already weaving although we're still far short of halfway to New York. For the rest of the day we lounge, eating large quantities of ice cream.

"Get everything out of the car?" I ask Robert on Monday morning, before locking it. Anne will be coming later to hook up the motor home and meet us in Lennep.

"Yes," he answers, and I lock the door.

"And where's your helmet?" Robert asks.

It's in the car, as are the keys I've locked inside for Anne to use later. At the same instant I see that my seat has gone flat overnight.

We walk across the street and fill the spare tube at the gas station. When I pull my sunglasses from the pack, they are broken. The gas station sells superglue and we stick the glasses back together.

"We're not even on the road yet, and we've already got three strikes," I complain to Robert.

Finally we are ready to ride. An American flag was hanging completely still when we arrived. It makes the slightest flutter as we ride away.

The sun rises to match our start east on Highway 12. Twenty minutes later it's joined by a strengthening headwind, just as we begin twenty-seven miles of unexpected climbing to get over the Big Belt Mountains—so much for everything being downhill after the Continental Divide. I'm on the four-inch cranks, and it's hard pushing. The headwind adds to the challenge.

A few miles into the climb, a pickup passes and panics us with a blast of its horn. A moving truck following just behind also blasts. We're frightened, vulnerable. I jerk off onto the gravel, just barely managing to avoid a fall. Robert reacts with shouted words that need no repeating. What a start to this day!

The next vehicle is a bull-hauler, full of cattle. The rear end of one cow and a vent in the side of the trailer must be lined up perfectly. A hundred yards ahead of us a spray of green crap explodes from the truck.

Robert laughs hard enough to threaten his balance. I join in, imagining a direct hit and the stories we would have to tell. The spell of the day is broken; now it feels bright with possibility. Pedaling toward the summit, we count nine other places where these cows had found breakfast relief and sprayed the road. There are endless miles of cows ahead and thousands of bull-haulers to enliven our travels.

Following Deep Creek up through pines, we reach the summit and bid our farewell to the Rockies. Cresting this pass we are greeted by a vast endless view. The Crazy Mountains are to the south. The road fades into infinity in the basin ahead. My own sense of significance fades to nothing. We get back on our cycles and begin riding into this land—one pedal stroke at a time.

The wind comes from behind for a few miles, but I am still tiring out. This is our first day without towns and services on our route, so we are carrying all our water and food with us, rationing it carefully. This is different from the thousand-calorie stops I've become accustomed to every fifteen or twenty miles. At mile thirty-three we reach the intersection with Highway 8 and stop for a rest. Robert and I decide on a roadside nap, the first one of the trip for us. The wind is blowing hard now, and when we turn south on 89 we will be facing it straight on.

"Hey look." Robert says after just a few moments of lying on the gravel. "I think that's my mom and dad…That *is* my mom and dad."

Religious conversions happen over lesser events. Loaded with water and muffins and bananas and more, Skip and Barb are our saviors in the desert. I stuff myself while they talk. Then we head on into the wind while Robert's folks drive off in search of Amy.

"Want me to ride with the wind for a minute and see how fast it's blowing?" Robert asks after a couple of miles.

"Sure, it's definitely getting stronger."

Robert turns around and rides with it for a bit, checking his coasting speed against his speedometer, then reports, "I'm guessing seventeen and gusting to twenty."

This is a gentle breeze compared to what comes next. Reaching Highway 294 we take another break. In the middle of this vast landscape the wind is now singing through the spokes on our wheels; it's difficult to hear each other while riding. When we get going, I start up a small rise as the wind gusts, knocking me off the unicycle. There are fifteen more miles to Lennep. We count them off by the slow progression of mile markers. By now the wind is so strong that the only solution is laughter. The annoyance has become a challenge to be savored. In the back of my mind is just one reservation. Wind like this may be normal around here.

At mile five we come to the "monster" hill that our evening's host, Kate Nichols, had described to us on the phone. Ahead we see the road cut the hillside. The grade doesn't look bad, but as soon as we reach it, the wind pounds me off the unicycle again.

"Lunchtime," I holler out, unable to ride farther. We pull off to the side of the road. "Let's just wait here until Anne and Amy show up," I suggest.

We start another nap with only sagebrush to shield us from the wind. Three minutes later Robert's parents again show up. "We didn't find Amy and Anne," they tell us.

"They're probably shopping for stuff this morning," Robert answers. "They'll come."

We feast on more good food. I am hoping Anne will show up soon, so I can switch to longer cranks to ride through this wind. When they don't arrive and we've eaten all we can, I decide to try again with my four-inch cranks. After a dozen attempts I finally manage a wobbling start towards the hill, make it thirty yards, and then get blown off again. Walking forward to where the road is cut into the hill I find just enough protection from the wind for me to start pedaling forwards.

"There they are," Robert points out over the valley, and we can see the motor home and the camper coming slowly out of the far distance. "That VW engine is going to be struggling today."

They join us at the top of the hill. When Anne opens Harvey's door, the wind sucks out a stack of colored paper the kids have been drawing on. Down the hill and over the sagebrush it flies, irretrievable colorful confetti.

I never expected to need my six-inch cranks on this trip, but today I'm thankful for the fifty percent increase of pedal torque. Hanging onto the motor home and using it for protection, I pedal to the front of the RV and get blasted off as soon as I leave its protection. Here at the crest it's hard just standing upright in the wind. Three times in a row the wind blows me downwind, off the road, where I fall. The fourth time I barely bobble up and around the corner; we are finally headed into our last ten miles. I had thought the biggest challenges might be over after the Rockies, but today proves me wrong.

"Great adventure," Robert and I agree when we finally reach Lennep. Wind weary, we are thankful for the gracious welcome from Kate and her family. Her pastor in Harlowtown, forty miles up the road, had told her of our trip.

There are just three families living in Lennep, which also features the second oldest Lutheran Church in the state, and a school with four students. Twelve years ago Kate and Nick left computer programming positions in Trenton, New Jersey and headed to Montana to make a life here. They bought a 1920s home with a good well; it had belonged to the owners of the railroad that once went through these parts. They are raising daughters here, Alice and Janis, while making a living programming computers for people across the USA and Canada.

"Why here?" I ask.

"My grandfather used to be a pastor in the Billings area. I visited when I was a kid. Tim saw the Crazy Mountains on his way to pick apples in Washington. We always wanted to come back."

Great dinner. Great company. As we eat I think of how many people dream of a life just like this. The Nichols enjoy a life of self-sufficiency here on the edge of the high plains, but the price is full time work split between gardening, long drives, business, and the children's education. Janis and Alice keep asking when we can come back. Visitors here are few and far between.

"Lennep's a good place to stop and visit," Kate tells us, extending an invitation to return.

As we walk out to the motor homes to go to bed, the stars are hanging thick in the sky. The wind has diminished.

Tuesday morning brings a complete calm. We head out into the most brilliant sunrise of the trip. Here on Highway 294 we can ride on the right shoulder of the road or straight down the middle. There are no cars. When the first one passes us we check my odometer: sixteen miles, an hour and a half, with the road all to ourselves. You can see miles ahead on these roads. We turn onto Highway 12, heading east to Harlowtown. For most of the ride, we can't see a car in either direction.

We do see a skunk.

"Whoa!" Robert cries out. The skunk is running fast, directly towards us.

I jump off my unicycle and start a quick retreat; this charging skunk has even more potential for calamity than yesterday's bull-hauler. Thankfully she turns off the road and heads for a clump of bushes. We proceed cautiously out of range.

After forty quick miles we're in Harlowtown, a small town that seems huge compared to Lennep. While we eat breakfast, the editor of the newspaper arrives as does Kate's pastor, Kristie Bummer. She brings fresh banana bread for us that she's baked this morning. The editor brings a camera and his years of experience covering the area's news.

"You must know everything that happens around here," I say, testing his interest in conversation.

"Not everything, but a lot." And he begins to tell me about the changing human landscape of eastern Montana. "Kids here grow up and move on to bigger places. Some of our schools have only two or three students. Someday the state will have to decide if it can continue to support these schools."

"I've been hearing that same thing in other small towns," I confirm.

"The next county you're heading into is the least populated in the state. Golden Valley County has only nine hundred residents in that whole huge space. Ryegate, the county seat, has only three hundred. Eventually these counties will have to be redistricted. It's too hard to afford a county government with less than a thousand people."

Kate and her family in Lennep are the exceptions to the rule of rural depopulation that we are witnessing. Down south on Interstate 90, towns like Billings and Missoula are booming. Up here on old Highway 12, towns are shrinking.

Back on the unicycle we ride back into more of this dry rural sage ranchland, mile after mile until we reach Ryegate. I'm tired when I arrive. The sign at the bar advertises "Testical Festival." Something looks wrong with this sign. Everyone is gathered a hundred yards farther on at the roadside park. When Robert and I stop I ask out loud, "How do you spell testicle?"

Amy, the contemplative of our trip, bursts out laughing. The rest of us join in when she explains. "I was just wondering today as I was driving, 'What does Lars think about when he's riding all day?'"

We get our thoughts and our spelling straightened out, glad that we're not heading in for any bull testicle hors d'oeurve this evening. Anne and Amy decide to drive to Grandma's home in Colstrip and get some extra time there with the children. Skip will stay to drive support for Robert and me.

I've been toying with the idea of seeing how far I can ride in a twenty-four-hour stretch.

"Are you going to do it?" Anne asks.

"Maybee," I reply

When Anne and I lived on the Seward Peninsula we often heard people say, "MayBee." I was used to the word being a polite way of saying, probably not. "MayBee," as said on the Seward Peninsula, seems to mean the opposite; we'll be there or we'll do that if everything works out, but you never know what will happen.

"Have fun," Anne encourages me. "Be safe. We'll see you in Colstrip."

These last few days have been fitting together well for an attempt:

- Guinness World Records finally got back to us confirming our attempt at the long-distance unicycling record and affirming their interest in a new record for the farthest distance in twenty-four hours.
- Robert's friend Dieth is coming to Ryegate and they are considering a 180 mile ride to Colstrip. "You should come too, Lars," Robert encouraged.
- Robert's dad has volunteered to drive support vehicle alongside of me if I try a twenty-four-hour ride. The rest of the family will be enjoying themselves in Colstrip.
- Robert's mom works for the sheriff's department. "I'll tell them to look out for you," she assures me.

The big question is what will the weather do? After Anne and Amy leave, the wind starts swirling and then rain comes; every drop is a small blessing against the four-year drought. "We'll have a tailwind in the morning," Robert predicts.

We talk it over for a while, and I finally decide to go for it. "Dawn's early light then. We'll see what happens."

Deith has arrived and scouted the town for a place to sleep so the four of us won't have to jam into the Westphalia. "We have an invitation at the Espresso Shop," he reports back.

The Espresso Shop is actually the new community center. David, the physics teacher at school, and Audrey the local physical therapist, joined forces to start this center a half-year before. The building was Ryegate's old meat freezer; inside it still has solid wood siding from floor to ceiling. Full of character then, it is full of kids now. There is weight-lifting equipment, a pool table, a tennis table, exercise mats, couches for chatting; it is one of the most inspiring sights I've seen on the trip so far.

David and Audrey are creating a vibrant community in the face of the surrounding decline. They graciously open the center to us for our overnight stay. We sleep on exercise mats. Waking briefly at one o'clock, I hear the wind howling. Which way is it blowing?

At 4:15, we are up and getting ready. The wind has quieted, but a stiff breeze still blows. The direction is right: out of the west and towards Colstrip.

"Okay, let's try this," I declare, shivering from the chill of the morning.

At 5:18, we take a picture at the *Welcome to Ryegate* sign. Deith and Robert head onto the highway with me, out into the rain and the pre-dawn sky.

"Do some coasting for me today," I say, and they streak off down the road while I pedal stroke by stroke, the wind pushing at my back. Skip is driving the van. He pulls in behind me, the little Volkswagen motor putting along, matching my pace.

"The only people that predict weather in Montana are either newcomers or fools," Skip tells me at my first energy bar break.

Ten miles. Fifty minutes. This is my fastest riding ever. I start thinking of how this day might go, and I begin to count on this west wind holding steady. Soon the stiff breeze strengthens into heavy wind. As I am passing under a power line, I hear the wind ripping through the wires sounding like a jet at the far end of a runway. I am moving at thirteen miles an hour, occasionally stepping it up to fifteen, shoved strongly from behind. The temperature hasn't warmed up. Hail falls at intervals, stinging my face whenever the road curves sideways to the wind.

When I reach Roundup after forty miles, the wind has fallen off to almost dead calm. After oatmeal, bacon and eggs, I step back out in the sprinkling rain. Soon the wind shifts and comes from my right side. I'm riding eleven or twelve miles an hour now. Then the wind dies again before returning from over my left shoulder. A man stops his van and runs out to get a picture of me riding by. "You've got fifty-mile-an-hour winds coming at you from behind," he shouts across the road to me. "Good luck!"

For the next hour and a half I ride with winds on my left shoulder. Eight of these miles are through road construction. Rain has turned the road to mud. It squishes under my big tire, mostly solid enough for easy riding but occasionally soft. Mud. Holes. Sidewinds. This is bad for speed. By the time I reach the end of it, I'm covered with mud that reaches halfway up my back. On pavement again, I resume my pace.

Sandstone formations and scattered pine make up the landscape here, beautiful even as I race through it. Huge ranches are the norm. From my left, riding along one of the small canyons I sense a distant roar. Minutes later the wind hits me. Blasting from the side it grows in the space of two more minutes to become the biggest wind I've ever faced. I lean far to my left and barely keep balance. I come to Musselshell a mile later where I stop to confer with Skip. "Could we go south here?" I ask.

"No, this cross-road won't get us to Colstrip."

"I'm not ready to give up yet," I tell Skip. "This wind has been changing all morning. Maybe it will straighten out and get behind us again."

I get back on the unicycle and soon the roar of the wind brings laughter. Maybe this comes from the challenge of big winds, or from how lively they make me feel, every bit of my energy concentrating on staying upright and heading forward, or maybe its just the reminder of how puny I am in the face of all this energy that seems funny this morning.

Up ahead the road takes a ninety-degree left and makes a gentle climb up a sandstone wall headed straight into the wind. Though this would be easy on a windless day, it might be more than I can handle this morning. I don't get a chance to find out. On the approach to the curve I dig in with my pedals and suddenly something snaps, throwing me from my seat. One of the bolts holding the bearings is broken. My spare unicycle is already in Colstrip with Anne.

"I've got a hundred of those bolts in my garage," Skip comments. "We could drive to the next town and see if we can find one somewhere."

"Okay, let's try for that."

I pack my muddy unicycle and muddy self in the VW and slam the door shut against the wind. As we start up the small climb, the camper is rocked from the wind. At the top it's even stronger.

With a side blast for the next ten miles, the camper is buffeted viciously.

"We'd better call it a day," I tell Skip at last.

"Whatever you want," he replies, "but, I think you're right."

"Maybee" turns out to be sixty-three miles on this day.

The wind turns to tail a few miles down the road. We are driving fifty-five, barely passing the tumbleweeds that blow alongside us. Cloud patches in the sky throw shadows on the road that race ahead of us far faster than we drive.

At a high point of the road, we just barely receive an incoming call on our cell phone.

"You're done riding for the day." It's Anne on the phone. "Robert and Deith had to quit up ahead of you. Deith's wife is going out to pick them up." Even with the bad connection, I can hear her relief to know we are heading back.

12
Devil's Tower

There are no buffaloes in America now, except Buffalo Bill…
I can remember the time when I was a boy, when buffaloes were
plentiful in America. …Great pity it is so.

MARK TWAIN

The wind is gone, but there is snow on the ground in the morning and no assurance of what the road will be like when we drive 117 miles back to start riding again in Musselshell. By 10 a.m. when Skip drops me off, the sun is shining. The temperature is cool; the wind has died. The hill that looked insurmountable in the wind is barely noticeable as I pedal over it into the experiences that this day will offer.

A white pickup truck stops ahead of me, a few miles into the day's ride. "I saw you out here yesterday in the wind and radioed back to the office to tell them. They wouldn't believe me." His name is Jerry, and his job is to take care of the oilrigs in the area.

"How often does it get so windy?" I ask.

"Not often. Yesterday was so windy that when I drove out to check the rigs I couldn't even hear them running when I was standing right beside them. How did you make out?"

I tell him how I got blown out for the day. Before I leave, he tells me about the wild asparagus growing in the ditch. "Supposedly a train dropped the seed on a trip west. However it got here, it's good asparagus."

A garage, a café, a hardware store and a dozen or so houses are all that make up Meltown, but I meet a woman here who handles cookies like sacred objects. Yesterday, in the wind, Robert and Deith stopped here to shiver and try to warm themselves. The good folks at the Meltown Bar and Café built them a fire in the fireplace. I stop in to tell them how much that fire had been appreciated. There are six people seated inside the simple café; an order counter is up front with no one behind it. Back in the kitchen, Judy is getting the lunch menu prepared. After passing on the thanks from Robert and Deith, I ask for a signature on a Guinness World Record slip.

"I always wondered how they kept track of these records," Judy says carefully, as if she'd given this issue long considered thought.

"May I get some water?" I ask.

"Of course you can. The water is here."

"Thank you for stopping in," she says, handing back the form and pointing, "This Tupperware is full of cookies. There are chocolate chip and oatmeal applesauce. Take as many as you can eat." She offers me the big canister like she's serving Holy Communion.

Forty miles into the day's ride, I come to Ingomar. The Bunk n' Biscuit is here, advertising itself as the only place to sleep in one hundred miles. The mileage is exaggerated by sixty miles, but the feel of that number is dead on. The Jersey Lilly café is also here, half a mile off the road. To get there I dismount the unicycle twice to walk across cattle guards. An old tin covered building sits abandoned across the street. This is all of Ingomar.

Amy is waiting inside the café. She's got a book along and is looking forward to an afternoon of unaccustomed solitude. For the rest of the afternoon she will be driving ahead in ten-mile stretches to provide my water breaks. The next forty miles to Forsyth offer nothing but an abandoned town and a couple of ranch homes.

"Order the beans," Skip had told me as we had driven past the Jersey Lilly on our way back to Musselshell. "They're the best ones you can find in this country."

"You've eaten here?" I had asked.

"Oh, yeah, people drive from Colstrip to eat here."

That's an eighty-mile drive. If you're ready to drive this distance for good beans, you may be ready for eastern Montana.

Three cowboys are sitting at the table next to Amy, talking with her. One of them is youngish, another middle-aged, the third a bit older. They all have their cowboy hats on, big ones. One of them wears leather chaps, too. So, I think, "At last, the real Montana."

When I join the conversation, I learn they are from Missouri, "…here for a week of playing cowboy.

"We've been coming here the last three years. We trailer our horses out and help the ranchers."

"Did you ride yesterday?" I ask, wondering about their experience with the wind.

"No, even folks around here said that wind was strong for these parts."

Our waitress, Patti interjects, "It was windy. It got to seventy-seven miles an hour gusting to ninety yesterday."

"Order the beans," the oldest of the three says, "if you're up for a recommendation. And you might also try the Sheepherder's hors d'oeuvre."

Neither he nor Patti will tell us what the Sheepherder's hors d'oeurve are, but for one dollar we order them. Back in Ryegate the bar had advertised the Testical Festival, and I have heard people arguing the merits of bulls' balls or pigs' as we cross the state. For just the dollar price of this hors d'oeurve, I'm hopeful that neither bull nor boar is part of the ingredients. As we wait, I realize I'm a long way from home.

"I hear you're a pastor," the middle-aged cowboy says as we wait.

When I confirm this, he continues, mixing reverence into his heavy Missouri accent, "That's why I come back every year, to be here in the middle of creation. We get out in places that hardly anybody, maybe nobody, has ever been before. When you first get here, you think there's nothing, and then after awhile you realize that everything is right here."

A desert father of the early Christian church couldn't have said it better. Here I am forty miles from anything resembling a church, and I find myself knee-deep in holy ground.

The beans do come, and they are great. A whole pot of them is set on the table for Amy and me to share. The Sheepherder's Surprise is fine, too, nothing to worry about.

Our Missouri cowboys teach us about Montana while we eat. A section of land is a mile square, 640 acres. It takes eighty sections here for a family to make a living raising cattle. A single cow takes fourteen or more acres, depending on whether Amy or I heard right. Land sells for something like seventy-five dollars an acre.

"That seems cheap," we are told, "but when you figure how many acres it takes for a cow, that's a lot of money."

One of the larger ranches in the area is four hundred sections. That would be a ranch ten miles wide and as long as the forty-mile distance I'll be riding to Forsyth this afternoon.

This is a long, long way from the Los Angeles suburb of my growing up. Patti, though, is right at home. "We sold our ranch in the eighties and moved to Ingomar until we could figure out where we wanted to live. Still here. It's a nice place, don't you think?"

I do. I really do.

Late starts make for late days. By the time I get out of Ingomar, it is after three. Amy does ten-mile breaks for me along the way: fruit, water, energy bars. Two of the rests are in wide-open country. One is at Vananda, which is now abandoned. The old brick schoolhouse is still standing, visible five miles before I get there.

"This is great," Amy said. "I've gotten a walk, a chance to read, some time to meditate, and a nap." For Anne and Amy, keeping the ride and our families on the road is full-time work.

Toward the end of the day I see a horse and rider atop a butte in the distance. I would have missed this if I'd ridden twenty-four hours yesterday. Perfectly still, the rider appears to be surveying the ranch below. Whatever he or she is doing brings to mind images of times gone by, times when Vananda was still thriving. As I come closer, I wave, but I see no response. Passing below the butte, the horse and rider suddenly become an inch thick, a two-dimensional steel sculpture fixed in place.

Fooled by a statue, I laugh at myself and finish the last ten miles through this holy land. The weather is cold again, but in Forsyth I end the ride with a milkshake. It's eight o'clock. Amy puts the heater on high and drives us home to the crowd.

These last two days hold another story, waiting only for us to name it. It might have been fun to ride for twenty-four hours straight, to conquer another goal. Instead the post-storm pieces have been filled with surprises and an earthy holiness.

At the very beginning of *The Adventures of Huckleberry Finn*, the widow Douglass offered to adopt Huck and "sivilize" him, to conquer his open attitude with the manners, customs, and morals of the day. Even dinnertime was a symbol of the predictability she sought, but Huckleberry resisted it.

> *you had to wait for the widow to tuck down her head and grumble a little over the victuals, though there warn't really anything the matter with them. That is, nothing only everything was cooked by itself. In a barrel of odds and ends it is different; things get mixed up, and the juice kind of swaps around, and the things go better.*

A barrel of odds and ends. The farther we travel on this trip the less we pray for performance, civility, and predictability; the more we look for the story of the road, the people and places that get mixed up together and which are the treasure of this journey.

Group Ride. At seven the next morning, Skip is driving us back to Forsyth with a big crew. Grandma Barb is watching the younger kids so Anne and Amy can ride along with us for the last miles left on our journey to Colstrip. KariAnna has decided to join us with her bicycle.

"It's thirty-six miles, a long way," I'd told her last night.

"I don't care; I can do it. I'm going to ride with you."

Sara Okleasik is also along with us. Yesterday she flew in to nearby Billings, and now she will be joining us for the next three weeks. Sara is from Nome. She is Inupiat Eskimo, and riding with us is her way of helping out the endowment fund this summer. When we had asked if she was interested in riding she responded, "Maybe this is an answer to prayer."

In Forsyth, we meet with both the newspaper and radio reporters. Sara gets a chance to add her voice to the Seward Peninsula story. Then we ride. After two miles we stop and shed jackets by a roadside spring.

"Best water around," Skip assures us. "It's tested every month." At roadside springs all over this state, people fill containers with fresh sweet water.

The day turns out to be one of the slower trips that Robert and I have made. We stop every two miles for water or chocolate. After five miles the frontage road turns onto Highway 39 heading south. A rumble strip on the wide shoulder warns motorists who drift too far to the right. KariAnna bumps her bike along the strip, singing out a loud and happy vibrato.

Our little girl makes thirteen and a half miles on her pink play-bike. I have begun thinking maybe she really will ride the whole way when finally she announces,

"Daddy, I'm tired of riding." At the next pullout we stop for another break.

"I'm dead tired," she says with emphasis on dead.

What a day it is for Anne and me to ride this distance with our daughter who is so quickly growing older and stronger. While we're resting, Skip drives back to check on us. We load KariAnna's bike in the back of the truck, and Skip drives her home.

"How was she?" I ask when we return to Colstrip.

"With the warm sun shining, she fell right to sleep in the cab."

Inside the house, I listen while Anne asks Sara how she's feeling after the ride. She is downing two pain pills.

"I wanted to see if I could still do it," Sara answers. "And I did." Sara has rheumatoid arthritis [RA]. Her joints were stiffening up as we rode today, but she kept moving along.

"There's a lot of grieving with this illness," she says quietly.

I can't even imagine it. My knees had been a touch sore yesterday from riding eighty miles, but today they are fine again. When Sara had first gotten RA she could barely move. She explains, "One time I had to open a door by myself. I couldn't move my arm. I couldn't even turn the knob. It took me fifteen minutes to get that door open. I was crying and my whole body was shaking just to get a door open.

"Mornings were the worst," she continues, "I used to dread going to bed because I knew I would have to wake up. But I kept going to school. If I just got through the mornings then the rest of the day was less painful."

We are sitting and talking at the kitchen table. Sara has been a good friend since we first met in Nome, always an inspiring person, but the challenges of these last few years have pushed her to her limit.

"Med's have helped and mostly now I get through the days without too much pain. RA is really hard until you accept it, but then when you do, you can move on, make some goals, and it's okay. So much depends on how you deal with it in your head. There are some people on the Seward Peninsula who have RA. Some of them are elders. They keep telling me, 'Sara. Keep moving. Keep moving.'"

On the next day, Robert and I get a chance to stop moving, our first rest day since Helena. After a late breakfast, Skip offers us all a tour of the Colstrip mine. He and Barb moved here in 1969, two years after the strip-mining began. Skip has been working ever since.

Eighteen miles by ten miles in size, the mine is bigger than the San Fernando Valley of a million people where I grew up. There are three draglines working to expose the coal. Some goes straight to the power plant, and the rest is shipped by railroad. After the coal is extracted, the land is filled back in. Topsoil, which is removed and stored before excavation begins, is layered back on top and the land is replanted so that ranching can be resumed. The company has won awards for their reclamation efforts. On our tour we see cattle and antelope grazing on the reclaimed land.

Mine it. Ship it. Use it. This is the energy intensive world of today. These days I pedal with just my legs for power, burning carbohydrates, fat, and proteins for my fuel. Traveling alongside of this simplicity, though, is old Harvey, sucking gas, a constant reminder of our energy dependence. Dig, Skip, dig, until we find new ways of living.

Lately I've been humming "Home on the Range."

> "Oh, give me a home,
> Where the buffalo roam,
> And the deer and the antelope play,
> Where seldom is heard a discouraging word,
> And the skies are not cloudy all day."

So far, we are scoring three out of five on the lines of this song

• Our homes are still rolling dependably along ahead of the unicycle

- Deer and antelope still play. We ride for miles and miles, seeing them close by or along the skylines. Sometimes they are alone. Sometimes we see them in groups of a dozen or more. Too often they are road kill.
- The skies are not cloudy all day. We've had just two days with rain and two short stretches with snowflakes.

Of the other two lines, the buffalo no longer roam, and the discouraging word is "decline." Decline is the consistent word out here in rural America. From way back in Wilbur, Washington, through every single small town, we've heard the same story of declining population and shrinking opportunities.

Wilbur had a population of 1,800 until the sawmill closed. Now there are 1,200 in town, with one hundred students in the schools. More teacher cuts are threatened as enrollment slowly dwindles. As Roger had said, "When kids grow up they leave for college or the university. They never return, except to visit."

Clark Fork, Idaho. Signs announced two gas stations as we rode in. We went to the second one for a snack. Mistake. It was boarded up.

Lennep, Montana, where we stayed with Kate and Nick: three houses, four students in the school. Kate is excited, because fifteen miles up the road the neighboring town has reopened its grocery. "I try and give them as much business as possible, hoping they'll make it."

Vananda, Montana. We'd picked it as an overnight on our route and ended up riding through. Abandoned.

Author Wendell Berry writes of what we've seen: "We are at present completing the economic destruction of our rural and agricultural communities...As the nation has prospered, the country has declined."

I try to imagine what it will be like for KariAnna or Kai to bike this same route in the coming decades. We've had a few forty-mile stretches between any habitations. Decades ago the towns were at twenty-mile intervals. Perhaps there will be eighty-mile stretches in the future as Ingomar, Meltown, and others work through their issues of survival.

13
Eastern Montana

There are those who would misteach us that to stick in a rut is consistency—
and a virtue; and that to climb out of the rut is inconsistency—and a vice.

MARK TWAIN

My unicycle pitches me off when I try leaving Colstrip on Sunday morning. I check it, but nothing seems wrong. Getting on I pedal twice and am thrown off again. Five houses away from Skip and Barb's home, I turn around and walk back to their garage.

"What are the chances," I ask myself. A broken unicycle could have taken up a whole day if it happened anywhere else. We've just finished riding through hundreds of miles of Montana; throughout much of it I was alone and out of cell phone range. Today, as chance or whatever would have it, I'm just a two-minute walk from Skip's well-stocked garage.

I am long past believing that prayers assure outcomes. There are too many competing interests, otherwise my prayers would have prevented the war in Afghanistan. Too many situations defy assurance. Yet, on this trip, every single thing we've needed has fallen into place. Whatever the chances, I am constantly thankful. We inspect the unicycle and find a broken bearing. Our 5 a.m. start is delayed until 6:30.

On our journey so far, we have traveled through Makah land, the twelve tribes of the Colville Reservation, and the Flathead Reservation. This morning we are riding through red rock country towards Lame Deer and the Northern Cheyenne Indian Reservation. At one point, six deer line out and bound along parallel to us, jumping gracefully over a fence and looking for all the world like they're training to be Santa's reindeer.

General Custer's monument is located just before we reach Lame Deer. His "Last Stand," the Battle of the Little Big Horn, took place here at Greasy Grass on June 25, 1876. Robert remembers coming here on school field trips. Even the Cheyenne students in his class had to come along and honor

Custer, the great American hero. In reality, over ten thousand Indians won the Battle of the Little Big Horn. Still, they lost the war to save the buffalo and save their lands. The ones who win the wars write the histories. Today the monument also honors the Indians who were at the battle. Finally.

The journey has been tough for the Northern Cheyenne, including slaughters at Sand Creek (1864), Washita (1868), and Summit Springs (1869.) Shipped to reservation life in Oklahoma, some escaped to return north. Many ended up as prisoners at Fort Robinson, Nebraska. Of those, many were killed trying to escape the fort in 1879. In 1890, the survivors were finally granted the Northern Cheyenne Indian Reservation, whose size is the same as the forty-square-mile ranch we'd heard about back at the Jersey Lilly Café. Hemmed in, and with the buffalo gone, this harsh and bitter land offered little hope for survival. Against all natural and political odds, the Northern Cheyenne are still here.

We ride into Lame Deer and stop at the corner store; our awareness of history is growing each day on our trip. The generous receptions are stark contrast to the histories that we learn each time we ride through reservation land. Folks greet us everywhere, inquire about our destination, and give heartfelt wishes for luck.

The owner of the little corner market, Ione, signs my Guinness World Record while we stop for chocolate milk. When we're back on the road, Deith, Carol and Amy cycle ahead. Robert and I ride side by side as we're used to doing.

"How did it feel going through Lame Deer this time?" I ask. Robert has told me lots of stories before our Colstrip arrival. When he worked at a tire shop in his youth, he learned where they kept the tires for white people, and the tires for Indians.

"This was the best experience I ever had here. I grew up believing there's nothing good in Lame Deer."

I tell Robert how the broken bearing got me thinking about the chances of our ride going so well.

"Riding through the reservation sure blows the prayer guarantee to bits and pieces. It hasn't worked for the Cheyenne, unless you think just the Christian prayers of the conquerors count."

"Shit happens," Robert says.

I laugh in affirmation. When I was in seminary, I saw bumper stickers with these words. I was, after all, studying in Berkeley. It was there I realized that theology, the study of God, starts with that bumper sticker: Shit Happens. Robert and I have talked about this since he shared his apprehension about riding with a pastor. It has become our theological shorthand for this ride. Over and over again we've met people who have suffered the fate that the bumper sticker implies and have good reason for bitterness, hopelessness, and vengeance. Yet in so many people, like Tim back at the Colville Museum, we've seen compassion win out.

This is why I love Huckleberry Finn. Talk about shit happening! His father locks him in an isolated cabin, chases him drunkenly with a knife and then locks Huck in alone while he leaves for days at a time in pursuit of more whiskey. Huck's experience is a lot like Jesus' forty-day trek in the wilderness. Their responses are about the same, as well. Jesus chooses compassion, healing and teaching even at the cost of persecution. When Huck escapes, he chooses to befriend the runaway slave, Jim, despite the risks involved.

In one episode, Jim and Huck narrowly escape murderers by leaving them behind on a sternwheeler that is sinking in the middle of the Mississippi. Almost immediately after their escape, Huck becomes concerned for their predicament.

> *Now was the first time I begun to worry about the men — I reckon I hadn't had time to before. I begun to think how dreadful it was, even for murderers, to be in such a fix. I says to myself, there ain't no telling but I might come to be a murderer myself, yet, and then how would I like it?*

That's compassion.

On the unicycle we go slowly through this land, getting a view of the uncertainties, the unknown, the possibilities and the damage. The view could make us cynical or hopeless. Instead we are riding with greater care and sensitivity as we get deeper into our land. I hope it is transforming us toward Huck's kind of concern for others.

We crest a seven-mile grade on the way to Ashland. For the twentieth time since the Continental Divide, Robert announces, "It's all downhill from here."

In town, people are out waving and cheering. "We heard you on the radio!" they shout. Barbara at Ashland Mercantile gives us a case of soda for lunch. Folks at the bar wobble outside and ask me for my autograph. We give them posters and take their well wishes.

Amy takes over driving after lunch, and Sara gets her bike out to join Robert and me for the next stretch. There are forty miles ahead of us to Broadus. The land is continuing to open up more and more. We're riding on Highway 212, a shortcut for trucks between Interstates 90 and 94. No one would call the road crowded, but folks are blazing by at high speed. All through Montana, roadside crosses mark where motorists have died.

We keep our eyes on our rearview mirrors, thankful when the shoulder is wide. Most vehicles cross over and pass us on the far side of the road. One truck that comes close actually blows me off the front of the unicycle for the first time on the ride. I hang onto the handlebars and run a few steps before I can stop.

Reaching Broadus, we find it has a blinking red stop light in town, the first one since Helena a week ago. We arrive at the Lutheran church after worship but in time for the potluck. They have evening worship here because they have no pastor right now. Paul, the visiting pastor, drives here from his parish in Gillette, Wyoming, a hundred miles away. This Sunday he has announced that he is accepting a new call to a church in St. Louis, Missouri. Broadus feels lucky, though, an old rancher tells me, "We've got a seminary intern for the coming year. "

Later, this rancher gives us a tour of his church and declares, "Survival. That's our biggest priority these days. Survival."

I haven't counted, but it feels as though half and maybe more of the small town Lutheran churches we've come across on this trip are looking for pastors. Seminaries are graduating far fewer than half of the pastors who are needed each year so the shortage of just a few years becomes more and more critical, especially in these small rural congregations. We've had many an invitation to come back and minister after the ride is over.

From Broadus to Alzada is sixty miles. Two towns are marked on the map. Hammond has a one-room schoolhouse and a post office serving the surrounding area. Boyes has only a post office. It is Memorial Day. Both towns are deserted, more rural atrophy in this wide-open land. Seeing long distances ahead makes the miles feel longer. We ride almost fifty miles before the motor homes catch up to us with lunch. We're all three out of water and snacks by then. The lunch burritos go down in a hurry, and then we break for a short nap.

"Let's sneak out, Kai," I prod him. Amy and Robert are still napping, and Kai has been begging to ride his bicycle. The shoulder here is wide, and the traffic is light. He grins as we get his bike ready for the sneak-away. Both Robert and Amy wake up in time, though, and when we get Kai all set for his big ride, we head off down the road together.

"Watch the white line, Kai. That's the only rule." He carries his shoulders proudly, and is smiling like a big-time biker.

"Listen for the cars and trucks." I add.

He nods. A mile and a half up the road, Anne is waiting. There's road construction and no more shoulder. Kai isn't ready to stop, but he is beaming after his first bike tour on the open road. As we load his bike, we agree to meet in Alzada.

"Must be the suburbs," Robert remarks as we approach scattered dwellings. The mileage is right for Alzada, though, and we find it consists of the Stoneville Saloon followed a half mile later by the Cenex gas station. In the gravel parking lot next to the saloon, Anne already has Harvey's awning rolled down.

"This is it," she says, showing off our campground with a sideways smile.

"Cheap Drinks. Lousy Food." is painted on the saloon's front. I walk past four Harleys and go inside for a signature on my ride slip. I pass lots of tattoos, leather and liquor. Signs here cover the walls.

"Customers are always first, but the bartender decides who is a customer."

"Showers are three dollars. Pay the bartender first."

Diane, the heavily tattooed bartender, signs my paper; the three men at the bar ask what I'm doing.

"Lots of climbing on the road to Hulet," they advise. "You'd be better off going to Belle Fourche." Everywhere we go, we're told about someone's big hill, big grade, or big mountain.

The kids are watching peacocks when I come back outside. We sit awhile, looking at the kids, looking at the birds, looking at the barren gravel parking lot. We sit some more. We look some more. Forty miles south of here is Devil's Tower National Monument, the reason we're making our jog south at this point. We look at the gravel some more.

"How about we go to Devil's Tower?" I suggest.

Without discussion, we immediately begin re-packing. Fifteen minutes later we're driving the forty-mile trip into Wyoming and to Devil's Tower. Someone will drive Robert and me back in the morning to continue pedaling. This is Black Hills country now, and the ranches are spread out over hills and rock outcroppings, so different from the flat Alzada we've just left behind.

Devil's Tower, a huge thumb of rock, is visible from a dozen miles away. It's the cooled magma from inside a volcano, all that's left behind after eons of erosion. According to Indian legend, the mountain was shaped by a bear scratching to get to the maiden on top of the tower. The kids spend the evening looking at the tower, asking questions about volcanoes and letting their imaginations work on the project. Nathaniel decides that there are jewels in it, and he wants to go digging for them.

14
Black Hills

There are many humorous things in the world; among them,
the white man's notion that he is less savage than the other savages.

MARK TWAIN

Wyoming

A t ten miles an hour, it is easy to study roadside markers. The first of them on Wyoming 112 is the marker for Camp Devin, just south of Alzada. It explains that the camp existed for just two months in the late 1800s while the military completed telegraph communications linking Montana, Wyoming and the Dakotas. This sign also announces that we are entering the Black Hills. In 1868, the Fort Laramie treaty guaranteed these hills to the Sioux people "for as long as the grass shall grow and the rivers shall run." However, the ensuing gold rush brought in the military, too, and a new treaty was drawn that removed the Sioux from their sacred lands to places far away. It's a sad sign to read on the day after Memorial Day.

The next morning, pedaling down a last steep hill into Sundance, I see what is beginning to seem like an endangered species—another bicyclist is riding towards me. The cyclist starts walking uphill just before I catch him. I see his old face and turn across the road to introduce myself. After a few questions about my unicycle, he starts telling me about himself.

"I've been biking for twenty years, since I retired."

I ask if he was born in Sundance. "No, but I've been here for seventy years." He barely looks seventy, so I figure his parents arrived when he was one or two, but no…

"I came out when I was twenty. I came here from Pennsylvania; I rode a motorcycle." That would have been 1932, during the Great Depression.

He is wearing an electrician's cap. I point to his brim. "Is that what you did for a living before you retired?"

"No, they just give these caps away free here. I ranched until I was 44, and then I worked for the park service after that."

We talk a while longer.

"How many miles are on your tire?" he asks.

"Seventeen hundred so far."

"I've got six thousand on my back tire," he lets me know. "People say biking is only good for the legs. It's good for the whole body. Keeps my belly from growing out too far."

When I ask where we should eat breakfast, he speaks well of all the restaurants in town.

"You've made my day," I tell him as he gets ready to resume his ride.

Robert and Amy are waiting at the bottom of the hill.

"Maybe you should get off and walk." Robert tells me, pointing ahead of us.

Earlier in the morning, we had passed a herd of Black Angus in their pasture and caused them to stampede. Now, we have just caught up to a cattle drive. A total of eight cowboys, cowgirls and cowkids are moving some hundreds of Herefords up the highway to a new pasture. Bawling cows block cars in both directions.

When the two cowboys riding point get to us, they say we can ride through, and we start pedaling. Despite the concerned looks of the cattle, they stay in file. A moment later we cross under Interstate 90 and arrive in Sundance, stopping for one of the recommended breakfasts.

Sundance is named after the mountain it backs up to. Sioux Sun Dances used to be held here. The Sundance Kid took his name from this place after spending eighteen months in jail and then hooked up with Butch Cassidy. The town wears this distinction with a romantic pride that is difficult for outsiders to understand. The Wild West was brutal, and so much of its history is only a hundred years old. That picture grows clearer with each passing mile of our journey.

Sara has driven into town to meet us. She switches with Amy, who drives the Honda back to camp. The hills were steep and long on Highway 14. After breakfast, the road gentles out on Highway 585, but the temperature starts rising quickly.

"My Eskimo blood isn't made for this," Sara says, laughing as she pedals up a rise. We're enjoying riding and remembering her work at the recreation center in Nome. She catches me up on the physical therapy degree she's working on in Oregon.

This is Sara's first time in this part of the USA. "The open country here reminds me of Nome," she tells Robert and me. Nome lies just below the Arctic Circle and has no trees; the biggest plants are willow and alder bushes.

The tailwind today exactly matches our speed, making the air feel even hotter as we pedal. We keep applying sunscreen. Above four thousand feet, we fry quickly.

"Here comes One Wheel," Robert calls out to us. Amy has driven back and helped Anne pack everything together, make breakfast for the kids, hitch the Honda behind Harvey and get everyone on the road. Whenever it's close to lunchtime our eyes are always peeled for when the motor home and camper van will catch up with us. They pull off the road up ahead, chain out our dogs, get food ready, and let the kids tumble out to start jumping and greeting our arrival.

Steam is rising from the engine compartment. Robert and I check things over but can't find a leak.

"Maybe it's just the hot day."

We make sure it's full of water and agree to check it later.

In the afternoon we ride through Four Corners. Once this was a major intersection. These days it's a T-junction; only three corners remain. Later we pass Salt Creek, where entrepreneurs used to gather 35,000 pounds of salt a day, most of it used for refining gold. Newcastle is the end of our day; like its namesake in England, it was once a coal mining center. We covered seventy-five miles through the Black Hills. Today, May 29, is exactly a month since we started pedaling from Neah Bay.

South Dakota

When we start out the next morning, we have only thirty-eight miles to reach Custer, South Dakota. After ten miles we reach the South Dakota state line. Our seventh state greets us at the border with the most highly refined road of our trip. We ride on brand new concrete that has all the feel of an interstate. Fifteen miles into the state, we pass a warning sign, and in the blink of an eye Highway 16 turns from the best to the worst road of our travels, winding its way past Jewel Cave National Monument in twenty-five-mile-per-hour curves and sharp grades. There is zero shoulder and more traffic than we are used to after all our Montana miles. I wave two trucks past me and manage to ride in the gravel at the side of the road to give them room, all the while ready to jump off if necessary. Later the road widens out again in new concrete. We pedal the last miles into Custer with a crosswind coming from behind us. This is the best wind, helping to cool us and speeding us on our way.

Custer is the central tourist town of the Black Hills. Named after General George Armstrong Custer, it is the site of one of his camps during his 1874 expedition of one thousand men, one hundred and ten wagons, and hundreds of horses and mules. Today, for miles before we hit town, campgrounds line the highway. We have gained one thousand feet climbing from Newcastle to Custer's elevation of 5303 feet. Even here, at mile-high elevation, the temperature is almost ninety in the mid-afternoon.

Back on that first fine section of South Dakota road, we had stopped at the U.S. Forest Service interpretive sign as we entered Black Hills National Forest. There's a quotation there from 1907 when Gifford Pinchot was the director of the National Forest Service. His words report, "this land is designated for multiple use. Each individual may have to give a little, but the result is a great benefit for everyone."

This road sign carries just the barest mention of the Sioux; no admission that all these hills, this land, once belonged to them. The loss and benefit to them is not figured in with Pinchot's statement.

In *Travels With Charley*, John Steinbeck wrote about being an "avid reader of signs," noting that the shorter and less dramatic the history of a state, the more signs it seemed to have. "I find this interesting," he wrote, "but it does make for suspicion of history as a record of reality...how the myth wipes out the fact."

How myth wipes out fact.

I find it all ironic. The Fort Laramie treaty guaranteeing these lands to the Sioux was signed in 1868. Chief Red Cloud achieved this agreement by defeating the U.S. Army in its treaty-breaking efforts to open the Bozeman Trail. All of western South Dakota and large parts of Montana and Wyoming are included in this treaty. By 1874, the Fort Laramie treaty was already being broken and the Sioux were being banished from their traditional homelands after Custer's expedition and the ensuing gold rush. Just two decades later, in 1897, these lands were declared a Forest Preserve by President Grover Cleveland to protect against fires, wasteful lumbering practices and timber fraud. The land, which had lasted thousands and thousands of years, was being destroyed in a matter of a few decades. It's enough to make a person think the land should have been left to the Sioux people.

This thought forced its way into my thoughts and stayed with me until Custer. How much of it was grief and how much was anger, I don't know, but some mixture of emotions makes me feel deeply the wrongfulness of what has been done here. I know that I am getting just the barest taste of this bitter pill. Many Native Americans have lived their entire lives in the shadow of these injustices. The ones who amaze and inspire me are those who have suffered these losses yet somehow find a way to harness hope and grace as they work for the sake of their communities. Somehow they manage to stay above despair. The challenge became clear to me from our own experience in Nome. Near the end of our time there, sitting together at the kitchen table, Anne had asked me, "Are you okay? Your eyes are far away from here."

"I'm not okay," I finally answered, "and I'm not getting better."

On call for twenty-four-hours a day, the burials and crises at last over-whelmed the laughter and energy of daily life in Alaska: of rejuvenating tea sipped in human presence, of winter's skis and dogsleds and summer's fish camps beneath the sky of nature's healing hand. By the time of Anne's inquiry, I had nothing left to give.

Sometimes an empty space like that can turn into sacred space. I came to understand that even if I made no difference, Nome was an appropriate place to try and be faithful. As big a revelation as this was to me, I could not deny that my sails were empty. The trade winds had brought me far from the safe harbor of Mark Twain's description, but I was drowning.

A week after Anne's inquiry, she said simply, "Okay, we'll go."

I had hoped to last in Nome at least ten years, long enough to live into the patterns of the place, and hopefully to be of some discernible use. We left after three-and-a-half years.

Today another inspiration is in store for us. After we pedal the last miles into Custer and set up our campsite, we pile into the VW and drive the four miles to the Crazy Horse monument and museum. In 1939, when Sculptor Korczak Ziolkowski was assisting Gutzon Borglum on the Mt. Rushmore carving, Chief Henry Standing Bear asked him to carve a monument so that "the white man will know that the red man has great heroes, too."

Once Korczak accepted the project, it became his life work, "to right a lit-tle bit of the wrongs that have been done to these people." Today his wife and seven of their ten children are carrying on the leadership of the proj-ect. Fifty-four years into the project, the face of Crazy Horse has been com-pleted. It was unveiled in 1998 for the fiftieth anniversary of the project. When the sculpture is completed, it will be the biggest in the world, 570 feet tall, bigger even than the pyramids. Just the head of Crazy Horse alone is bigger than the entire Mt. Rushmore monument.

In the monument, Crazy Horse is riding his horse, emerging from the mountain with his arm outstretched, pointing as he answers the question of where his lands are, "My lands are where my dead lie buried."

Crazy Horse lived at the time of the Oregon Trail, the building of forts on Sioux land, and the destruction of the buffalo. His father was a medicine man, and Crazy Horse was himself a contemplative and deeply spiritual person. He was also a great warrior who fought and won battle after battle, a leader with incredible charisma. In 1877, he arrived voluntarily to speak with the army commander at Fort Robinson. When he realized he was being led to the fort jail, he tried to escape, but a soldier's bayonet through his back killed him. He was only in his thirties. Almost two thousand years earlier, another charismatic leader, also in his third decade, was crucified in his quest for justice and peace.

"When the legends die," Korczak said as he carved into the stone mountain, "the dreams end, and when the dreams die, there is no more greatness." Before his own death, he told his wife and children that it doesn't matter how long it takes to carve Crazy Horse, just as long as the work continues.

In the morning we pedal south from Custer on the George Mickelsen Trail. An old railroad track covered with limestone, it stretches 114 miles through the Black Hills. Part of the national "Rails to Trails" project, more and more abandoned railroads are being converted to cycling routes. We ride forty gentle, secluded miles on the track as we ride towards Hot Springs. Back when we were planning this trip, we included Hot Springs on our route, hoping that its name is descriptive of local opportunities. In fact we do find a creek where the water is warm. The kids are soon naked, splashing through the water and getting sunburned. We spend the rest of the day here.

The ride seems to be working well for everyone at this point. KariAnna has told us a number of variations of her goal. In one version she is married with a son and a daughter and is riding across the country on a unicycle.

"I'll do the riding and the cooking," she tells us.

In another version she's not married, but she's still riding her unicycle across the country. I offer to drive the support vehicle for her.

Three-year-old Caroline is caught up in the ride, too. She knows our destination, and she's ready to tell anyone and everyone, "Weuw going to the Statue of Libowtee."

Day by day, we're getting closer. Our total trip mileage is nearing two thousand. Tonight we park Harvey and the VW in a grocery store parking lot. The kids can barely stay awake until it's dark.

15
First Corn and First Peoples

Knowledge of Indians and humanity are seldom found in the same individual.

MARK TWAIN

Nebraska

Chadron is next on our route allowing us to dip down and get a few miles of riding in Nebraska, our eighth state. We're covering all the northern states just in case things keep working out for a fifty-state attempt. Immanuel Lutheran Church in Chadron has been offering encouragement to us for months.

The weather is already warm as Robert and I start from Hot Springs at 4:30 on Saturday morning. Ten miles out we leave the Black Hills behind and look out on endless plains ahead of us. At mile twenty-three we reach Olerich, a town of some fifty homes. The water tower has been visible from miles away, but we find no café for breakfast. A woman named Carla sees us from her garage door, and we stop to ask for a signature and guidance. She tells us she has grown up in the area and done both ranching and farming. When she and her husband got "too old to farm anymore," they came to town.

"We're mostly retired folks here. There's no restaurant in town. Just a store that's slowly going out of business, a gas station and a bar." Then she adds, "There used to be a lot more here. We used to have a barber shop and everything a little town would need. Now everyone drives to Hot Springs or Chadron. On weekdays, this town empties out. Everyone young enough to work drives away to jobs."

We ride four blocks on dirt streets and find a store. The owner is friendly and large. The selection is tiny. We find donuts, bananas, M&Ms and old-style tin of V8 Juice on aisle shelves that are mostly bare. Munching the donuts on a bench outside the store, Amy inspects the "sell by" date on the package. It reads May 3, the day that we arrived in Chelan, Washington, almost a month earlier. It takes the whole can of V8 juice to wash them down.

A dozen miles up the road, at a roadside rest, we read about Buffalo Gap National Grasslands. Ranchers settled this land in the late 1800s and early 1900s, but the living was sparse, hard on both land and people. When the depression hit in the 1930s, over two million people ended up leaving this land that couldn't support their efforts. Much of it had been seriously eroded in its few years service as farmland. To help out the farmers and ranchers, the government offered to purchase the land, which ultimately became these National Grasslands. Millions of buffalo lived here for thousands of years, yet it couldn't support even a few decades of farming. This mythic Wild West is showing more of its brutality and transience.

A strong headwind whips up and turns Chadron into a difficult goal. Arriving at last, we meet our hosts, Carlene and her granddaughter Sarah, at the parking lot of Wal-Mart, the first one we've seen since way back in Helena, Montana. They show us the way to Chadron State Park where we'll be staying. The entrance sign tells how this land was the site of fierce fights, first when the Plains Indians were dispossessed of it, and then later between ranchers and farmers. Today it's a state park with electrical hookups and the welcome relief of a swimming pool.

Pastor Chris has invited me to preach on Sunday morning. *Change* is the subject on my mind. This land can look timeless at seventy miles an hour— at ten mph, history races.

Lewis and Clark made their trip west in the summer of 1804. The fur museum here in Chadron reports that trapping lasted thirty years or so, beginning in the 1830s. A second generation brought the gold seekers. Ranchers and farmers began settling in the next generation. Native Americans were moved off their lands beginning in the 1850s. Then the droughts came, then the migrations to bigger cities began, and then the small towns began dying.

Each change has seen new "winners" and new "losers." Current winners seem to be the middle sized and larger cities that can attract businesses and chain stores for the people moving off the land. There are now so many generations of accumulated losses in this rapid-fire history that the most common theme would seem to be grief.

I preach about change and loss and grief during my sermon, sharing these wonderings with folks. Afterwards a woman from a family ranch comes to say her thanks: "Someone needed to say those words to us here." Tempted as we all are by the hopes of winning, it's difficult to imagine us binding ourselves together in the common denominator of grief. The story is here, though, written all over the West through which we've been traveling.

The winner for this day is Kai. He's been pulling his 16-inch unicycle off the rack once in awhile, giving it a try. Today, suddenly, he zips off and gets three revolutions.

"Really?" he beams when we shout the number out. "Yippee, we get ice cream!"

As with KariAnna, we're treating ourselves to celebration ice creams when the kids reach their unicycling goals. Kai's next goal is five pedals. We're just around the corner from having another unicyclist in the crew.

On Monday morning, Chris is up and ready to pedal the day with us, starting from Chadron at 4:30. Just east of town we see our first cornfield. We're now on the western edge of the Great Plains. The weather will start getting humid somewhere up ahead. Today we also reach the 2,000 mile point on our journey.

Our destination is the Pine Ridge Indian Reservation, back up in South Dakota. I've seen a few pieces on TV about Pine Ridge, the poorest county in the nation; everything I've heard has been dismal. I feel anxious as we ride closer. Cars drive carefully as they pass us. Most are full of adults and children. All of them are waving big friendly waves. Horns toot. We relax. It feels almost as if they're expecting us.

And then we see two people who really are expecting us. Charlie and Betty Downs from Michigan are driving to their granddaughter's high school graduation in Puyallup, Washington. They step out of their mini-van wearing purple "One Wheel" shirts they ordered before the ride began. After all the miles of following our own little map lines, it's a bright moment to end up sharing the same space here at the side of the road.

"Pine Ridge is just a few more miles," Betty tells us. "Can we have lunch together there?" We agree to meet at Big Bat's Texaco.

Just before Pine Ridge we ride through Whiteclay. This town is in Nebraska, just outside the southern border of the reservation. Its solitary purpose is to sell alcohol, millions of cans of beer each year. There are lots of people standing along the road. Some are sober, some are not. One pretends to push me over as I pass close, the rest are clapping and cheering. Then we're past Whiteclay, into South Dakota, riding the last two miles into Pine Ridge.

I remember that people often asked us about alcohol use in Nome and on the Seward Peninsula. It was always a complicated question to answer. I remember a time with a good friend from Nome.

"Seal oil?" my friend would ask, whenever I went to visit. Along with the oil, which had been rendered from seal blubber, Pilot Bread Crackers and dried salmon were always on the small kitchen table next to the window. In the summer, bright sunshine came in across the plastic tablecloth, checkered red and white. In the winter, icicles hung from the roof down over the windows.

"Sure," I'd answer, and we'd sit silently, or talk together about ancient things, the day's weather, church, or plans for a new hunting camp up the Nome River.

One Sunday night this strong and vibrant elder showed up noisily at our back door. He came in fast, snow falling from his boot soles onto the brown carpet of our living room; the alcohol on his breath unleashing the deep rage that he normally contained. Anne quickly gathered one-year-old KariAnna and took her to the back bedroom.

"Why?" he shouted at me, coming closer across the carpet. Each desperate cry echoed the breaks in the world that were cracking his life apart: tradition, faith, family, work, past, present, and future. Reaching my side he grabbed my arm, digging deep into my flesh with his nails, locking us eye-to-eye. "Why?"

It seemed a long time—this rage expressed in circular shouts and sobs—before at last he made a slow, spent, stumbling departure, heading back into the black night where the melted snow on his boots and clothes would quickly freeze.

"Is there alcohol in your community?" people asked of Anne and me when we lived in Nome.

Yes, alcohol is there—not as cause, but as the result of things gone desperately wrong, of lives and communities gone desperate.

The icicles hung long the next afternoon. The checkered table had Pilot Bread Crackers on it, a cup of steaming Lipton, and dried salmon,

"Seal oil?" he asked.

"Sure." I answered, taking a seat next to the frosted window.

✳

"Buffalo Burger?" Charlie asks when we get to Pine Ridge. We're in the cafeteria line at Big Bat's.

"Sure," I answer.

After our visit, Charlie and Betty drive on for Casper, Wyoming, and we stay at Big Bat's, waiting for our families. The woman who served lunch sits down with us. We find out that she has grown up here, is twenty-eight, has two children, and wants to talk. She and Sara strike a chord, so they spend the rest of the afternoon together.

"I mostly just listened," Sara tells me later. "She's dealt with a lot. But she has dreams. I hope she can make them happen."

Larry Petersen is our contact in Pine Ridge. He's a Lutheran pastor who has been here for ten years. He tells how he was advised by an elder, "If you're going to do this, you should stay for twenty years."

After nine years here, Larry still laughs all the time. He is welcoming to all of us as he explains, "From now until September, every day is going to be like this one. People will be coming and going all the time."

Just the thought of hosting so many people makes me tired. Larry seems to get a charge from it. He takes us downstairs where it's cooler and gives us a brief introduction. "A lot of people come here with expectations," he begins, "and that often causes frustration. I can't promise you how many people will be at your presentation tonight. People here don't make those kinds of commitments. Planning for what will happen a week from now is foreign to the traditional way of doing things here."

I don't know how similar or different things are at Pine Ridge compared to Nome, but this aspect of life, this "maybee," sounds very familiar. Larry tells me they have a word here that means the same thing, "doksha."

We get settled in our motor homes and get baths for the kids and showers for the adults. Larry even makes us sloppy joes for dinner after his daily afternoon session with the children. We hear laughter coming up from the basement. It's crowded with kids who've come to play table tennis, pool, board games, and to be with Larry and each other.

"That's the future," he says, pointing a free elbow downstairs toward the kids.

A few folks show up and visit with us. Three young girls stay for the presentation in the evening, and they tell us about the dancing they do, and the differences between traditional, fancy, and jingle dancing. Everyone's tired, so folks head to bed after the presentation.

"Thanks for the day," I say to Larry, wishing him a goodnight, intending to head out the door. Instead we end up talking for another hour.

"I don't know if I could go back to a 'regular' parish again. I feel like I belong in a place like this," he tells me. When I'm here, I never forget that life is a gift."

Our church talks a great deal about the grace of God, but for many, faith still comes across as a performance requirement. Larry is a treat. He laughs when I tell him about the bumper sticker Robert and I are using for our theological shorthand on this trip.

"Our schools are performance-based. Our work is performance-based. It's no wonder so many of us figure that God's main job is counting our good deeds."

"When people come here to do service projects," Larry explains, "I always insist on spending time with them first. If they don't understand they're receiving as big a blessing as they give—if all they believe is that they're going to go and fix things for someone else—they don't get to go."

"The things people can accomplish are amazing and great," he continues. "But what about people here who don't or can't have great accomplishments? That's where compassion comes in. And that kind of real sympathy has to be a response to knowing that life is a gift. Living here at Pine Ridge reminds me of it every day."

"I'm always thankful when I meet a person like you." I tell him.

Larry laughs yet again.

The next morning we ride fifty miles; Sara picks us up in the Honda and has us back in Pine Ridge before 11. We've agreed with Larry that we'll spend some time with the Bible School children.

The kids clap when I ride my unicycle down the aisle of the church where they are gathered. Sara is with me, and she answers questions about how cold it is in Alaska, informs them that she doesn't live in an igloo, and that she does like basketball. Larry was right when he predicted that spending time with a native person from Alaska would generate a lot of excitement.

"Alapah," she teaches them, "that's the word for cold." She's been teaching our kids a few words too along the way. They are running around these days, saying thank you—"Quyanna"—more often than before.

After lunch, we have the afternoon to visit more of the reservation. The heritage center is four miles out of town, and we head there first. There is artwork, historical clothing, books, and information here. We walk outside to the cemetery and see where Chief Red Cloud is buried. He is credited with winning a war against the U.S. Army, securing treaty rights covering all of the Black Hills and extending into the neighboring states.

Wounded Knee is a dozen miles out of Pine Ridge in the other direction. We drive there next and take ourselves back to a desperate time, the climactic month of December 1890.

Two days after Chief Sitting Bull was assassinated by Indian police on December 15, the *St. Louis Republic* editorialized his death,

> *The death of Sitting Bull removes one of the obstacles to civilization. He was a greasy savage, who rarely bathed and was liable at any time to become infected with vermin. During the whole of his life he entertained the remarkable delusion that he was a free-born American with*

some rights in the country of his ancestors… He will now make excel-
lent manure for the crops, which will grow over him when his reser-
vation is civilized.

A similar editorial in the *Aberdeen Saturday Pioneer* advocated genocide.
The writer was Frank Baum, who would later author *The Wizard of Oz*.

With his fall the nobility of the Redskin is extinguished, and what few
are left are a pack of whining curs who lick the hand that smites them.
The Whites, by law of conquest, by justice of civilization, are masters
of the American continent, and the best safety of the frontier settle-
ments will be secured by the total annihilation of the few remaining
Indians. Why not annihilation? Their glory has fled, their spirit bro-
ken, their manhood effaced; better that they die than live the miserable
wretches that they are.

Some speculate that newspaper writings like these helped to incite the
Wounded Knee massacre. Long-standing issues were also in abundance. In
December of 1890, even army officers and South Dakota legislators were
petitioning the U.S. Government to fulfill its treaty requirements. General
John Schoefield's telegram to Washington D.C. is representative; it was sent
on December 19, four days after Sitting Bull's assassination.

One point is of vital importance—the difficult Indian problem can not
be solved permanently at this end of the line. It requires the fulfillment
by Congress of the treaty obligations which the Indians were entreated
and coerced into signing. They signed away a valuable portion of their
reservation, and it is now occupied by white people, for which they
have received nothing. They understood that ample provision would be
made for their support; instead, their supplies have been reduced, and
much of the time they have been living on half and two-thirds rations.
Their crops, as well as the crops of the white people, for two years have
been almost a total failure. The disaffection is widespread, especially
among the Sioux, while the Cheyennes have been on the verge of star-
vation and were forced to commit depredations to sustain life. These
facts are beyond question, and the evidence is positive and sustained
by thousands of witnesses.

Today at Wounded Knee there is a tiny community of homes and families, the American Indian Movement Museum, and the simple site of the
massacre. Here, just ten days after General Schoefield's urgent appeal, some

three hundred Lakota people were slaughtered on December 29, 1890. Two-thirds of the massacred Lakotas were women and children. The report of American Horse, one of the survivors, was preserved in the 1896 report of the United States Bureau of Ethnology.

> *They turned their guns, Hotchkiss guns [breech-loading cannons that fired an explosive shell], etc., upon the women who were in the lodges standing there under a flag of truce, and of course as soon as they were fired upon they fled…There was a woman with an infant in her arms who was killed as she almost touched the flag of truce [which flew over the Lakota camp], and the woman and children of course were strewn all along the circular village until they were dispatched. Right near the flag of truce a mother was shot down with her infant; the child not knowing that its mother was dead was still nursing, and that especially was a very sad sight. The women as they were fleeing with their babes were killed together, shot right through, and the women who were very heavy with child were also killed…After most all of them had been killed a cry was made that all those who were not killed or wounded should come forth and they would be safe. Little boys who were not wounded came out of their places of refuge, and as soon as they came in sight a number of soldiers surrounded them and butchered them there…Of course it would have been all right if only the men had been killed; we would feel almost grateful for it. But the fact of the killing of the women, and more especially the killing of the young boys and girls who are to go to make up the future strength of the Indian people, is the saddest part of the whole affair and we feel it very sorely.*

An army photographer was along on the day of the massacre at Wounded Knee. Graphic pictures were taken after the killing. We view them at the site. The weather that day of the massacre was freezing cold. Bodies in the picture are shown frozen in contorted position. Wounded Knee ended with a mass burial.

Or, more precisely, it never ended. We've gotten just the barest taste of Pine Ridge. Real faces with the complexity of hope and despair have replaced one-sided memories from TV shows we've seen. The people live on despite the genocidal editorials and actions of the past. History and the present story mix in ways that are difficult to understand. We've seen another of the many spokes to this one wheel that we call the United States of America.

At the end of the day we are given a gift, a vision of hope and determination. Our last stop is the SuAnne Big Crow Boys and Girl's Club. A star basketball player, SuAnne once scored sixty-nine points in a game, the record for South Dakota women's high school basketball. She averaged over thirty-nine points a game, and she brought her team to the state championship. Along with basketball, she was a spokesperson for drug and alcohol-free living. At the end of her high school career in 1992, she fell asleep while driving on Interstate 90, and died in the accident.

Some time later SuAnn's mom, Chick, started a small recreation center in town where kids could come and play basketball and learn healthy lifestyles. After it was established, the Boys and Girls Club organization visited, and Pine Ridge was chosen to become the first site for developing a Boys and Girls Club.

We arrive the weekend following the new Boys and Girls Club dedication. Becka gives us a tour. Even the richest suburbs would boast of a center like this one. A six million dollar facility houses gyms, workout rooms and game rooms, plus a full-size competition swimming pool, and a restaurant called "Happy Town." Five full-time staff will work here, plus the pool staff and attendants and more. In this place where poverty is evident everywhere we turn, this club is stunning; nothing has been spared. Becka explains the complex mix of federal, state and private grants that have made the center possible. Coca-Cola, Nike, Tupperware and others were major contributors.

SuAnne's memorabilia occupies one room, and there we see a video of her life. In it is a clip of the end of the state championship game. With seconds left, the game is tied at forty. SuAnne takes the ball all the way down court to her basket. She misses the shot, gets her own rebound, and pumps the ball back up at the hoop. It drops in at the sound of the buzzer and the spectators erupt in cheers and hugs. Watching it, I get the shivers.

16
Double Century

Apparently there is nothing that cannot happen.

MARK TWAIN

"I'm freezing," Robert says every time we ride downhill into a low spot. We are on the road at 4:45 a.m., heading east from Martin. By 7 the day is warm. Sixty miles ahead is Mission; with no towns or services along the way, we pedal along patiently.

"I just zoned out," Robert says, somewhere around mile thirty; he is tired after a poor night's sleep.

"Me, too," I reply. "I was just thinking about whether we'll get a chance to try a twenty-four-hour ride again for the Guinness World Record—I doubt we're going to get another shot."

"Why not?"

"Well, we've got more evening presentations the farther east we go so we won't be able to ride through the night. Sara is going home on Sunday, so we won't have an extra driver. The roads are going to get more crowded, and the weather is going to get hotter. The chances are slipping fast."

We ride farther in the bright morning sun.

"I've started thinking about the other record that Guinness says they're interested in: How long a person can ride a unicycle without dismounting."

"How are you going to pee if you do that?"

We ride along a few more miles.

"Hey, why don't you try for the twenty-four-hour record today?"

"You think so? Everyone is back in Martin, getting the Honda fixed; that may take all day. We haven't talked to Anne and Amy." The Honda is having trouble with the steering. Yesterday it wasn't tracking right when we towed it to Wounded Knee. We have no idea why.

A few more miles.

"I guess we could just keep riding and see if things work out..." I offer.

"I'm up for it," Robert replies.

Maybee. It is intention tempered with all the unknowns that might interrupt the course of events.

On we ride. No big deal. No pressure. We're just pedaling, waiting to see what might happen. Rolling farm and ranch land keep the ride interesting. This grass is longer and deeper green than the gray-toned shortgrass of Montana and western Nebraska. There's a gentle crosswind coming up out of the south; it tails us very slightly from the west.

Eventually we get to the Rosebud Indian Reservation. We see Bureau of Indian Affairs housing on the ranches here, indicating that much of this ranch land is being cared for by native people. There seem to be many more native ranches here than on the Pine Ridge Reservation. Old pieces of roofing tin, spray-painted with names like Thunder Cloud, announce who lives on these dirt roads that trail back into the hills.

We make Mission at 11, sixty miles into our ride. We have been on the road six hours and fifteen minutes. The fastest hundred-mile unicycle ride was done in six hours and forty-seven minutes by a Japanese unicyclist in the 1980s. He averaged almost fifteen miles an hour. I can't keep my Coker going that fast. I am hoping that a Double Century, two hundred miles in twenty-four hours, will be enticing enough for Guinness to establish a new record category.

A few weeks earlier, on our Montana attempt at the twenty-four-hour ride, I'd envisioned the ride in reserve time. I average about ten miles an hour when I'm riding; so if we go the whole way, I'll be on the unicycle twenty of these twenty-four hours. That gives four hours of reserve time. When we reach Mission, I've got three hours and forty-five minutes of reserve left. It's an encouraging start.

Guinness Records asks that witnesses be noted officials or well-known people in the community. Two police cars are pulled up next to one another as we ride into Mission. Merlin gives us his signature and recommends the Antelope Motel and Restaurant where we meet Damien, our waiter.

"Sit here," he points, "or sit here. Which do you prefer?"

The place is full so Damien is pointing us to seats that share the table with other customers. We choose the ones closest to the buffet.

"Take good care of these two," he tells the cook who is serving the buffet line. Roast beef, sausage and kraut, and turkey are the choices for lunch.

"What would you like?" she asks.

"All of it," we reply in unison.

Several thousand calories later, we're back out on the road, our water bottles filled with cold ice tea thanks to Damien. It is noon on our watches.

The Rosebud Reservation uses Central Time, even though the actual line isn't for another twenty-five miles at the tiny settlement of Carter. We decide to stay on Mountain Time until this ride is over. We leave Mission with two hours and forty-five minutes of reserve time left.

Our original destination had been Okreek. We reach it at mile seventy-five without any sign of our support crew catching up.

"Wonder what's happened to the Honda?" I ask Robert.

"There's a pool in Martin. Maybe the Honda is fine and they just went swimming."

Cell phones don't work here, so Robert stops to wait for Anne and Amy to catch up in Okreek. I keep riding. The day is warm but not hot. The breeze is still gentle and beginning to pick up. I ride alone until the motor home and van pass me near mile 90. I flash them sign language for "I love you," as I always do when they go by. The Honda is trailing the RV, a good sign.

Hugs for the kids. A kiss with Anne. She cuts fresh watermelon, and as I slurp it down, we share how the day has gone for each of us. The mechanics found nothing wrong with the Honda. Anne and Amy both agree to this twenty-four-hour foolishness.

"I was hoping you were going to do this while I was still along with all of you," Sara tells me, her basketball competitiveness coming to the foreground. "You can do it."

"Everything feels good so far," I answer her.

Robert catches up. Sara gets her bike off the rack to pedal with us. A dozen miles ahead is the town of Winner. At mile one hundred I get off the unicycle for a picture. Actually, I get off the unicycle at mile 99.83. There's a billboard here, which says, believe it or not, "Are You Hurting? Jesus Cares."

Ask me again at midnight…

Robert and Sara take a signature slip and ride ahead into Winner, looking for a policeman to verify the ride. I catch up to the motor home parked in front of a market. The door is unlocked, so I climb in for more watermelon, a pop and a handful of nuts.

Anne comes out of the store with our ride supplies for the night. A Styrofoam cooler for the Honda is filled with two half gallons of chocolate milk, a half gallon of orange juice, a dozen candy bars and a six pack of soda. With all on board for riding through the night, I become more focused. Ninety-eight miles to go. We still have two hours and forty-five minutes of reserve time left. I am back on the road as quickly as possible. Everyone else will head over to Pizza Hut for dinner. All of us are now involved in this attempt.

"We'll bring you dinner soon."

The warmest part of the day is now, somewhere in the mid-eighties. I pedal east on Highway 44 for another eight miles, drinking water and electrolyte mix, knowing I have to keep enough energy coming in. I wonder how my body will fare as the miles add up.

When I turn north on 49, the crosswind is at last at my back after a full day of having it as a sidewind. Robert and Sara catch up just after the north-bound turn. We flag down a highway patrol car. The trooper signs our sheet and wishes us well for the night. We keep expecting the pizzas to show up, but we get to mile 125 before the RV and van pass us to serve dinner. The kids are jumping up and down with greetings when we arrive. Pizza boxes and drinks are spread out on the shoulder of the road. We lean up against the cars, eating and resting. Amy rubs birch oil on my knees, gives me an anti-inflammatory pill, and tells me to take some homeopathic Arnica tablets through the night. Robert and Sara will catch up after they hook up the lights on their bikes. Anne and Amy get ready to drive ahead for a campsite at the Missouri River. Anne will drive back with the Honda as soon as they're set up. Then I take off again. It's 7 p.m. Now we've got two hours and fifteen minutes of reserve time.

Ouch. During dinner my knees seized up. They were tender before I stopped. Now they feel stuck. It takes a full thirty minutes of painful crank-ing before they spin easily again. No more long breaks tonight. No nap for sure.

The countryside is wide-open ranchland. The sun goes behind a cloud, making the land look gray and dreary. I am tired, and suddenly with a full night of riding ahead, I feel lonely and small. I keep hoping Robert and Sara will catch up, but they must still be packing their bikes for the night ride. A bit later a rainbow appears to my right and lifts my spirits. Actually, it's a double rainbow. The northern end reaches up somewhere towards my destination. The southern trails my path, out across the fields, so bright that its reflection shimmers over the field.

"That's a sign, Lars," Sara says, catching up and pointing to the rainbow.

The rainbow fades just before the sun sets. We are expecting Anne back with the Honda anytime. It gets darker and darker. Cars have their headlights on. Soon we turn ours on. Crossing the White River we climb a steep grade to get out of the river valley. Five more miles and we're at the underpass to Interstate 90. It is completely dark now, and stars are showing in the sky.

"We need a Honda," Sara begins chanting.

When the infrequent car comes our way, we can see its headlights far into the distance ahead of its approach. Robert and I join Sara's chant.

"We need a Honda."

Finally, one vehicle slows and turns. It's Anne and the Honda. We have reached mile 151.

"You've come far," Anne exclaims. "Sorry I'm late. We got all set up before the attendant came and told us that we were in someone else's spot. They helped us move, but it took a long time. What do you want? I've got pizza, chocolate milk, OJ."

It is a quarter past ten; we have six hours and thirty minutes left, an hour and a half of reserve time. Sara rides a few quick circles in the headlights of the Honda to get in the last three tenths of a mile and reach sixty miles for her day. This ride is her longest ever, and she's felt well the whole ride. She packs her bike up and gets in the Honda to help escort us through the night. Guided by the headlights, Robert and I ride alongside the car. Country music comes out the open windows.

At 11 p.m., we have enough cell phone reception to call WCCO radio for our regular Wednesday evening update with Al Malmberg.

"I'm sorry you have to stop," he apologizes.

"Don't worry. You have no idea how good it feels to rest."

We tell about our day, and he tells his audience how they can support the endowment, then wishes us well for the ride through the night. Midnight. 164 miles. We ride into June 6 with a bit more than an hour of reserve time left.

Miles 160 to 170 are the slowest ones yet. We're riding across the Lower Brule Indian Reservation, headed towards the Missouri River and Fort Thompson. For a long stretch, I'm riding only eight miles an hour.

"Is that the dam up there?" I ask.

Robert laughs at me.

"No really, is it?"

"Of course it is," he replies.

The lights are swimming together in my vision. Then finally we're riding over Big Bend, a long earthen dam that is lit by streetlamps along its full length. It is our last intersection with Lewis and Clark's route. Wherever they were 200 years ago, at this time of day they were probably asleep.

"We're camped down there," Anne points to the lower side of the dam. "Just a few more hours and you can come back to sleep."

We ride through Fort Thompson, then follow the sign for East 34.

"You're doing great, guys," Sara calls, cheerleading out the window.

Now it's Robert's turn to zone out. He misses when he tries to return his water bottle to its carrier and it drops to the ground. When we pass a flashlight back and forth to check my odometer, it requires our full concentration to keep from dropping it.

"Shine the light on that sign," I tell Robert, "I think it says west on it."
West.

Somewhere in our grogginess we've missed a turn! Sara hands the map out the window of the Honda. We're under an hour of reserve time now, and nervous minutes tick by as we try to figure out where we are, in the middle of the night, all alone. We are lucky. We are on West 34, but right here the road is jogging north for twenty miles. It will meet up with Highway 14 where we can continue east. No harm done. There's even a benefit to our mistake; in this direction the gentle breeze is still behind us.

Mac's Corner is on the map, too, but all we find here is a single gas station, closed for the night. We stop for another piece of pizza. Amazingly, two cars with children and dads are waiting for us.

"We couldn't believe it when we passed you back there. What are you doing, trying to set a record or something?"

"Yeah, we are," I reply. "What are you doing here at two in the morning?"

"Oh, we're just coming back from taking the kids fishing. I work here. I'm the head of security at the Cherokee Tribal High School."

Another official on our path to sign the Guinness Record slip; what are the chances of this in the middle of rural South Dakota in the middle of the night? We have nineteen miles to go and fifty minutes of reserve time.

We check the odometer when we're convinced we've covered another five miles. Each time the flashlight shows we've only gone another mile, sometimes two. We're almost there, but nineteen miles is still a long ride on its own merits. I visualize riding down the block from home, passing each house, turning each corner, riding past my high school, the mall, and then out Tujunga Canyon Road towards the beach. This is a six-mile trip. I ask Robert to check the mileage. We've pedaled just two-and-a-half.

Anne is sleeping now. Sara is driving. She looks tired, but she's our sparkplug these last hours.

"This is great. You're doing great."

At last we reach 190 miles. We have just ten to go, with thirty minutes of reserve left.

With five miles remaining we see a light ahead, shining in the darkness. Reaching it we find two sorry-looking drunken cowboys standing outside their broken-down car, a lantern on top of the hood.

"We need a ride;" the tall one tells us and declares, "we'll ride in the car."

We all try to focus our fuzzy minds on solving this problem. We have four miles to Highmore and the two-hundred-mile mark. The Honda is full of stuff. We're traveling nine or ten slow miles an hour. We don't want Anne and Sara riding with two drunks in their laps for the next hour. It's a balmy pre-dawn, so they are in no danger of freezing.

"Sorry," I say, "we can't give you a ride. The car's full. We'll go to Highmore and call someone to come and get you."

"We can fit."

"No, we can't give you a ride."

"We'll ride on top."

"No." If we weren't so tired and in such a hurry, this conversation would be interesting.

"Keep an eye on them," I tell Robert. "I'll try to get going again, and you catch up when Sara and Anne get by."

Mounting has grown increasingly challenging with my weariness. Adrenaline helps now, and I make it back up on the first try and pedal off. Sara drives past our cowboys and we continue on.

"Well," Robert says, "that woke me up."

In a moment the sky begins to lighten, and we see Highmore in the distance. Pedal, pedal, pedal. With twenty-three minutes of reserve time left we hit two hundred miles just south of Highmore. For five minutes we stop to share hugs, take pictures, and get a drink of orange juice. Then Robert and I get back on our cycles one last time for the last few minutes. We ride through town and make the turn out on to Highway 14 East, ride a mile or so out of town and stop finally at 4:45 a.m. The sun is just ready to crest the horizon. We've covered 202.78 miles. That distance is:

- a bit longer than Seattle to Portland (189 miles)
- a bit shorter than New York to Washington D.C. (233 miles)
- more than halfway from Los Angeles to San Francisco (379 miles)

I never would have dreamed a day like this could happen. It never would have without Anne and this team of friends. Who you're riding with makes all the difference.

17
New Heads

You can't depend on your judgment when your imagination is out of focus.

MARK TWAIN

It was all I could do after the twenty-four-hour ride to get up, eat, drink, and feign interest in the children's sandcastles while relaxing on the lakeside beach. What I forgot to check during our day of resting was Harvey's radiator.

"Remind me to check the water when they catch up," I ask Robert as soon as the oversight flashes through my head. We are back riding again.

My legs are creaky. Both of us are low energy. But, hey, we're on the road again. Yesterday we e-mailed the two-hundred-mile ride details to Guinness. Today we're back to our regular routine.

The motor home never catches up. Instead Anne arrives in the Honda.

"It's steaming again," she tells us. "I left it just outside of Highmore."

We won't know for many weeks whether Guinness accepts our ride for a new record, but we immediately find out that my oversight has fried the big 454 engine in Harvey. South Dakota, never-ending South Dakota, becomes a test of our group's resourcefulness and $1,500 drain on our mechanical budget.

We manage to hobble Harvey almost two hundred miles to Brookings where the Stiegelmeier's live, Anne's college friends.

"Three days," John's mechanic estimates when we take it to his garage. "We'll work as fast as we can, but we've got to rebuild the heads."

We all decide Robert and I will ride on alone until the motor home is fixed. Anne and Amy will wait for the motor home and get Sara to the airport. She's become such a part of our group that we all try and pressure her into staying.

"I've got to get back to Nome, " she answers. "I'd like to stay, but it's berry-picking season at home. I need to be there."

Before we leave Brookings, I change my tire for the first time on the trip. After twenty-five hundred miles the plies are just starting to show through the rubber. With full water bottles and cash for motels, we pick up our route again at Huron. It's a quarter past one, Monday afternoon, the muggiest day of our riding so far.

What a struggle. The land is totally flat. Roads are true to the compass directions, an obsessive land planner even built the roads straight across lakes instead of jogging around them. There is no wind; we're baked by heat and steamed by humidity. After five miles we stop under the shade of an oak tree and look at our map. It will be a long afternoon. We reach Carpenter with no water and no more energy. A small hand-carved sign reads simply, "Café." We try the door and find two women inside playing cards.

"Come in. It's hot out there."

"Look, Lars," Robert points to the menu on the wall, "milkshakes." We order two along with burgers, pop, and chips, and savor the blessed coolness from the air conditioner that hums in the background.

The women play another hand and then ask us what we're doing. I tell them about the ride, the 5,000 mile route, and the 3,300,000 pedals we're racking up on the way to the Statue of Liberty.

"We're trying to raise a dollar-forty-nine a pedal."

"I'll buy one," says the owner. The other woman comes over and gives us money for two more.

"How many people live in Carpenter?" I ask.

"Thirteen," replies the owner. "Not too busy any more. You should have seen it, though, when we had our centennial celebration. We had three thousand people here for the weekend."

The other woman continues, "We had big tents set up for the celebration, and we cooked and cooked and cooked."

"Perfect weather, too. Everybody was talking about how perfect the weather was."

The descriptions are so vivid that I'm sure we just missed South Dakota's biggest event for the summer. "When was the celebration?" I ask.

"In 1994," they answer together. "It was such a wonderful weekend."

Talk about living history. Small places seem to make for long memories. We're thankful for the rest and the conversation. With re-filled water bottles, we get back on the cycles, heading north and east for Clark. It's a quarter past five now, the worst of the heat is starting to ease.

An hour up the road we stop for a break. There's no traffic. We stretch out on the road.

"I'd be careful about that water." Robert advises. "Did you see how rusty that sink was?"

As thirsty as I am I take a big mouthful. Instantly I eject the water, spitting it half way across the road, sputtering a description of its treachery.

Robert laughs at me. I ride dry for the next three hours until we make it to Clark—sixty long, sweaty miles for the day.

A line of six bright-red Lincoln Continentals is in the middle of a field as we approach town. They are old, immaculate, someone's version of art. Over a rise we descend into this beautiful town of almost 1,300 people. Trees in every yard and along every street make a sharp contrast with the open fields of the country. The Playhouse Restaurant is still open, and we get BLT sandwiches to go with endless refills of soda and water.

The McCain Potato Processing Plant in Clark employed more than four hundred people until it shut down just a week ago. After all we've seen of rural decline, it's hard to imagine Clark surviving this blow; over half the town's jobs have suddenly ended. Amazingly, folks in town are as kind and generous as can be.

"We'll see how things work out," our server at the restaurant tells us. She buys our dinner for us.

An old truck-driver visits with us while we eat. He retired just a week ago when there were no more French fries to haul to Alabama.

"Here's something for your project," he says after we talk, handing us twenty-five dollars.

We are directed to a motel up the street, right next to the silent McCain's. Checking in, we get our showers and are soon asleep.

People from Clark might end up moving to Watertown. Like other feeder towns for rural population, Watertown grew by more than ten percent during the 1990s. It now exceeds 20,000 people. Reaching it by breakfast we stop to eat at the 121 Café. We have come to the first route intersection with my bicycle journey of fifteen years before.

While we eat, I tell Robert how I loved visiting Watertown when I was a kid. We didn't go there for natural beauty or American history. An aunt, an uncle, and three cousins lived here. We visited often, because, having been born into a Danish immigrant family, these were my only cousins living in the United States. Our times together brought connection that I sensed nowhere else. All my relatives have moved away, but I still have many memories.

On my bicycle trip across the country, I had pedaled into Watertown on a weekday in the late afternoon.

"Do you want to come to church with us?" my aunt asked.

"Sure," I answered. This was new. My family always went to church. These relatives hadn't during all the time of our growing up.

Speaking in tongues, falling on the floor in ecstasy— this was far differ-ent from the emotion-wary Lutheran worship of my childhood. But dinner was good after we got home, and being with relatives, supreme.

"Tell us about your trip," my uncle asked.

I told them about the route, the miles, the camping, the people. I told them about riding through Hopi Land, the Navajo Nation, and visiting a Winnebago elder. I told them of my appreciation for what I was experi-encing on Native lands, and my growing sense of connection between my Christian background and Native ways of knowing.

My uncle heard me out silently. I still remember the kitchen table where we were sitting, a bowl of popcorn between us, his intensity of expression, a stubborn Danish accent still on each syllable when at last his words came with passion in his voice, "Lars, I'm telling you this because I love you. If you believe what you say about the Indians, you better get an asbestos suit because it's going to be hot for you. You are going to burn in hell."

"So," Robert comments, "That explains our hot weather." We head out from the restaurant and start riding north in the heat, making the junction of Interstate 29 and Highway 12 in time for lunch at tiny Summit.

At a lone Conoco station, we ask if there's a restaurant in town.

"Well," the counter person hesitates to share the information, "there is a little restaurant if you ride on into town."

We give her our thanks and leave the deep-fried options at the gas sta-tion to look for the Eagles Nest Café. The sign out front is hand-lettered. Inside nothing is new, but everything is neat. We're seated in a comfort-able booth. Rosemary, our server, is owner, waitress, cook, and developer.

"We moved into town after living in the country for lots of years. My husband runs the service garage down the block, and I'm running this place to make a living."

The burger is big and hearty. The milkshakes are thick and cold. Summit is an oasis from the heat and length of the day, the highest point of these glacial hills that we are riding through, named back when the railroad used it as a stop for water and fuel.

While we eat, we read a copy of the commemorative publication for Summit's Centennial and learn about the land rush of 1889 on the nearby Lake Traverse Reservation of the Dakota people. Wounded Knee and the Cheyenne Trail of Tears are perhaps the most well-known events of Native history, but the themes of those stories have repeated time and time again.

1. Tribe originally lives on land covering a vast area: For the Dakota this land stretched through Minnesota, north to Manitoba and south into Iowa.

2. Tribe forced to a reservation with promises of compensatory pro-
visions from the U.S. Government: In 1851 the Dakota were con-
fined to an area near Mankato, Minnesota.
3. Tribe must learn to live with broken promises.

In the case of the Dakota, when they were suffering from starvation, they
rebelled, declaring war in 1862. General Sibley squashed the revolt, and three
hundred leaders were sentenced to be executed. President Abraham Lincoln
commuted the sentences for all but thirty-two, who were hanged on the day
after Christmas, 1862—the largest hanging in the history of the United States.

Congress then abrogated all treaties with the Dakotas. They were banished from the state of Minnesota. After five years of starvation and death,
the Lake Traverse Reservation was established just north of Summit.
Allotments were to be made for each Dakota family during the next twenty-
five years. On December 12, 1889, all unallotted land was to be opened to
homesteading. On that day, just about one year before Wounded Knee, the
land rush took place. Of the million plus acres given by treaty to the Dakota
people, today only 27,000 acres remain in Indian possession.

The day is still steaming after lunch, and we have thirty more miles to
Sisseton. Riding on the Lake Traverse Reservation we can't tell any difference from non-reservation land. There are corn, soybeans, and cattle as far
as the eye can see. We follow Highway 81. It is small and poorly main-
tained, a frontage road to Interstate 29. A ragtag paving crew is putting on
the thinnest layer of asphalt we've ever seen.

The hot and humid weather has us exhausted by the end of the day.
Sisseton is the largest town in northeastern South Dakota. At a Dairy Queen
with air-conditioning, we order Blizzards and cool down. We've done
ninety-three miles of riding for the day. I'm relieved to get off the unicycle.

Talking to Anne on the phone, we find out that the mechanics have had
trouble locating replacement heads for Harvey. "They finally found a pair
from a boat motor that a guy is rebuilding."

Now the estimated time for completing Harvey is Wednesday afternoon.
We're on our own again tonight. Robert calls the I-29 Motel which was recommended by the DQ staff. It has no vacancy. We ride instead to the Viking
and find it full, too. Harry and Meeka are at the desk, apologizing. "This
is only the second time that we have had no vacancy. We have a lot of construction workers staying here. Forty miles south to Watertown there is
nothing, and ninety miles north to Fargo there is also nothing."

We talk for a moment. They seem to be considering our plight as we speak.

"You could stay in our garage," they offer, almost apologetically. We roll
hide-a-beds into the garage and when we are set up, they offer us showers

in their home. It turns out that Harry and Meeka purchased this motel only last August. Both of them were born in India. "The previous owner here was also a Sikh. I used to travel a lot and stay here often. He offered to sell me the hotel last year. A person has to try and make it sometime in life," he adds as explanation.

While Robert showers, I go back outside to show their two young children my unicycle. Maheela and Neal are excited and gracious. They get out their bikes and we ride laps around the parking lot until Robert has finished showering. After a full day out sweating in ninety-degree weather and putting on sunscreen and picking up road grime all along the way, one of the best parts of the day is a simple shower.

Harry says, "Go ahead," when Robert and I offer to take their kids with us to dinner. French fries and salad for them. Barbecue ribs for me.

"We don't eat meat," Maheela explains to us. "I really like Sa-ladd; please order it with cheese on top."

The kids bubble and talk to us throughout dinner, giving us a child's-eye view of Sisseton.

"Do you want to own a hotel when you grow up?" I ask Neal. He has been telling us about the relative merits of the three hotels in town. One of them has beds that he estimates to be much too short for us.

"No," he answers, "I want to be a scientist."

Back at the garage we hand the kids back to their parents and settle in for as comfortable a night's rest as if we'd gotten the Viking's finest room.

The next morning is June 12, and when we wake up Robert greets me with, "Happy Birthday. You've made it through your fortieth year!"

Fargo is ninety miles north, and today will probably be one of our last really remote days of riding. South Dakota's state map notes it is legal to bicycle on the interstates, and we assume it is the same for North Dakota. I-29 is the only straight route to Fargo so we decide to spend the day riding the interstate to avoid jogging back and forth on county roads. The traffic is light and the shoulder is wide as we leave Sisseton and begin my birthday ride.

"I don't mean to disappoint you, Lars, but I bet North Dakota will look a lot like South Dakota," Robert says when we are five miles from the border.

North Dakota

"You wait; it will be different," I joke. I expect no change, but when we cross into our ninth state, it really is different. Yesterday we rode through hills created from debris pushed into place by the glaciers of 10,000 years ago. Today, as soon as we cross into North Dakota, the land is as flat as a pancake. Other than the Magic Casino at the border where we have breakfast, there is nothing on this highway all the way to Fargo, sixty-five miles north.

Today we gauge our progress by the freeway overpasses. They are spaced every two or three miles, so we can see from one to the next. Every ten miles we pull up under the shade of one for a rest and a snack.

As we near Fargo, a camera crew from Channel 6 News meets us on the highway to capture our arrival. They spend forty-five minutes driving back and forth, taking our pictures as we pedal closer to town. "A reporter will come over to your house tonight for the interview," they tell us as they finish filming

Fargo has a boomtown look as we ride into it. Together with adjoining West Fargo, the population is over 115,000 people. It grew twenty-two percent during the last decade, and it's still growing; we see lots of new construction as we approach.

Anne and Amy have called. There's another delay, so now they aren't expecting to arrive until Thursday. We are wearing the same riding clothes we started with back in Huron on Monday. When the wind blows over us today, it's hard to tolerate our smell. We stop at Saver's thrift store to find shorts and a shirt to put on after our next shower. We've gotten here a day early. With the long miles we've been putting in, we're glad for an extra day of rest.

"Come on over anytime," our hosts invited when we called them yesterday from Sisseton. "We'll be having a fiftieth birthday party for our friend Linda, and we would love to have you join us."

The house is full when we arrive at Peter and Vicky Schmidt's home. We try to avoid welcome hugs until after we've showered. The house is full of good company and good food, but it's my forty-first birthday and I miss Anne and the kids.

In my fortieth year I rode 2,700 miles from Tillamook, Oregon to Sisseton, South Dakota. Today on my birthday I've ridden ninety-six miles to Peter and Vicky's home. After dinner I turn to Robert.

"Are you game for a four-mile ride? I'd like my birthday present to be a century ride, a hundred-miler."

"Let's do it."

Our story on the ten o'clock news is followed by the story of flooding in nearby Minnesota. In Ada and Rousseau, it rained twelve inches in twenty-four hours. After these thousands of miles of riding through drought-parched land, the pictures of flooded communities look terribly out of place.

"Make yourselves at home," Vicky tells us over and over. We have gotten up late and are enjoying an uncharacteristic morning of doing nothing.

"Are you sure this is okay?" I ask her. Fargo is becoming a gathering place for "One Wheel – Many Spokes" friends from all over the country. Anne and Amy finally get the motor home back from the shop. With the new heads on they start north and arrive at 10 p.m. on Thursday. Robert's parents have driven here from Montana with their fifth-wheel trailer. A slowdown at the coal mine has given them a week off to drive here and join the ride again. Soon afterward, Mike and Leslie Swenson arrive. They are best friends from Nome and are joining "One Wheel – Many Spokes" for a week. KariAnna and Kai have been eagerly awaiting Rachel, Sara, and David, their children.

Brant Thomsen also arrives. He's been training to ride his unicycle across Minnesota with me, and we've been e-mailing for months before finally meeting here. He has come from St. Paul and plans to unicycle home.

To each arriving person, Vicky extends her gracious offer, "Make yourself at home."

Others will be joining us in Minnesota. This is becoming the biggest family reunion I've ever been part of.

Friday morning five of us are riding together. We'll have Mike and Brandt along for a number of days, and for the first time since the kid's parade back in Sultan, I'm riding alongside another unicycle. Brant has been training for months, and he's a fast rider, faster than I am. He's jazzed for this ride, so off we go.

Christof, Peter and Vicky's son, has volunteered to guide us through Fargo and Moorhead. "Check this out," he says a few miles into the ride. We stop at a monument on one of Fargo's main roads and see a statuette in the likeness of our goal.

"We've done it! We've made it to the Statue of Liberty!"

Minnesota

Next we are guided through downtown Fargo where devastating flooding occurred in 1997. That year the Red River rose out of its banks and covered miles and miles of land in deep, dirty water. Anne and I lived in Minneapolis that spring, and each night we watched the flood on TV. I am sure the Red River is a mammoth like the Mississippi, but it is tiny on this summer day, no wider than a two-lane road. As we cross it, we enter Minnesota, our tenth state. Christof stops, "This is where the Viking ship is."

We are too early to get into Moorhead's Heritage Hjemkost Interpretive Center, but we look in the windows. The center's stated objective fits our

State signs.

One Wheel – Many Spokes. Near Avon, Montana.

Unicycling on six feet of Bering Sea ice. Off the coast of Nome, Alaska.

With Robert Martin. Starting out at Neah Bay, Washington.

Stevens Pass, Washington. Elevation 4061 ft. (Nathaniel on the left).

Old unicyclists never die, they just go to the "Busted Ass Corral."
Near Arlee, Montana.

KariAnna, Sara, and Amy riding along near Colstrip, Montana.

Skip Martin helping us change a broken bearing at 5:30 a.m. Colstrip, Montana.

Midwest historical farm. Decorah, Iowa.

Breaking the long-distance Guinness World Record. Near Toledo, Ohio.

With Keith Cash. Kai's first day unicycling. Schenectady, New York.

At the Appalachian Trail. Near Bennington, Vermont.

Shampooing Katie and Luther after the skunk. Pine Haven, New Hampshire.

CROSS-COUNTRY! York Beach, Maine.

Times Square, Manhattan.

Made it! 5,032 miles.

Three generations on unicycle. KariAnna, Lars, and Kai, riding with Grandpa. Tyler, Minnesota.

Shenandoah National Parkway, Virginia.

At the Gulf of Mexico. Grayton Beach, Florida.

Troubles with Harvey. Little Rock, Arkansas.

KariAnna learning to ride the giraffe. Dalhart, Texas.

Just a few more inches for Kai to fit KariAnna's unicycle. Albuquerque, New Mexico.

Replacing Harvey's heads in Albuquerque, New Mexico.

At the Grand Canyon. Arizona.

9,000-mile mark. A sandstorm in the Mojave Desert. Near Victorville, California.

The last 100 yards. Santa Monica, California.

With KariAnna on the Santa Monica Pier. 9,136 miles. Los Angeles, California.

Last ride. Kona, Hawaii.

summer: "Dare to Dream." The centerpiece is the Viking ship, built by Robert Asp, a guidance counselor at Moorhead Jr. High. He started his dream in 1971, and was able to sail it on Lake Superior in 1980. Later that same year he died of leukemia. In 1982 a crew of his family and friends completed his dream, sailing the Hjemkost all the way from Duluth, Minnesota, to Bergen, Norway.

At last we are out of town and riding past farms. Stopping at a convenience store for refreshments, we all thank Christof for the tour.

"We'd never have known a bit about all this without your guiding us."

I originally expected a fifty-mile day from Fargo to Frazee, but it is turning out much longer. The tour through town and the curving route through Detroit Lakes add miles and time. We've already ridden thirty-two miles by the time we reach Barnesville for breakfast. As Brant jumps off his unicycle, I ask him how he's doing.

"Fine so far. My legs are a little tight."

"Looks like this day is going to be long."

We finally make it to Frazee in the late afternoon—traveling eighty-five miles instead of fifty. Brant has pedaled through every mile. I'm amazed, and I'm hoping we haven't pushed too hard on his first day of riding across Minnesota.

18
Midwest

Man was made at the end of the week's work when God was tired.

MARK TWAIN

"What should we tell them?" I ask. We have pedaled eighteen days and 840 miles since Fargo. It is evening and we are with our friends Jenn and Mark in their living room. They are hosting us in their Chicago condominium on the shore of Lake Michigan. A week from now we'll meet them again in East Lansing for their wedding.

Iowa

"Tell them about the corn," Anne says.

"There was lots of corn in the fields these last three weeks since Fargo. Lots and lots of corn in the Midwest."

"And corn means heat," Anne fills in. "And humidity. I've decided that I am not meant to live wherever corn grows."

"But you grew up in Iowa," Amy responds.

"That's why I was a lifeguard. So I could spend my summers at the pool."

"Tell them about the pool," Amy says.

"You tell them, KariAnna." Anne says.

"Decorah has the *best* pool. They have a slide, and I went on it myself. And they have a big mushroom that you can walk under. We went there every day."

Anne and Amy and the kids were in Decorah for a week with Anne's mom. First Lutheran Church hosted our stay and set a $10,000 goal for the endowment. Robert and I pedaled from Rochester, Minnesota, to Cobb,

Wisconsin during that time. Except for one night in a motel, we got rides back and forth to sleep in Decorah.

Even with all our riding amid Native American lands, people, and history on this trip, after arriving in Decorah we paid no attention to the native story, focusing instead on family and community events. This, after all, is Anne's home, going back four generations to when her great-great-grandfather helped found Luther College in 1862. For all this time, Decorah has been a national center of Norwegian immigrant heritage. Hardly a trace of native influence remains, even though the town is named after Chief Waukon Decorah, and the county is named for Chief Winneshiek of the Winnebago tribe. Like most non-native people, when we are in a familiar routine we forget that virtually every place in North America is suffused with the roots of hunting-gathering people.

The Winnebago people were in Iowa for only half-a-dozen years, as part of the journey of their removal from traditional lands in Wisconsin. Beginning in 1832 with a treaty they claim was fraudulent, the Winnebagos were moved successively through Iowa, Minnesota, South Dakota, and finally to Nebraska, where their reservation is today.

Today, the Winnebago tribal name is best known as a motor home, another reminder of Steinbeck's observation, "how myth obscures fact." In the familiar space of our family and friends here in Decorah, we are not attentive to this history.

"Tell them about your birthday, Kai," I invite.

"I turned six."

"Why did you say it was your best birthday?"

"Because we were at Grandma's house. And she had a birthday, too."

"She turned eighty-five," Anne says. "We were so lucky to have our trip coincide with her birthday."

"Remember to tell them that Iowa is not flat," Robert suggests.

It's not all flat, and it's not all corn. Some of the steepest hills and longest climbs of the last thousand miles were in southeastern Minnesota and northeastern Iowa. After so many flat miles, the hills were a big change of pace. Decorah Cycles gave us riding shirts when we visited there. It warns right on the shirt, "Iowa is not flat."

"Tell them about the unicyclists," KariAnna says.

"That's right. We met a lot of unicyclists. Brant rode with us from Fargo to St. Cloud, but then he got the flu. He says he'll finish riding across Minnesota on his own when he feels better. And in St. Cloud we met a group in a unicycle club and rode together for a few miles."

"Tell them about Vaughn and Ben," Robert says.

"We met Vaughn in Minneapolis. Together with his bicycling partner, Vaughn had just finished unicycling all the way from Portland, Oregon. They were finishing in Iowa, so we rode together for a few days. Last summer they did the first half of their trip, from Boston to Iowa, so this was the finish of a two-summer, cross-country ride for them."

"Remember how much they liked getting a ride in the motor home?" Amy recalled.

"They were amazing," Robert added. "They did the whole ride, just the two of them, no support vehicles."

"What are the chances we would have met up with them on this trip?" I say.

"Remember that day leaving Minneapolis with them? Elijah, from the Twin Cities Unicycling Club, joined us. We had three Coker unicycles on the road."

"That was the day," Robert remembers, "when you popped five inner tubes on your seat and ended up using my bicycle tube for padding. That was one hot day, and the headwind just about knocked us out. I was glad when Anne picked us up in Kenyon."

"Remember how big a crowd we were back in Minnesota?" Amy reminisces. "Remember way back in Menahga, with all of us parked in Sandy's backyard, and that RV pulled up and asked if there was any more space? They thought we were a public campground. And that next night we were all in the Sebeka parade, circling around the camper on bicycles and unicycles. For a few days we were up to twenty-nine people and two dogs."

"That's right," Anne says. "Carl and Nelia took our dogs for a little vacation in Pennsylvania. We'll get them back when we arrive there in a few weeks."

"I liked playing with my friends," KariAnna says.

"Me, too," Kai chimes in.

"Me, too," repeat Caroline and Nathaniel.

"You did get to play with a lot of kids these last few weeks," Amy says.

"Tell them about the Honda." Anne says.

"Do I have to tell them?" I ask.

"I'll do it," Robert says. "When we were in St. Cloud, Lars and I forgot to put the Honda in neutral when we were hooking it up to the motor home. Towing a car in gear is a terrible thing. The next morning Amy was following Anne and saw it start throwing steam and gushing radiator fluid. We hauled it to Decorah where the mechanics thought we'd blown the whole engine. We were lucky; it works again with just a new radiator."

"When we get too tired, we seem to make more mistakes," I reflect.

"But we're making it," I continue. "We've crossed the Mississippi River, that's a highlight. And we broke through 3,000 miles back in Northfield, Minnesota. Janey McCauley from the Associated Press called that morning and got a news bulletin published. The Seattle Mariners game even announced our ride that day. And we've been to church headquarters."

Anne tells about the presentation she and I made at the church's national office in Chicago. "Lars even got to pedal through the office hallways and hand out posters with two other unicyclists. A lot of people came to our presentation. Everything went fine, but Lars is definitely more comfortable on the edge of the road than on the 10th floor of church headquarters."

"That's true enough," I agree, "but I still keep wondering how we can help the endowment fund reach its goal. It's only at $200,000 so far."

"You've gotten some good press coverage," Robert comments. "That Lutheran insurance company did a great photo shoot at the capital in St. Paul."

The best interview was certainly by Orlon Love, back in Spring Grove, Minnesota. He drove a hundred miles from Cedar Rapids to talk with Anne and me for the *Gazette*.

"I like to make things happen rather than report history," he told us. "I want people to be able to find you when you get to Decorah."

Orlon had followed our web site all along the way, and we talked for a long time over milkshakes in the town café. He made us feel good about what we are doing. "You are going to write a book, aren't you?"

"I'm keeping notes," I answered. "Maybee."

We made a special point of going to Spring Grove, because Helen Frost once lived here, and she was a beloved leader in the ministry of the Seward Peninsula from 1926 to 1961. We are carrying copies of a new book created from her journals, *Frost Among the Eskimos*, edited by Ross Hidy. Long before women were ordained in the Lutheran church, Helen was on the Seward Peninsula doing every task of ordained pastors, registered nurses, and orphanage directors combined. She is still revered by elders there.

> *That winter [1927] the temperature stayed between 30-40 degrees below zero for a month. One early morning I happened to look at the thermometer and it read fifty-two below. I knew I had been shoveling a lot of coal into my stoves but did not realize it was quite that cold.*

In her journal, Helen writes of asking her father's opinion after she was requested to serve in Alaska.

"What do you think I should do?"

Suddenly he was very excited. His eyes were shining as he told me something I had never known. "I am so pleased Helen, that you have this invitation, this call to go to Alaska. The government asked for a Lutheran pastor to go to Alaska to minister to the Lapp reindeer herders and to the natives. I volunteered and so did T.L. Brevig. They chose Brevig for he had been a teacher and was better in English as well as Norwegian...Perhaps, Helen, you are to go and do the work I wanted to do when I was a young man. Perhaps you are to go in my place. I could wish no greater joy than that one of my children be a missionary."

Every time I read this passage and imagine the scene, shivers run down my spine.

✳

Memories. We're building them up as we travel along. For Robert and me, our longest ride between Fargo and Chicago was in Wisconsin from Cobb to Racine.

Wisconsin

By the time we reached Decorah, the heat was getting so bad that we bought night-lights from Decorah Bicycles. We envision starting at three in the morning to avoid the hottest parts of the days. Instead we start on Sunday afternoon, hoping to keep cool with a night ride across Wisconsin.

First, we drive back to Cobb where we left off on Friday, and we leave the Honda there for Anne to pick up the next day. We start riding at 3:30. If we can get to Janesville by midnight, we'll get a motel room for some hours of sleep and meet our families in Racine on Monday afternoon.

Our first stop is in Dodgeville for a root beer float and a quick visit with Kathy Franzenburg, a pastor friend from Alaska. While she and I catch up, Robert rides out to buy bread and jam for the night's riding.

"They closed at five," Robert tells us upon his return.

It's 5:15, so I think we've just missed closing time for the day.

"No," says Robert, "you don't understand. They just closed that store forever. I missed their last moment of existence by five minutes."

Kathy heads back to her friends, and we ride on toward Janesville. It's hot, but not blistering. There's a good westerly breeze. Weather could be a lot worse for riding. We head onto Wisconsin's country roads: D, 39, W, 92, E, C, 14, A, 12, D, 36, 20. The roads wind through hilly country, taking more miles than we expected. Right now I don't mind; the Wisconsin country-side is a welcome place for riding.

As we pedal into the early evening, a one-ton truck pulls up and stops in the road; the driver rolls down his window and reports to me, "Hey, you're missing a wheel!"

"Thanks," I reply. "I've been looking for it all over the country. If you find it, let me know."

He drives away, the fourth person in the last two hours to tell me the same joke. In Hollander we stop at the gas station, the only place open on Sunday evening. A man gets out of his car and asks what we're doing.

"You must be sick in the mind," he says and walks in the mini-mart.

We follow him inside for ice cream and see him repeating our story to an old man eating his soft serve.

"Sick in the mind," the old man mutters, "must be sick in the mind."

Humor seems consistent in these parts—as do the farms. Everything here is in place, immaculate. Even the big round hay bales are packed with a precision that sets them apart from anyplace else we've seen. A few miles farther on, we see a sign describing this area as Little Switzerland.

"That explains it," I tell Robert, "Anne and I traveled in Switzerland on our honeymoon; it was the most orderly place I've ever been."

We reach New Glarus just before ten. The town is a perfect Swiss repro-duction. Off the cycles for a moment, we walk and pretend we're strolling through Europe. Everything is closed except the Sportsman Lodge Bar, so we get a soda from a machine, make ham sandwiches from the bread we bought at the last stop, and rest before riding into the night. Darkness is complete by the time we leave, so we turn our night-lights on for the first time: Night-Sticks for Robert and Fireballs for me. Flashing LED blinkers shine backwards. This is new adventure.

County Road W is our route now; traffic funnels in from a nearby detour. A car passes and then the taillights climb abruptly into the sky. In a moment we're on the steepest hill we've encountered in weeks. It is hard to keep bal-ance in the dark; I strain against the handlebars. Both of us start laughing. We can't see the top of this hill, and by night it feels giant; somehow I stay balanced, and we get over.

Janesville seems farther and farther distant. Mosquitoes interrupt the two naps we attempt. A police officer standing outside the station in Evansville at 2 in the morning signs our Guinness slip and wishes us well.

After midnight, a half-moon rises, and we turn our headlamps off to ride by its light. Huckleberry Finn comes to mind. To avoid capture, he and Jim did their rafting by night.

> *Sometimes we'd have that whole river all to ourselves for the longest time… It's lovely to live on a raft. We had the sky, up there, all speckled with stars, and we used to lay on our backs and look up at them, and discuss about whether they was made or only just happened.*

Whenever paddle-wheelers approached on the river, Huck and Jim lit their lantern. For Robert and me, whenever the rare car light appears in the distance, we turn on our headlamps for safety.

Our odometer reads ninety-two miles when we reach Janesville at 4 in the morning; the ride has taken us all night. Crossing under Interstate 90, we stop at the only place open, a Wendy's Restaurant at a twenty-four-hour truck stop—so much for a night's sleep in Janesville.

"Maybe we can get a nap at the table after we eat," Robert suggests.

While we order, five teenagers come in, made gleeful by a full night of drinking and partying. One drops his soda. As he attempts to pick it up, the rest laugh loudly—so much for napping in Wendy's.

"Another all-nighter," Robert remarks as we walk back to the cycles, "and we've still got sixty-five miles to Racine."

"And it's hot," I add.

The temperature all night has been in the seventies. The humidity has stayed high. We've sweat gallons and smell badly. Each of us pedaled through weary spells when we wanted to fall asleep. Now it's morning, and we're in poor shape for the ride ahead. We start east on County A. It is 4:30 a.m., and we've been on the road thirteen hours.

Two hours later we are relieved to find chocolate milk and something to eat. A hand-lettered misspelled sign on the store's front window explains in lengthy detail how bikes are dangerous to customers and an inconvenience to their shopping. We park our cycles at the back of the store.

"No restrooms," the man answers my question.

"No phones," he answers my next question.

We ride on in search of hospitality, and find it at the next town of Abell Corners, at a family-run restaurant. The eggs we order all have double yolks.

"Can we take your picture?" Mom asks after a back-and-forth conversation that lasts throughout our meal. She gives us detailed directions for the route to Racine.

"I feel lousy," Robert says after breakfast.

There's a big shade tree nearby, and under it we take the first of four necessary naps to get us the last forty miles to Racine.

The temperature quickly works its way to the day's peak of ninety-five degrees. The heat index is 105. At times the tailwind matches our speed exactly and the road scorches like a furnace; this is the hottest day of the trip. We're riding on the verge of heat exhaustion each pedal of the way. Every five miles we head for the shade of a tree, which feels cool compared to the road. Force of will is the only thing that gets us back in the saddle.

On our approach to Rochester, we pass a gravel quarry, and the little county road on which we've been traveling turns into an anthill of trucks speeding back and forth with their loads. They don't slow down for us. We ditch off the roadway twice to avoid getting smashed. Our rearview mirrors are saving our lives today.

In Rochester we stop for lunch and air-conditioning. Again when we cross under Interstate 94 we duck in out of the heat for a root beer float. At 4:30 p.m. we finish the ride at Racine; it's been twenty-five hours since we started our plan to avoid the heat of the day. It was a brilliant plan gone bad. On this hottest day we're chafed raw from humidity, tired from lack of sleep, and smelling impossibly bad. After 152 miles on the road we're thankful to be finished. I check phone messages and end up giving an interview. Robert is smarter. He gets a nap.

Mt. Pleasant Lutheran Church is known in town as the flying saucer church. It was built in the 1960s. In the round means there are no stairs. Hallways slope up and down around the circumference of the building, taking you via this maze to any of the three floors of the church. It is unique, inviting, and air conditioned. In the winter the congregation shelters homeless people, so we have access to a shower, a washer, and sleeping mats. We were considering a hotel with a pool for the night to get relief from the heat, but this church is cool and lots of fun for the kids.

Anne and Amy have had their own trials during the day. They finally make it in at 5. The motor home has over-heated again, twenty miles west. We all have dinner together, then Robert and I drive out to see what's happened. This time it's a heater hose. While we're fixing it, darkness comes, and so do the mosquitoes. We're bombarded every time we walk outside. What's worse is we don't notice an open window and before we realize it, the inside of the motor home is as buggy as the outside. Mosquitoes suck blood all the way home. Ten minutes after we get home, we take a final scratch at the bites and fall fast asleep.

✳

Another memory arises for Anne and me from these last three weeks. Just south of Minneapolis, near Red Wing, we had our second crossing with my bike ride journey of fifteen years before. It was two days after the first crossing that I'd spent with my relatives in Watertown, South Dakota.

Perhaps the winds of hell were pursuing me that day after my uncle's warning. Whatever the true reason, I rode a monstrous tailwind from Watertown almost all the way across Minnesota. I rode until eleven o'clock that night, twenty-six miles an hour with my fully loaded touring bike, hour after hour, until I toppled into a cornfield at the instant my odometer reached two hundred miles

Five years before that bike ride I had met a really cool girl while I volunteered at Holden Village. I was just finished with my undergraduate degree at Berkeley; she had just finished two years of teaching in Iowa. We hiked together constantly, talked lots, and did calligraphy together for the village signs. I had another girlfriend at the time; she had another boyfriend. We exchanged Christmas cards the first few years after we met.

As I bicycled closer to Iowa, I had written to her parents' address, wondering where she was. On a phone call to my parents, my mom told me a letter had arrived. I asked her to read it.

"I live in Red Wing now. Sure. Please come and visit. Love, Anne."

Arriving the morning after the two-hundred-mile ride, I learned Anne had spent the previous year living in Norway, working on a farm that did Christian outreach. That same year I had been living in Denmark, working for a windmill company. Neither of us knew at the time that our arrivals and departures in Europe coincided within a week of one another. We found this very interesting. I stayed the night. She had a different boyfriend by then. My former girlfriend had found a different boyfriend, too. Alone that night, I didn't sleep much, because a longing for love was growing inside me.

I delayed my normal sunrise start until three o'clock the next afternoon— as close to declaring love as I could get without naming the words. We committed to writing letters again. My parents started forwarding more mail to general delivery sites ahead of my bicycling journey. That visit in Red Wing turned out to be the most important day of the whole ride across the country.

Today our unicycle route crosses close to Red Wing. Anne is piloting 10,000-pound Harvey. I'm pedaling the unicycle, more amazed than ever at our good fortune to find each other and share this life. And together, in KariAnna and Kai, we are raising the next generation of experiences, memories, and stories.

During that day back bicycling across Minnesota…those definitely were the winds of love.

19
Around Lake Michigan

The first thing I want to teach is disloyalty
till they get used to disusing that word loyalty
as representing a virtue.

MARK TWAIN

Illinois

Boom!

Approaching downtown Chicago, all of us are startled by this explosion. I fall off my unicycle.

"No problem," I yell. "My seat tube just blew up."

This is not the typical slow leaker. Most times a tube will last about a hundred miles, more or less, and then a very slow leak will start until the tube goes flat over the next two or three miles of riding. We've tried duct-taping around the whole tube to prevent rubbing, but that doesn't help. It seems as though the holes start from the inside. The combination of being over-inflated and pounded all day by my rear-end does a number on them. The explosion is a dramatic variation on tube failure, but I'll gladly keep paying $3.95 a tube to stay comfortable. We put another one in and continue south.

At 6 a.m. the traffic is already building, but we pick up the Lakeshore bike trail. Downtown we stop to look across the famous Chicago skyline. Amy's brother Todd is visiting from Seattle, and he takes in the sight with us.

For the first time I feel overwhelmed by how far we've ridden.

"Can you believe it?" I ask Robert.

"We've come a long way," he agrees. After a quiet moment he adds, "I'm no city person, though. Let's get going."

From downtown we ride along the lake to South Chicago, mindful of the many warnings people have given us about this part of the city,

"You'll be riding over lots of glass on that bike trail…You be careful there…I'd never go to South Chicago myself…"

We encounter no broken glass. The only difference we can tell between north and South Chicago are the number of greetings we get. We have grown accustomed to the lack of acknowledgement up north, ascribing it to the high population density. Yet, as soon as we get south of downtown, we are suddenly greeted, cheered, waved, and encouraged by the majority of people on the bike trail. There's some kind of an organized walk or run going on this morning, and the trail is crowded. Temps have cooled down, so everything feels perfect. We're in Gary, Indiana, by 9:30 a.m., eating breakfast at the Purple Steer restaurant, fueling up for the second half of the day. This is our fourteenth state. Gary is another area where people have warned, "It's the murder capital of the country…the armpit of America…you be careful…"

Indiana

We've gotten a lot of warnings on this trip, and they correspond closely to the number of African Americans or Native Americans in the community. "Watch out," we're told.

Our experiences always turn out to be the inverse of the warnings we receive. Our unicycles and bicycles continue to be non-threatening wherever we ride. Three young African American men are at the gas station where we stop for refreshment before noon. They talk loudly to others who stop for gas, gesturing, posturing, fitting stereotypes we've heard over and over again about black men. I pick up my unicycle and get ready to continue.

"Whach'alldoin?" asks the biggest of the young men.

"Riding across the country," we answer, telling them where we've come from and where we're going.

The man inside his car exclaims, "I heard about you on the radio! I'm going to keep listening for when you get there, and when you do, I can say, 'I know that guy!'"

"We're planning to be there August 10," I tell him. "One more month to go."

We ride on past the buildings of Gary, some of them abandoned, all in the shadow of the big steel producers that line this part of Lake Michigan. In the long, deep history of our country's racism, perhaps it makes no difference, but the waves, cheers, and gas station greeting have turned South Chicago and Gary into welcome parts of this ride.

A lot of doors have opened to us on this journey. People keep asking about KariAnna and Kai. As much as anything, I'm thankful they are experiencing this hospitality, day after day after day. I pray it helps them grow up with a wide welcoming embrace of our rich and diverse world.

Soon we are in Portage, rolling in for a two-day stay with Steve and Karen, friends of Amy's parents. Todd pulls in with us after fifty-six miles of the most urban riding we've yet encountered.

In the four years that we lived in Michigan, we often found ourselves driving this route to Chicago, or else all the way to Anne's mom's home in Iowa. Michigan people are not kind in their description of this stretch of road bordering the southern shore of Lake Michigan. When we used to drive it, we were always thankful to get through this area of heavy industry and heavy traffic.

"The busiest truck traffic in the whole nation is right here," Karen tells us. They live just off of Highway 20, half a mile south of Interstate 94 and a mile north of Interstate 80/90. These three interstates cover all of the northern part of the U.S., and here every road funnels together to get south of Lake Michigan. Off the highway in their home, you'd never know it's such a busy area.

I get one afternoon alone to input Guinness World Record documentation from all the places we've been since Montana. It is time to get the records straight and figure out where we'll break the current distance record of 3876 miles. After calculating our route through Michigan, we estimate we will break the record on Wednesday, July 17, twenty or thirty miles east of Toledo, Ohio. My dad has shown up to be with us for a few weeks again. If all goes well, he'll get to see us break the record.

Anne and I have begun talking more about what to do after New York.

Whenever KariAnna is in hearing distance, she insists, "We have to unicycle back." She's loving this trip.

"Kai seems to be up for it, too," I say.

"He seems to be," Anne replies. "He seems happy wherever he is."

People are becoming more persistent in their questions of what we are going to do next. Both Anne and I believed we would have some inspiration when we got this far into the ride. The main purpose of the year off was to explore directions for our future, yet neither of us has gained clear insight. As much as anything, the lack of a clear vision for the future makes staying on the road, continuing with these experiences, our most attractive option.

"We've still got a long way left," Anne says. "Let's wait and see."

Michigan

From Portage we ride east. Just before the Michigan border we see the work of an unusual surveyor. A circle is painted around a rotting raccoon and lettered, "Roadkill." Twenty yards farther on another carcass is circled and lettered "Mikes Dinner."

Other signs here make us sad. Many gas stations in the area boast "American Owned and Operated," barely disguised reminders that the fears of terrorism are overflowing onto innocents such as Middle-Eastern service-station owners.

We cross into Michigan, our fifteenth state, following the Red Arrow Highway that takes us north along the lake towards St. Joseph. The man who signs our Guinness slip gives us good directions and then adds a warning about not riding through Benton Harbor at night, another predominantly African American community.

At Union Town we stop for fresh cherries; good ones, but this year they are imported. Almost all the local blossoms froze earlier this spring.

A few miles before Stevensville, Alice Schinkel pulls up behind us. Alice is a member of University Lutheran Church, where I served as a campus pastor. She treats us all to lunch in Stevensville, and afterwards we ride on to Lisa Hirsch's home, another friend from church and campus. On our first day in the state, Michigan is already starting to feel like a reunion.

In the morning I suggest to Robert, "Let's skip the shortcut and keep riding along the highway. We need the extra miles since yesterday was so short."

We're trying to stay on track with the mileage estimates through Michigan so that we'll end up breaking the Guinness long distance record on Wednesday the seventeenth. This morning we get our miles in with no problem; for the first time on the trip we get lost to the tune of a dozen extra miles. It's frustrating to be retracing roads and wondering where to go. We've been lucky so far with staying on course.

"This reminds me of when Anne and I did our tandem honeymoon tour," I tell Robert. "We got lost on the way to Stockholm. It was a foggy day, and after a whole hour of riding lost, we ended up right back where we started. Bicycles weren't allowed on the freeway there, but we couldn't figure out any other way to get out of town. Trucks honked at us the whole time."

Kalamazoo is our destination now. We encounter more and more vehicles as we approach. Chicago's traffic was congested, but Kalamazoo is different. Everywhere in our travels, cars have given as much space as possible when they passed. Not in Michigan, especially not in Kalamazoo. Maybe ninety percent of the drivers give us space, but that leaves one in ten, which doesn't budge for us. Moving right down the center of their lane, seemingly oblivious to our presence, they drive past us without slowing down or edging over—staying close enough to feel threatening. We keep our eyes constantly in the rear-view mirrors. Even as we pass by Western Michigan University, there is no bike path or bike lane or even a shoulder along this major thoroughfare. As we approach a stoplight, a black Toyota barges past us only to stop immediately ahead of us in the line of traffic. We have to re-pass it on our way to the red light. "What's the point of this driving?" we wonder. The drivers seem to be wondering what the point is to our cycling: Why would anything other than an auto be on the road? Heading south on Westnedge Avenue, we experience more of the same. A woman leans over her young son on the passenger side and yells out, "Sidewalk!"

"Most states don't let you ride on the sidewalks," Robert says to me.

I look at the cars lined up in driveways to enter and exit the gas stations and stores. I look at the corners of streets where we'd be invisible to cars if we were approaching from the sidewalks. No place seems safe for us here in Michigan, the car-capitol of the United States.

Local culture is showing through. Prince of Peace Lutheran Church is our destination. We need that peace by the time we arrive. Thankfully, we find it.

After the evening presentation, Anne and I make plans for the coming two days. More logistics. She and KariAnna fly out in the morning for a presentation to the Women of the Lutheran Church's Triennial Convention in Philadelphia. KariAnna will be riding her unicycle while Anne speaks at the convention. They'll take my dad's car to the airport. He'll drive the RV. We'll meet Friday night again in Lansing.

When Robert and I start pedaling out of Kalamazoo at 5:30 a.m., traffic is already building. We carry our blinking red lights that should be visible at least 3,500 feet. Still, a car comes close, swerves to avoid us, and then blasts us with its horn.

"Here we go again," Robert says.

"Last night I was thinking that biking through Kalamazoo is like being Native in America."

"What do you mean?" he asks.

"Even if the law says we have a right to be here, it doesn't do any good unless people give us room on the road; it's just like the treaties that have been broken over and over again."

"We definitely don't count for much here," Robert agrees.

"On the Seward Peninsula people have to decide how they're going to respond to the culture challenges. It seems the same for bikers here on the shoulder of the road."

A stoplight turns red ahead of us.

"We've got options. We could flip the drivers off, ignore the cars, or give up cycling and get our own cars," I finish.

"Or join a biking club," Robert adds, "and try to change the way people drive. You don't have to think much about it until your space is taken away."

We get a few miles of this experience. Native people get an entire lifetime.

After breakfast in Richland, we ride up around Gull Lake. The country here is heavily wooded, and the land has a bit of a roll. The Kellogg family summer cottage is here. Nearby Battle Creek is the town the Kelloggs established as "cereal city."

Soon we ride through Hickory Corners. We're sitting on the ground, leaning against the wall when a very large man in Carhart overalls stops to greet us. After introductions he tells us, "I just got back from eighteen years of traveling this country. I rode it all in a covered wagon."

"Wow," I said. "Really?"

"Yes, I did. Pulled it with four one-ton draft horses. Did you see that girl who just walked in?"

She had greeted us, thirteen or fourteen years old I figured.

"She was born in that wagon."

"So you didn't have to buy gas, but what did you do for food?"

"I'm a blacksmith, a tree cutter, and a mason. I had my tools in the wagon. Altogether it weighed 12,900 pounds."

"How far was a long day of traveling?" I find myself asking the same questions of this giant of a man that people always ask of us.

"Twenty-eight miles."

"Four, five miles an hour, or how fast did you travel?"

He holds up four fingers. Our trip feels like a stroll in the park compared to imagining this man's journey.

He enters the store and his daughter comes out carrying a soda. She smiles at us, dressed in her old blue jeans and flannel shirt, "Y'all have yourselves a good day now."

We get back on our tiny steel steeds and head east through more beautiful, rolling wooded land.

"Twelve thousand and nine hundred pounds? That's more weight than Harvey!"

"I wonder if his wagon ever broke down like Harvey?" Robert says.

Wheat fields here are ready for harvest; we've pedaled through an entire growing season. Back in Wilbur, Washington, the first blades had just been rising from the fields.

Robert and I are running on low energy again today from heat and lack of sleep. We see a home with a lawn that reaches to the highway. Ten minutes of napping under a big shade tree leaves us feeling refreshed, and we're back on the road to Eaton Rapids.

We spend our night with a couple who found our ride on the Internet, and we speak at her church in Jackson. Friday morning, July 12, starts our homecoming ride to East Lansing. A dozen folks from church have come to greet us at Eaton Rapids. The mayor gives us a tee-shirt and greeting from the town. Some friends bike with us, others follow by car. At the Lansing city limit, we're met by a police escort, and from then on, we've got a whole lane of traffic to ourselves. Three news stations are leap-frogging ahead and taking video as we ride.

After a stop at the capitol, we ride down Michigan Avenue and the police trade off at the border with East Lansing. Friends meet us along the way. Then we're on Grand River, along the northern edge of Michigan State, until we finally turn onto campus.

Michigan State University is about two miles wide and six miles deep; most of the land is used for agricultural studies. It is the oldest land grant college in the country, founded in 1855. Today a campus police car and a bicycle cop escort us the last two miles to the church. We are greeted there with overflowing kindness. There's a story in the Bible about the prodigal son, the son who gets his inheritance and goes out to see the world. When he returns his father's greeting is far better than he deserves. Now I know how the prodigal felt.

We have two days here. It is so easy to settle into the friendships of a year ago that we almost forget we're riding. If KariAnna and Kai have wished for one place to arrive on this trip, it has always been Michigan. They've spent most of their years here.

Jenn and Mark, with whom we stayed in Chicago a week ago, are in East Lansing with us too. Former campus ministry students, early this year they decided to marry. What a surprise it was when they called before our tour to ask if I would officiate at their wedding.

"Sure," I had answered. "We'll do our best to be there. That's three thousand miles of unicycling, though, and I can't guarantee we'll keep our schedule or even for sure that we'll make it that far."

"We'll take our chances," they had replied.

Now Friday evening we are gathered for the wedding rehearsal. Maybe I enjoy marriage ceremonies so much because of being kicked out of seminary those dozen years ago: During weddings, I get a chance to talk about hearts and hopes winning out over hard-and-fast rules.

Similarities exist between a unicycle journey and getting married. Both feature vulnerability as an asset: We are learning that our exposure on the open road helps us in our willingness to offer and receive hospitality and care. Both contain enduring imperfection: We could have used another year to get ready for this ride, but the shortcomings haven't stopped us from pedaling onwards. Finally, neither marriage nor this trek guarantee an assured outcome, but hopefully there is the growing sense, as on this journey, that we are on a good path with good partners.

The kids go non-stop on this busy weekend: swimming with friends, meeting at the children's park on campus with long-time best friends, and playing at the church. Nathaniel and Caroline hop right in. On Saturday evening, after a big picnic, KariAnna says to me of her first grade classmates, "They've changed a lot."

I reply that she has, too.

"Not like they have," she repeats. "They've changed a lot!"

When Sunday comes, the church fills up. Worship is filled with favorite songs. I get to preach again, and I include the story about Kalamazoo drivers helping us feel Native. After worship, two friends tell me the newspaper has run recent articles about the danger of cycling in the Lansing area. Apparently the problem isn't limited to Kalamazoo.

A huge potluck follows worship. A local news crew shows up again. A kid's rodeo has me unicycling with a bunch of bicycling, rollerblading, skateboarding kids in the parking lot after church. Everyone is invited to add money to the "thermocycle." It was at $6,500 on Sunday morning. By the end of the afternoon, the red thermometer is colored in above the congregation's $10,000 goal. What a homecoming!

At the presentation our friends ask us the question that we hear all the time now, "What are you going to do next?"

I look at Anne. Anne looks at me. She signals permission for me to share our thoughts. "Our family is having a good time on this ride," I say, "so we're thinking we'll keep riding after the Statue of Liberty. Maybe we'll make it all the way back to the Pacific Ocean."

I speak with hesitation, uncertain in my choice of words. That's the way of new adventures for me: first a dream, later an uncertain voicing, and then finally learning the language of the experience as we go along. Being here in the company of friends helps spur us on.

20
Guinness Record

What is it that confers the noblest delight? ...Discovery!
To do something, say something, see something, before anybody else
...Lifetimes of ecstasy crowded into a single moment.

MARK TWAIN

One hundred and forty-four miles remain to reach the Guinness World Record. On Monday morning we ride away from East Lansing. Five children accompany us for the first miles on our way to Ann Arbor.

When we leave Ann Arbor the next morning, just seventy-seven miles remain to the record. Today it is Robert's turn to start riding with only three hours of sleep. The weather has turned scorching again, and he couldn't fall asleep. Both of us perk up after a few miles. In Milan we find a bakery but no café. Donuts aren't on the top of our power food list, but they taste great. The miles roll by easily. Jeremy from the *Toledo Blade* meets us on the road with his camera. He catches up to us just after we cross the border into Ohio, the sixteenth state of the ride. We're at the outskirts of Toledo by 11:30, so we stop at a gas-mart for something to drink and to study the map.

Ohio

"Sly, the Seven-up Guy," wants our signature before he drives his big beverage truck to the next stop. A man pumping gas walks over to us and invites us to stay overnight at his house.

"My kids would love to meet you. We've got a pool and a pond, too."

From the generosity of those we've known well in Michigan we are back to the generosity of strangers. It keeps happening, this kindness and caring. I know this hospitality is changing our lives. Fox Television finds us riding along the route and a reporter stops for our story.

"I heard about you on the scanner, and I had to see what you're up to."

At the evening presentation at Hope Lutheran Church, we learn that people from the congregation have been making frequent mission trips to help folks in Central America and other places. They are interested in comparing their experiences to ours in Alaska.

"Everything you said sounds familiar," one member tells me afterwards, "even though the places are so far apart. Going on that trip to Central America changed the way I look at life."

Joining us this evening are Al Lieffring and his family from Athens, Georgia. They have timed their vacation to meet us here in Ohio. Al has a unicycling e-group that I get updates from, and the latest news is that Al was stopped for riding his unicycle the wrong way on a one-way street. He received no mercy from the officer, and ended up with a thirty-dollar ticket. He and his son Nick have their unicycles along and will ride the last miles with me across the record line.

Before we go to bed I call FOX, ABC, and CBS with our route for the morning, asking if they can share the story, "A lot of folks we've met along the way would enjoy seeing us break this Guinness World Record."

Finally the day comes. July 17, 2002. We leave Hope Lutheran at 8 a.m. for the final 18.76 miles to the Guinness World Record. CBS News follows along as we head out the driveway.

Two miles down the road, a cyclist makes a U-turn to join us. "I'm one of the ones who sent you route directions in the mail. Four of us were waiting at the church at 5:30 for you," she states as she falls in line with us.

I apologize. "I'm sorry. We made an 8 a.m. start so the news cameras could catch us if they want to come out."

Pat Squire has joined us; she's been bicycling for twenty-five years. "I grew up in this town. I live right here in the inner city. Even the few years I've been away from Toledo, I've always lived in the inner city. Wouldn't live anywhere else. You have to know how to bicycle in the city, though. Positioning yourself on the road, that's what matters."

I don't know Pat's age, but I'd like to follow in the footsteps of her years and experience. She rides with us for the first five or six miles giving us history. "This here is one of the largest Victorian-home neighborhoods in the country. All of it is on the national historic register."

Down a few more blocks, "This is the neighborhood my husband grew up in," and around the next corner, "See that sign with the bicycle and the number twenty? This is our county's first bicycle route. We just got the signs put up six months ago."

Pat gets us onto Highway 2, and after wishing us well, she turns around for the ride home. We pass through an industrial area and start seeing farms again. Corn plants are withered and browning. Soybeans are stunted, many of them just six inches high. The drought is deepening as summer goes on.

At mile twelve the motor homes catch up. We unload KariAnna's bike, and Al and Nick get their unicycles out to join the ride. They are riding twenty-four-inch unicycles, and while they pedal madly, I ride slowly to match their speed. If I had ridden my original twenty-four-inch wheel on this trip I'd still be back in the Dakotas. The thirty-six-inch Coker is working well.

At mile fourteen, CBS News is there again to take pictures and ask questions. The cameraman has done long distance cycling. The reporter asks what this morning means to me.

"It's a lot of fun," I tell her. "A Guinness World Record is every twelve-year-old's dream. Mostly, though, I hope it will get more attention for Seward Peninsula Lutheran Ministry."

KariAnna decides the day is too hectic for biking and packs her bicycle on the car. Al and Nick do another two miles with us; then Robert and I are back on busy Highway 2 alone. With a mile left he jets ahead to get ready for a picture. Al and his family are there at the line at 11:02 a.m. The imaginary line turns out to be just past the intersection of Teachout Road. I throw my arms in the air as I cross it.

We have been wondering if we will see an interesting sign near the Guinness World Record mark, like the "Etcetera Just Ahead" sign at the thousand-mile mark or the "Do You Hurt? Jesus Cares" sign at the hundred-mile mark of our 24-hour ride. This is a pretty plain section of road with a lot of truck traffic, but a few hundred yards earlier we saw an ice cream shop. Al's wife Rosemary asks if we want anything, and we answer, "Yes, please," to vanilla shakes.

When they catch up to hand us the shakes, we've got our sign.

"You're always writing about all that you're eating. Here. Try these!"

Out the window Al hands each of us a sixty-four-ounce vanilla shake.

We ride along, recounting all the shakes we've had on the road to get here, and soon we make it to the bottom of these half-gallon tubs too. I decide to keep the cup as a souvenir of the morning. A half-hour later both Robert and I have stomachaches.

Everything today takes much longer than a regular morning of riding down the shoulder of the road. Newspaper reporters from Cleveland and Sandusky find us for interviews and pictures.

In the evening we check e-mail. Already we have a message disputing the breaking of the record, asking me to stop spreading "a cloud of misinformation." The note has come from another unicyclist who has been dreaming of breaking the distance record.

Certification of our distance won't happen until we finish our ride, but the details for the Guinness World Records listing of the long distance unicycling record are well known. When Hans Peter Beck unicycled across Australia and set the record at 3876.1 miles, he averaged 74.5 miles a day on the trip. Our trip's daily average will be somewhere around fifty miles a day, but for a longer distance. Thus the contention with our record, that our pace is slower than Beck's. Guinness records okayed our itinerary prior to the ride, and we reconfirmed it a couple weeks before reaching the record mark. They make the determination of the attempt, so I assume this will be a record, subject to verification of our ride and route. We have collected three to four signatures a day from people we met along the route, and we recorded our route each evening, with highways numbers and mileage. When we reach the Statue of Liberty, we'll submit all the information to Guinness for the final decision.

Perhaps a half dozen people have unicycled across the USA. Vaughn Murray, whom we rode with near Minneapolis, completed his ride over the past two summers. Tyler Bechtel rode from near Oregon to Florida in 1997. In the mid-nineties someone from Japan completed the ride. Keith Cash did his solo ride from Los Angeles to the East Coast in 1983. That same year Pietro Biondo started a fifteen-month adventure, unicycling twelve thousand miles around the perimeter of North America. Five years earlier, Wally Watts completed his own two-year trek, unicycling twelve thousand miles on a course around the world. The record we broke today is the record documented by Guinness World Records. Every one of the long distance riders who has talked with us has been generous with encouragement. People who have accomplished a journey like this know the ride isn't really about the numbers, the technology, or the record. It's not even about the unicycle. Once you get your routine working, the journey is about the people and the places and the experience, which is proving richer and fuller than anything we could have imagined. If for some reason Guinness doesn't certify the ride, the experience will be no less.

An hour after the ice-cream shakes, the temperature is up in the middle nineties, we're passing withered corn and we're withering too. We finally get to Port Clinton and are shuttled across the Sandusky Bridge because cycling on it is forbidden. On the other side of the bridge we're riding closer to water; the temperature drops into the lower nineties, and we feel much better. We pass Cedar Point, an amusement park which boasts the most roller coasters of any park in the nation. The road isn't very wide, but drivers are considerate.

We reach Huron at 5 p.m. after sixty-six miles. A sign at the city limits tells us that Huron was the biggest steamship builder on the Great Lakes in the 1830s. Before that, the Wyandotte Indians lived here.

The kids arrive earlier than we do and are swimming in Lake Erie. Our hosts have an outdoor train set in their yard, and the kids announce for the umpteenth time, "This is my favorite place." Wherever we are is often their "favorite place."

At the presentation tonight, we are asked a question that comes up often. "Should we even be supporting Christianity in native communities? It seems to have done so much harm to native culture."

"It's a good question," I answer. "There certainly has been a lot of harm. Here are two thoughts.

"Back when Lutheran Ministry started on the Seward Peninsula, they had to deal with two major disease outbreaks. The first was measles, brought to Nome by two miners during the gold rush in 1900. The second was Spanish Influenza in 1918, a flu that killed some twenty million around the world that year. When diseases first come to Native communities, they are devastating because people have very little resistance. I've been told that something like two-thirds of Native Alaskans died in the years when the people first contracted outside diseases. Oftentimes whole communities were ravaged, and many children were left without parents. After the two outbreaks on the Seward Peninsula, the Lutheran church took in the orphaned children and raised them. That reputation of care and service still survives for the Lutheran Church on the Seward Peninsula.

"My second thought is that the endowment doesn't tell the people on the Seward Peninsula what they have to do. For any harms that have been done, the endowment fund is a good answer. The reality is that after one hundred and eight years of Lutheranism on the Seward Peninsula, people are both Christian and Native. The endowment gives full freedom for people there to put together their faith and their tradition for the most hopeful possible future. This is what motivates Anne and me to keep sharing the story of Seward Peninsula Lutheran Ministry."

After the presentation we are served root beer floats, just what Robert and I need after the half-gallon shake.

21
Under Lake Erie

Where was the use, originally, in rushing this whole globe through in six days? It is likely that if more time had been taken in the first place, the world would have been made right, and this ceaseless improving and repairing would not be necessary now.

MARK TWAIN

Our guide through Ohio knows more about the Inupiat ways of food preparation than almost any other non-native person in the world. Back when we lived in Nome, Zona Spray came to visit. Her letter of introduction told us, "My parents were once teachers in Alaska, and I spent my first five years in western Alaska. I would like to come to the Spring Conference in Nome and study the ways that people prepare traditional food."

Zona has since made many trips to the Seward Peninsula and developed close friendships.

"What you are riding for is *so* important," Zona e-mailed to us during our preparations for the ride. "Whatever I can do to help, I'll do it."

Along with planning our route, our destinations, and media coverage for the state, Zona has a gourmet breakfast arranged for us on the shores of Lake Erie. At Lake Front Park, a white linen tablecloth is spread for us at the park's bandstand. Fresh fruit, blueberry bread, a silver coffee decanter, and flan are set out. Our friends Bill and Annelise have joined us for a few days of cycling. We haven't seen each other since I officiated their wedding last September.

"So this is why you like unicycling so much," Annelise jokes.

"Oh, yeah," says Robert, "we get this every day."

"We made the flan last night in class. It's your eggs for the day," says Marcia DePalma, a former student of the Zona Spray cooking school. She now has her own school, the Laurel Run, in nearby Vermilion.

An hour after breakfast, I take my first grounder of the trip. Distracted by a car pulling out of a driveway, I hit a bump at that instant and fall to the ground. For a second there's a race as my legs try pumping fast enough to stay under my body. I lose and finish the fall with a roll on the pavement, a scratch on my hip, another above my right knee. I've fallen many times on this trip, but always before I've landed standing up. After almost four thousand miles of riding, one fall is not bad.

Population density is continuing to increase as we travel east. Earlier we passed the factory that builds Ford vans. Power plants, farms, small communities in varied states of repair vie for ground space. Mansions dot the lakeshore.

Today is a short day of riding. After only forty miles, we arrive at Westlake. A CBS cameraman follows us to church. The sign at the city limit announces that Westlake was voted the number one suburb in the Cleveland area for 2001. At Prince of Peace a local reporter is waiting.

Zona and Grant, her husband, arrive in the afternoon. We all meet at the pastor's house where Zona prepares a feast, We have too little time to catch up on our friendship that began with eating her good food in Nome.

Pastor Sherman Bishop and I have an opportunity to talk when he drives me back to church. He worked as an assistant in the synod office before becoming pastor at this congregation. Listening to me talk about all the dying congregations I've seen on this trip, he tells me, "We did a study of our Lutheran Churches in this area. Most of the congregations were built where people lived at the time. But now the people have moved, and many of our older congregations aren't located where their members live, work or shop. If there is to be a Lutheran Church in the future, we need to do two things. One is to start new churches where people are living today. The other is that many of our congregations either need to relocate or redesign their ministry. As it stands, their ministry model or their ministry plan is about eighty years out of date."

"You used to work in the bishop's office. Do you ever think about being Bishop Bishop instead of Pastor Bishop?"

"You're the thousandth person who has joked about my name. I'm not interested. I want to be in a parish working with people and their lives."

I phone Anne at the end of the day. She and KariAnna are in North Carolina on their second conference of our road trip. Our church body's Global Mission Event is in session, and Anne will tell about the ride and about Seward Peninsula Lutheran Ministry. KariAnna will be the unicyclist. She's taking to this new role with enthusiasm.

"Four a.m. start tomorrow?" Annelise asks, when the day is done.

I nod. Westlake is a dozen miles from Cleveland, and we want to make it through the downtown area before Friday morning rush hour. In the morning Robert and I strap on our headlights, but we never need them; streetlights provide light all the way into town.

Skyscrapers, old churches and historical buildings all share the downtown. We're through it just before 6 a.m., while traffic is light. At the Rock and Roll Museum, we stop for pictures next to ten-foot tall guitars. Riding farther east, we pick up bike paths that contour the lake and Interstate 90. Traffic here by the freeway makes it too noisy to talk. We follow Lakeshore Drive past small communities until we come to Mentor-On-The-Lake. There are bike paths all over this town, a swimming pool, a nature center, and lots more. From our brief ride through we're impressed. We pick up more inner tubes for the seat, and stop at AAA for maps. For thousands of miles in the West we traveled without maps. Now we're lost without them.

"How far until four thousand miles?" Annelise asks as we're riding along. I check, surprised to see only four more miles left. We see dozens of signs all around as we hit this milepost of our trip, but none of them feel significant. Annelise jumps off the bike and asks the dealer at Cord Camera to come out and take our picture.

"We'll be the sign," she says, forming a four with her arms and directing Bill, Robert and me to be zeroes behind her.

Then up the road we ride to Ashtabula. We stay at Messiah Lutheran Church, which holds several highlights, including Pastor Elizabeth Eaton's energetic welcome. "I can't believe it. I can't believe you're doing this. You must be exhausted. Come in and rest. I can't believe it."

The congregation members are as lively as Pastor Elizabeth. Today is the eve of my dad's seventieth birthday, and during the presentation, in this congregation with no Danes, I teach them to help me sing, "Han Skal Leve!" It's a fine rendition.

After the presentation, my dad helps Kai with his unicycling. Kai scoots out from the wall time after time and finally runs over to me.

"I did it! I got eleven pedals."

Ten was his goal.

"We get ice cream now!"

Learning to unicycle was one of the hardest things I remember doing as a kid. Watching KariAnna and now Kai learn to ride are highlights for me. If I had to make a choice, I'd choose this over a Guinness Record any day.

Everyone is tired. The 4 a.m. start has us itching for bed. We check maps first and decide we'll try for Erie State Park in New York, some miles past our original destination of Harper's Creek, Pennsylvania. We estimate it to be about seventy miles.

We receive good news about the endowment fund today. The Global Mission Event that Anne is attending took an offering totaling $5,000. And while we were riding today, Bill shared another story. The best man in his wedding has been following "One Wheel – Many Spokes" all across the country. He's a member of Bear Run Church of the Brethren, a small church in rural Ohiopyle, Pennsylvania.

"They have maybe fourteen members, just a couple of farming families. No one there has a lot of money," Bill told me.

"They took an offering for the endowment last Sunday. It was five-hundred-and-twenty-eight dollars."

Pennsylvania

Saturday, July 20th. We follow Lake Erie from Ashtabula to the border of Pennsylvania and start pedaling through the Keystone State. It is state number seventeen of the journey. When we stop by a cornfield for a drink, we see a cyclist approaching on a big wide bike. As it gets closer, we see how fully loaded it is. The cyclist is spinning fast. I hold out a cookie in the palm of my hand and he grabs it on the fly, apparently intending to continue. He changes his mind, stops, and turns back to us. He's from Japan, riding from Los Angeles to New York.

He is the first cross-country cyclist that we've encountered on the trip. In all our miles we haven't met a single other one. He tells us his Japanese name and adds, "You can call me Rocky."

We visit until he sees my unicycle, and then his eyes bug out. He pulls a tripod and a camera from his stack of gear, then a roll of duct tape.

"Broken," he laughs, pointing to the tripod and taping his camera into place.

"Should I give him my license plate?" Robert asks.

Back in Michigan, Robert found a motorcycle license plate. In Toledo he was given an old Ohio plate that he strapped on his bike and has been riding with ever since.

"Yes," says Annelise, "Ohio means 'Good Morning' in Japanese."

Rocky thanks Robert with a big smile, then fastens the plate under the bungee cords as he repacks his tripod. I ride off with him for a quarter mile before he heads for Buffalo, riding fast, bringing back good memories of my own solo bicycling trips.

A few miles later we pass a white painted barn with Penn State logos covering it.

"Take a picture, Robert," I ask heading over to pose with the painted Nittany Lion mascot.

The farmer comes out to visit with us.

"Lots of people stop for pictures," he tells us, "but never anyone on a unicycle."

When I ask for water, he walks me to his house where I fill bottles at the sink.

"How's farming these days?"

"Not good," he answers.

"Do you have to work off the farm, too?"

"Not yet," he replies.

I ask about the drought.

"See that corn there that looks grayish? The leaves curl up and show the underside. That is severe drought stress. When they get to that point you don't get much for harvest. The soybeans quit growing last week. They got to knee-high. They're supposed to get waist high. Now they are just waiting to see if any water comes. We need it soon."

Things had looked even worse back in Ohio.

"The problem with farming, " he continues, "is that for anyone to do well in one place, some other place has to have a drought or have something else go wrong."

I thank him for the visit and the water. Back on the road I recall a breakfast conversation a month earlier in Pine Island, Minnesota. The person at the next table signed my Guinness Record slip, and we had begun talking. The problem in Pine Island was not drought, but rather, flooding. I asked if he knew whether the corn would survive. Many of the fields we'd passed were still submerged, and there were still sandbags at the end of town.

"That corn will be O.K. It can stand under water for at least a week. But corn can't stand a week of drought. Then the top opens up like a funnel to collect water, and you lose the crop.

"I used to farm," he continued. "I grew up on a farm and I owned a farm. This flood was worse than it had to be. Too many farmers have put drainage tiles in their fields; when a big rain comes, the water gets dumped into the rivers so fast the flooding can be terrible. We need more wetlands to protect the land when these big rains come."

"So you aren't farming anymore?" I asked.

"No I'm not. All that corn out in these fields costs more to plant and grow than the farmers get back for it. The only way it works is with government subsidies. The only solution is for us to pay more for the food we eat.

"I had a dairy farm with a hundred milk cows," he shared. "My wife and I have three sons, and any single one of us could run that farm. We all grew up with farming; it's part of who we are. One year, with all five of us working, I did the books and found that for the entire year we cleared one thousand dollars. That was for five of us, all working full time. That's when we sold the farm and I got into construction. My boys are all working for computer companies, making good money. One in Minneapolis. One in Rochester. One in New York."

The flooding in Minnesota was a strange interlude to the drought that we have been experiencing everywhere else. We're soon in Erie, sitting at another restaurant table for breakfast, this time eating Greek omelets.

Annelise and Bill have been great promoters this morning. We've packed posters and flyers in Robert's pack, and everywhere we pass a church, they put a poster under the door. Everywhere we stop in a store, they hand out a poster. We could have used them along on the whole ride, paving our way with publicity.

The New York border seems to keep fading into the distance ahead of us. When we finally do come to the sign that welcomes us to the state, our energy soars.

New York! Our eighteenth state. We're here!

We have come 4,106 miles. One thousand to go.

This is only the far western edge of a big state—but we're here! All the way across the country we've been shouting "New York!" whenever people ask where we're going. That won't do any more.

Twenty miles later we are at Erie State Park. We decorate Harvey with red and white streamers for my dad's seventieth birthday. We have some leftover cookies from our last presentation, and we top seven of them with candles and sing "Happy Birthday." The kids have been collecting twigs to get a small campfire going. We're in bed by 10 p.m., and there's no need to get up early.

Sunday morning in a state campground: no church, no riding, and no schedule. Kai and I roll out of bed at 8:30—what a luxury. It's been so long since we've been camping that Amy is spoiling us. Annelise and Bill help her make bacon and eggs and pancakes for breakfast. We've still got local cherries from yesterday. After breakfast, everyone heads out. Robert and Amy load their van for their family trip to Niagara Falls. Annelise and Bill get ready to head back to Michigan.

"Come on, Besty," Kai says to my dad, "Let's go for a bike ride." Besty is short for Bedstefar, the Danish word for Grandpa.

Kai and Besty go for a long bike ride. KariAnna calls on the cell-phone while they are bicycling.

"Guess who's riding your bike," I ask. When I tell her it's Bedstefar, she's surprised that he can fit it.

"You're getting to be a big girl if Besty can ride your bike."

I sit down on the picnic bench to the most solitude I can remember in months. Talk about busy days. We've been going full speed since Fargo, North Dakota. Here in New York we have few arrangements for the coming days. A month ago we were trying to schedule presentations for the state. Now we're glad for some unscheduled restful days before we reach Manhattan and the Statue of Liberty.

Anne and KariAnna return to us at 10 in the evening. KariAnna tells me her highlights and then falls asleep. Anne and I curl up together, thankful to be with each other for this last stretch to the statue. On Monday morning my dad packs up and begins his drive back to California.

22
Upstate New York

By trying we can easily learn to endure adversity—another man's I mean.

MARK TWAIN

On Saturday we saw a ridge as we entered New York; it was the first real bulge of land since the Black Hills. It looked pretty, but we thought no more of it.

For six weeks we have chosen routes through this flat land based solely on distance and traffic density. Other than getting around the Great Lakes, we haven't given a thought to topography. We have just one presentation evening in Alfred as we cross Upstate New York; so from Lake Erie State Park, we plot a course that will get us to Keith Cash's home two days ahead of schedule. This will give us the weekend and Monday to visit the cross-country unicyclist who has encouraged us so much. The extra time will also help us plan out our arrival in New York City. Instead of fifty-mile days, we map eighty- and ninety-milers all the way across.

The first indication that we have charted poorly comes on Monday morning. In Dunkirk I settle for a chocolate milk, assuming that we'll have breakfast in Lawton after riding through Cataraugus Indian Reservation on Highway 438. The reservation looks little different from other land in the area, except for the signs in support of or opposing a proposed casino. We're on small roads that don't show on our state map, so we're depending on directions from folks we meet or drivers we flag down at stop signs. After a quick error we get to Lawton, but there is no restaurant and no store. Continuing east on Genesee Road we see no towns, but here we first encounter the evidence of ancient glaciers.

Ridges pattern themselves in north to south lines. In other places, roads might switchback up and down the inclines. Here the road is paved straight up, across, and down each ridge, over and over again. In the West our steepest grades were seven percent. These hills outdo anything we've met so far—wow! It's also hot again, and we're riding this challenge on a single quart of chocolate milk.

Through East Concord we ride. Again there's no store, no gas station, and no café. "We've ridden all the way across the country, and now we're being tested," Robert remarks.

We're carrying no food, because we've gotten used to towns being closely spaced. Finally, in Yorkshire, after fifty-eight miles and lots of up and down, we make it to the air-conditioning of Earl's.

"It's hot out there," our waitress sympathizes as she seats us. "The temperature is supposed to be ninety-four degrees."

It's humid, too, a real steamer. After all those miles without any food, we're delighted that Earl's serves up real home-style cooking with great chicken. Drinks are served in Ball canning jars. We get the one-quart size, and each of us has two refills after guzzling the first.

"We're making it," Robert notes as we eat. "What a ride today."

"I'd better remember to change my four-inch cranks for longer ones. Who knows what's ahead."

Filled from lunch, we head out, ready for more heat and hills. Instead we walk into the first raindrops of a thunderstorm. Big pelting drops soon follow. We get drenched and the dry cornfields do, too. We've had so little rain it's a novelty, and we are instantly cooler.

While we are getting soggy, Anne and Amy have been searching without success for the state campground at Silver Lake. We meet them in Silver Springs at 6 p.m. Usually we finish riding by mid-afternoon. The hills have slowed our eighty-five miles today. By the time we drive over to Letchworth State Park and set up, it's late.

For the first night in a long time the eight of us are all alone. We can count only three nights on this trip without other company. Otherwise we've enjoyed hosts or traveling companions the whole way across the country. The night turns cool, good for sleeping. The air is so thick with moisture that it feels like we're in a cloudy jungle.

Our days are more flexible whenever we get a stretch without presentations. We are ahead of schedule and decide to use Tuesday for business. Robert and Amy take the kids so that Anne and I can head to town to make calls and find maps. AAA has great detail maps of Upstate New York. What a help to have every road marked out as we travel.

We get back and after quick hugs all around, Anne and I head out again. We've got an hour-and-a-half drive south for an evening presentation in Alfred. Anne and I haven't had this much time alone together in a long time. There is always something to do on this ride, one more thing to attend to, one more person to talk to. Today is not exactly a scheduled date, but we make the most of it.

Nearing Alfred, we pass a man and a woman touring by bicycle, and stop our car to greet them. They are hauling bike trailers adorned with license plates from many states.

"We've heard of you," the man says. "What are you doing driving a car?"

We tell them about the presentation and invite them to join us for dinner. They decide to keep riding, since they are now just two days from home. The woman of this duo just graduated from college in Portland, Oregon. Her father flew out for graduation ceremonies, and together they are riding home to eastern New York. What a graduation gift to have this time together.

When I see someone else doing a long tour by bicycle, the road seems newly magical to me and their accomplishment extraordinary. When we are doing it ourselves, we settle into a daily routine so that the ride seems unremarkable. Visiting with these cyclists reminds me of why we get so many surprised reactions.

In the college town of Alfred, our hosts are Tim and Jane Cochran. One day Tim was searching the web for information about the Tour de France and came up with a link to a cross-country unicyclist from Nome. He e-mailed us: "We used to live in Nome. Can you come and visit us when you come through New York?"

Tim had worked for the radio station in Nome. Jane worked at the hospital where I often spent time visiting patients. Before our presentation at the Catholic Student Center, we devour a huge dinner of tofu spaghetti, local corn on the cob, and ice cream with fresh strawberries. A few international students from Asia are attending, and I notice that one of the women begins to look uncomfortable after we begin our presentation. While Anne is talking, I go over and tell her it's okay if she needs to leave. Her answer surprises me. "I just begin contractions." A few minutes later the couple heads for the hospital to everyone's good wishes.

Anne and I drive back to our campsite in the dark. A full moon has risen by the time we reach Letchworth Gorge. We stop at an overlook for a full view of this Grand Canyon of the East. Just Anne and me, a full moon, and one more chance to confirm how much we love each other.

On Wednesday morning Robert and I return to the road to face more hills. We've put food in our packs, but today towns dot our route, including a wonderful breakfast in Geneseo. Our cook speaks little English, but she makes some of the best home fries we've had. She and the waitress come out to watch our departure. As we leave she shouts, "Maybe by car. Never by bicycle. You be careful!"

Just before breakfast we'd seen another reminder of our native history. In the late 1700s, a 4,000 person military operation was sent through the Finger lakes to destroy the "hostile aggressors," the Seneca and the Cayuga and others. Along the route today, we see other signs noting when white settlement started, and where the main village of some tribe or another had been destroyed.

Hills and grades define our day again. And again I forgot to change my cranks; I'm still riding on four-inchers. Fortunately these hills are slightly less steep than Monday's, still it takes until 7 p.m. to finish our eighty-three miles to the Cayuga Lake State Campground. Anne and Amy have set up right by the playground, and a dinner-feast is waiting. The showers are hot. The sleeping is cool. My only wish would be a few more hours of sleep. Heat and hills are sapping our energy.

We're up for a sunrise start on Thursday. Leaving the park we pass by a dozen signs posted in front of private homes and farms.

"No Reservation."

"No Sovereign Nation."

The bottom of the sign informs that they are protesting the Cayuga Native Land Claim.

We ride into the morning, into our ultimate hill day. They're big enough already, but whenever we stop, people tell us, "Wait till you get farther down the road." This time the warnings are right. Near Lafayette and Pompeii, the grades look like walls. On two of them, my legs are quivering, and I lose balance. I fall off before I get to the top, and I need to rest before I get back on and pump over the crest. We're thankful it's cool, but I'm maxed out. I wish I'd changed to longer cranks the night before. After almost three thousand miles on these I keep forgetting.

It takes us nine hours to make fifty-eight miles and reach Cazenovia by mid-afternoon. Our average speed is just barely better than five miles an hour. Usually we're above eight, including rests. Anne catches up with us and tells us, "We saw Rocky again. Amy stopped to see if he wants water."

When Rocky catches up with us, we all laugh. Back in Ohio we had talked about the flat terrain. Now when I ask Rocky if this is more like Japan, he shakes his head. "Japan like this," he says, making a snaking motion with his hand to show switchbacks. "Today is like going up Niagara Falls!"

An hour and a half slips by in the parking lot, and I get my cranks changed while we talk. Rocky decides to look for a nearby campsite. "Too tiring today," he admits.

Robert and I need another twenty-five miles if we're going to make Schenectady tomorrow, but I'm ready for the last stretch. The five-inch cranks give twenty-five percent more torque, making it easy to summit each hill. We find no more grades to match what we've already come through.

We had planned our route through Upstate New York, assuming that every road was equally easy. Looking at the map during a break, we see how much easier the route is up north along Lake Erie. We could have followed the shore of Lake Oneida and then paralleled the historic Erie Canal to Albany. Oh, well. Live and learn. We're on a beautiful ride, and pushing our limits is not all bad. Ahead of us lie the Green Mountains of Vermont and New Hampshire, and lots more of the Appalachians when we head south from New York. We may see more days like this one ahead; this ride isn't over yet.

The day is done before we reach our campground near Bridgewater. After ninety-three miles, the last half hour is pitch dark; we walk our cycles off the side of the road whenever a car passes. Anne apologizes for the campsite, which is right next to the highway. After I get my shower, I come back and the kids are in bed reading with Mommy.

"I love this campsite," I tell them.

"Why Daddy?"

"There's a rule for everything," I joke.

Anne already told me about signing a waiver for the kids to swim in the pond, about getting permission to park both vehicles on one site, about paying for electrical hookup, about paying three dollars extra to plug in our air conditioner, and about paying extra person fees for four of us.

"Why do you like it, Daddy?"

"KariAnna and Kai, this is the perfect way to find out what happens when you want a rule for everything. You end up not being able to do anything."

Before they fall asleep, the kids spend a few minutes designing the campsite of their dreams, telling Anne and me how they would do things. On the whole route, we've encountered just a couple of places like this one. They make me sad, and they make me laugh, both at the same time. Thankfully, and far more often, we find folks who delight in meeting others and in making sure that everyone receives hospitality.

The next morning we start out tired. When we stop to ask someone what the road to Schenectady will be like, we are encouraged.

"It's mostly downhill from here. We're at 1,800 feet. You're going all the way down to eighty. Still lots of hills, but nothing like you've come through."

"I'm a trucker," he adds. "Trucks don't go where you've been."

23
Unicycling Hero

One must keep one's character.
Earn a character first if you can,
and if you can't, then assume one.

MARK TWAIN

In 1981, a failed attempt at an acting career turned into a cross-country unicycle ride. That journey changed Keith Cash's life forever, moving him from depression to an unshakable gratitude for all things lovely in life.

Before the ride, my brother read an article about Keith and encouraged me to contact him. Ever since that first e-mail, Keith has been the most enthusiastic supporter of our family's unicycling venture. This afternoon we'll finally arrive at his home. What are the chances? He lives only four miles from the route that we had planned across the United States.

"There will be days that are tough," he advised. "Just remember your goal and you'll make it."

Whenever I've had a tough day on this trip, an image comes to mind of a twenty-three-year-old, unicycling across the United States, all alone and with no support crew, riding a twenty-four-inch unicycle. No way was I going to miss meeting Keith Cash on this trip.

"Hey, hey, hey!" Keith shouts from his front driveway and runs out to welcome our arrival after the long day of pedaling. Harvey and the Volkswagen have preceded us.

"Welcome home," Anne says. "These people feel just like family."

"Man that's a big unicycle," Keith says to me after a big welcome hug.

My thirty-six-inch Coker dwarfs the unicycle on which he did his ride. I never knew how much faster a big wheel is. What a difference! Keith traveled the country at five, six or seven miles an hour. He did it all with forty pounds of gear strapped on his unicycle, even including a small SVEA cook stove. He never had an air seat either. Ouch. He did it without shorter cranks, or anything extra except a set of handlebars. And off he went to the most life-changing experience of land and people he'd ever encountered.

"The best thing I've ever done," he says. "I was free! And I knew it!"

Craig, Keith's son, tells us, "You should see what my dad bought at the store. He filled the shopping cart all the way."

"You eat a lot when you're on the road," Keith counters. To his son he says, "You watch these guys eat while they're here."

"You must be hungry right now," Keith says to us. "Come in. Eat. Dinner's ready. This is the first chance I've had to pay back another unicyclist for everything that people did for me when I rode." Keith continues, "Some of those people saved my life."

On Saturday we get all our unicycles and bicycles unloaded. The kids are having a ball here. The front lawn is strewn with unicycles. KariAnna is getting assistance with the five-foot-high giraffe unicycle that we were given in Chicago. Robert is helping Nathaniel as he works to get a feel for his unicycle. Kai keeps asking someone to hold his hand while he gets started, then he takes off and rides on his own.

"Fourteen pedals!" We count for him. He beams. "Really?"

A few moments later it's twenty-four. "Yippee!" he exclaims. "Ice cream!"

He's met his next goal of twenty, and we'll all celebrate again with ice cream. A few moments later, he gets sixty-two pedals.

A moment comes for every learner when all of a sudden everything clicks. I still remember that day and that feeling when I became a unicyclist.

For two weeks I had been out in the alley behind our house. Except for dinner breaks, I was hanging onto the neighbor's wooden fence from the time I got home from school until bedtime. My dad had demonstrated for me on the day I got curious and asked him about his orange unicycle that had been hanging for so many years in the rafters of the garage. He had learned in college, during the long nights of working at the campus fire station. After his pointers I was alone with the challenge, the frustration, the study, and the imperceptibly slow learning. Along the fence I would struggle, hanging on tight, pedaling one foot-stroke at a time. When a week passed, I started trying to pedal away from the fence. Pedal, fall, pedal, fall, fall, fall, fall. I had a temper when I was young, and learning to unicycle brought it to the fore. Finally, after two weeks I headed away from that fence and got three pedals. Then five. My mom and dad and brother came out to watch the magical moment. Two days later it all felt easy. I was a unicyclist. My brother soon followed. That year two brand new Schwinn one-wheelers appeared under the Christmas tree.

I remember watching KariAnna learn last year. Now Kai's pedals are the highlight of the day for me, and he wants to be on his unicycle all the time.

"Hey, Lars," Keith says, coming around the corner from his garage, "this is for you."

Keith is pushing a huge forty-eight-inch diameter unicycle out onto the lawn. We have gotten used to thinking of my Coker as big. This is really big.

"Try it," Keith offers. "When you get your momentum going on this one, you really fly."

"I was hoping to break the one-hundred-mile speed record with this after I finished my ride across the country, but I never found a flat enough place to make the ride. I want you to have this. You can break that record, too."

I tell Keith I can't take his unicycle. We go back and forth between his insistence and my reluctance to accept his generosity.

"Lars, one of the most important lessons I learned on my ride was to accept the generosity of people who wanted to help me. Take this. I want you to have it."

"Okay, then. Thank you."

He and Robert assist me getting up. I hold on to their shoulders for the first fifty yards and then take off on my own. Every unicycle feels different. This one lopes down the block in huge pedaling strides. With enough practice, I could do a fast one hundred miles on this thing.

"Isn't it great traveling on a unicycle," Keith says after I'm back, "the way people treat you?"

"Everyone should be treated that way," he continues seriously, "every day. Wouldn't that be great? What a world it would be."

Keith uses the words *love* and *care* a lot. He's one of the most positive people I've met. Watching the news on Saturday and waiting for a newsclip about our ride, we see piece after piece about terror and war.

"They're still showing this stuff?" I ask.

"All the time." Keith replies. "If we could just figure out how to love each other instead of fighting and warring, what a world it could be."

"I like to think we're the good guys," he adds. "But when you watch this all the time, you start to wonder." A few minutes later Keith is laughing again. The news has just named me "The King of Unicycling."

Keith and Vicki's home overflows with our crew, but they don't seem to mind. We've taken up all the room on the couch, in the chairs and on the floor. When Carl and Nelia and their children and our two dogs arrive, Keith and Vicki stretch their welcome to include them, too. Katie and Luther appear to be thriving after being with the Jenkins since our time together back in Minnesota.

For most of the weekend, we are a crowd. Every once in awhile Keith talks to me alone. "That ride was the best thing that ever happened in my life," he tells me more than once.

"I was in a bad place before that ride. I don't tell people how desperate I was feeling. I was ready to give up. After that ride, everything started getting better. Now I'm the happiest guy in the world," he continues. "I met Vicki and we've got Craig. Life is wonderful."

On Sunday Kai reaches 107 pedals. He's really good at this unicycling, bobbing and weaving along, recovering well when he pedals too fast or leans too far to the side. He and KariAnna will be riding the block together soon. Kai is already working on his next ice cream goal, a figure eight.

In the afternoon the Jenkins head back for Pennsylvania. "We'll see you next weekend in Maine," they assure us.

Monday morning, while the rest of the family is still sleeping, I get up to do more preparation for the finish of the ride in New York City. Media calls, a check with police about a possible escort, phoning churches: There's a long list of things to do, and we just scratch the surface of the possibilities. We could have used a media and film crew on this trip, a logistics crew, and an endowment development crew, too. But then, who really thought we would make it all the way across the country? Keith did. And he's right, "Unicycling across the country is the best experience in the world."

On Tuesday morning we say goodbye and ride to Watervliet and Troy on the Hudson River, first settled in 1649. Compared to Native American history, the date is recent.

Cycling books often warn that "The steepest climbs of a cross country trip may well be the Green or the White mountains of New England." We head straight for them. The climb out of Troy is hard. Rising straight up out of the river valley, Highway 9 is also the main route through the city. Trucks pour smoke at us and wedge us into the gutter of the road.

Vermont

Soon we cross into Vermont, our nineteenth state. In Bennington we stretch out on the lawn by Bennington Tower and end up with an hour nap. The tower, a monument to the Revolutionary War, stands 308 feet high. Here the Green Mountain Boys helped turn the tide of the war, preventing the British from capturing a munitions store.

In this tower visitors can ride up to an observation deck to see New York, Vermont, and Massachusetts all at once. KariAnna has recently developed a fear of elevators and declares, "I'm not going."

I don't know how or why her fear developed, but we have a long conversation before she agrees to ride up.

Amy has been trying to explain the Revolutionary War to Nathaniel. He asks a good five-year-old question, "If both sides are the good guys, why were they fighting?"

Kai's concern is to get back down on the ground. It's not fear that drives him but anticipation. "You said you would unicycle with me Daddy. Let's go."

In the afternoon we officially enter the Green Mountains. The grade the ranger warned us about turns out to be easy. At the top we look back and see the hill marked at eight percent.

"Not nearly as steep as New York," Robert remarks. None of the New York grades we rode were marked. We'll forever be wondering exactly how steep they were. At Woodruff State Park we finish for the day, and get a campsite overlooking the lake. The weather is cooler and the forest has more evergreen, because our elevation is above 2,000 feet.

On Wednesday morning we ride out of the Green Mountains heading for Brattleboro. These mountains are tiny compared to the Rockies, but the feel of wildness and enchantment is back again after the farmland of the Midwest. The morning's challenge is an eight-mile construction section. We're worried for the first mile, climbing a steep grade on a dirt road, the shoulders bermed with gravel. Cones in the middle of the road leave no space for cars to pass us. I jump from the unicycle twice for passing trucks. A policeman is doing flagger duty at the top.

"Never seen that before," he points to the unicycle. "The road is better up ahead." For a while the road is paved again, then a sign announces, "Scarified Pavement Ahead;" it sounds like Halloween. Our costume will be dust and grit. Arriving for breakfast, we are two shades darker than usual.

At breakfast Robert and I often talk about our future plans. "Hiking the Appalachian Trail would be nice someday," Robert will suggest. Other times he will dream, "When the kids get older, we should all hike the Pacific Crest Trail together."

This morning the person sitting behind us at the Back Street Café has hiked the Pacific Crest Trail. "I did it when I was seventeen, back in the eighties. That was before lightweight equipment was light. I still miss those Sierra Nevada Mountains."

After Keith, and now this man, I remember back to the start of the ride, my conversation on the ferry with the bicyclist, "The best things I've ever done in my life, are the ones I can't explain."

New Hampshire

Back on the road, we cross into New Hampshire, our twentieth state. Traffic is picking up on this side of the mountains. The foothills still go up and down, up and down. At a mom-and-pop store, we stop for a soda. It's far more expensive than we've paid elsewhere, and "mom" exudes negative energy, telling us flatly, "We have no bathrooms for the public."

I'm reminded of a similar place back in Wisconsin and resist asking if she has relatives there. We have traveled a whole month since last experiencing this kind of reception. Every time I see it, I'm amazed at the power of an attitude and the effect it can have on me. We step outside to shake off the negativity, resting in the old Suburban seat which serves as a couch.

"Looks like a restroom right over there," I say when we finish our soda. We step behind trees and relieve our bladders.

Keene is crowded. AAA Travel is in a shopping area where cars are thickly congested. The woman who helps us starts to tell us about her father who was training for a Maine to Florida bike trek.

"He was seventy-two…"

Her voice catches in the middle of the telling.

"He was hit by a car…and killed."

The drivers of most cars we meet are great; a few would do well to hear her story and its terrible pain.

"AAA told us there's no camping at the Otterview State Park," we tell Amy and Anne when they pull up.

"Okay," Anne responds. "After lunch we'll go ahead on Highway 9 and start looking for a campsite after we pass South Stoddard."

In the hot afternoon Robert and I push on, riding another twenty miles. We find the motor home and van parked at Pine Haven, an old-fashioned place with cabins for rent, advertising breakfast. The kids are playing outside. Kai is unicycling.

"No campsites ahead," Anne says as we pull in. "We've got permission to park here overnight."

When I step inside to visit the owner, she is taciturn as she queries me, "What are you doing this for?"

I explain.

"How are your children doing?" she interrogates.

"Fine."

"You should take them swimming. There's a lake down the road." She says, softening. "What the kids will remember about New Hampshire is the lovely water. You are taking them swimming aren't you?"

It takes some wrong turns to get the directions sorted out, but on our wandering path to the lake we see stone fences everywhere. Building them used to be the best solution to the endless supply of rocks picked out of fields. Some of the fences are decaying, reminders of when this was farmland. Like the West that we traveled through earlier, transition has been constant here. Next to the old fences are new expensive ones: stylized, perfect, surrounding elaborate homes. The recommendation for the lake is a good one. The water is warm, and the lake is surrounded by trees.

Back from swimming, Amy makes another great dinner. Today, she found meatballs at the store, so we have spaghetti. While she's cooking, Anne and I take the dogs for a walk. Katie and Luther seem to like the traveling life, exploring every new place we come to. We eat outside for dinner. The adults are sitting on new lawn chairs that Keith and Vicki insisted we take along. The kids put their plates on the hood of the Honda; it ends up decorated with spaghetti sauce. Anne found ice cream and root beer at the store, so we all have floats before bedtime.

"New Hampshire," Anne says as we fall asleep. "We're almost there."

"Everything still going okay?" I ask.

"Everything is still fine. I'm glad it's cooled down a little bit."

In the middle of the night, the dogs scramble from underneath the motor home, the chain clanking as they move. I hear a surprised yelp.

"What's that?" Anne asks.

"Don't know."

"No way." I say a moment later. "It can't be." We open the window shade to look out at the dogs. In the moonlight, Luther is pawing at his nose, rolling himself in the dirt, intensely agitated.

I can usually live with the smell of skunk. On this trip we've had ample opportunity to smell these guys in every stage of decay. This is different. This is more than odor; it's force, penetrating deep into our very being. It is impossible to sleep. As we reel from the smell, we envision scenarios and solutions. Midnight hours are the time for the most dire worries.

"We'll have to shave the dogs."

"We'll have to get kennels and strap the dogs on top of the Honda for them to travel."

"Everything we own is going to smell like skunk."

"Can you imagine finishing at the Statue of Liberty, smelling like this?"

Thankfully, we are thirty miles ahead of schedule, so we can skip riding in the morning to find solutions. Somewhere around 3, we waft back into sleep, finally saturated by the skunk's contribution to our ride. The kids haven't stirred.

The next morning, in Keene again, the vet assistant asks Robert and me if we want "the magic recipe." We've already scrounged half a dozen cardboard boxes to protect the floor of the motor home where the dogs will lie. While she's writing, the veterinarian comes out. His name is Lee, and he is surprised by our presence.

"You lived in Nome? I've been to Nome. I went there to see the Iditarod."

"We used to watch the race every year."

"You're really riding your unicycle across the country?" Lee asks if we can wait a minute. "I'll write you a check for the endowment fund." What are the chances of finding this benefactor? I wait for him to return and thank him for his gift.

"So this stuff works pretty well?" I ask, holding up the recipe.

"It's good," Lee replies. "You'll still smell skunk a little bit, and if you wash them in two weeks, you'll smell it again when they get wet, but it helps a lot. We see bunches of skunks around here."

Off to the store we go for dog shampoo, a quart of hydrogen peroxide and a quarter cup of baking soda. Directions:

• Shampoo your dog.
• Mix the peroxide, baking soda and a tablespoon of liquid soap and wash your dog in this. Work it into the fur, especially on the face if that's where the skunk sprayed. Let it sit a bit, then rinse.

Anne and Amy and the kids are having breakfast on the porch of the main cabin when we return. Pine Haven lets us use a hose and I get to the task of washing dogs. Huskies have a lot of fur, so I triple the recipe. Every time they shake, I'm showered. Fortunately, I am wearing only my underwear. Katie and Luther are patient, though; maybe the washing relieves them as much as us.

Anne and I thought the skunk sprayed from behind the motor home. Robert sniffs out our site and reports, "The aroma will be coming with us. That skunk sprayed underneath the motor home."

24
Statue of Liberty

Distance lends enchantment to the view.

Mark Twain

"The dogs smell okay," Anne reports when we arrive at our next campsite, just east of Concord. There's a pool, so we all cool off. Temperatures once again reached the mid-nineties.

After showers, Anne and I head off to town for dinner together and to pick my mom up from the airport. She's joining us for the last two weeks. Robert and Amy are taking the kids for the evening.

Time to celebrate. We're reaching Maine and the Atlantic Ocean tomorrow. In our focus on the Statue of Liberty, we've almost forgotten how much of a highlight tomorrow will be. We have now gone coast-to-coast.

"We've made it, Anne!" We lift Margarita glasses at the Applebee's restaurant.

Skunks, heat, mountain passes, motor home challenges, wind…land, people, friends, surprises, family…it has all really happened.

"Still want to go back by unicycle?" I ask.

"Let's do it."

After dinner we drive to the airport in Manchester, pick up my mom, and return to the campsite at midnight. Twenty-three hours after the visit from the skunk, there's only a gentle reminder of how the day started out.

Everyone is sleeping when Robert and I start out in the morning for the Atlantic Ocean. New Hampshire, the first state in the Union to hold presidential primary elections, the state where the "shot heard 'round the world" was fired to start the Revolutionary War, is also flag land these days. In the wake of 9-11, some houses are decked two and three deep in flags and posters. We figure the red, white, and blue will get thicker and thicker, but later in the morning when we cross into Maine on Highway 101, the amount of color drops again. We have reached our twenty-first state. Now we have twelve miles to the ocean.

Maine

Nearing York, Robert calls out, "Ocean air!" It is our first whiff since Whidbey Island.

York is crammed with cars and people. Incorporated in 1652, the town is celebrating its 350th anniversary. At a fruit stand, three moms yell out an invitation for free lemonade. Sunday is "Children Appreciation Day," so moms are handing out lemonade and cookies. "My son wants a unicycle," one of the moms tells me.

"Talk to your bike store or check out 'unicycle.com,'" I tell her. Many people are asking about unicycle information for their kids, especially when they see KariAnna and Kai riding.

Two more miles and we're at York Beach. The day is July second. We have been on the road for 103 days. Suddenly, at last, we're at the Atlantic Ocean!

York Beach is horseshoe-shaped with rocks on both sides that protect the wide sandy shore. Huge mansions are visible to the north. A bike cop is visiting with the lifeguard as we ride up.

"Can we leave our shoes under your stand?" I ask as we get barefoot to push our cycles across the sand to the water. "We've just ridden all the way across the country."

"You're nuts," the bike cop tells us.

"I see your sign about alcohol on the beach," I continue. "I suppose we have to leave the bottle of champagne in the bike bag?" Robert had purchased a bottle at a convenience store back in York. It was their finest $7.59 champagne.

We start walking onto the beach and he calls to us, "Leave your shoes here. And yes, you can go ahead and drink the champagne. Congratulations."

The bottle pops when we get the cork pushed up. After getting our picture taken we toast the ride and each other, pour champagne on our wheels, and look out at the water.

Anne and Amy call on the phone. The roads are too busy for them to join us here. We decide to meet a dozen miles south in Kittery. Sitting for a few last minutes we finally stand and walk up the beach.

"Better start heading for New York City."

Soon we cross into Portsmouth, New Hampshire, a zoo of a road system, crazily congested. I make it through on my one wheeler, weaving between stopped cars. How will Anne do it with the RV, pulling the Honda? She calls later to report how challenging the driving is. The land is now densely populated, and the roads bend, fork and change names often, making them hard to follow. It's Friday afternoon at the height of the tourist season; finding a campsite is difficult. Our support crew is experiencing all this while Robert and I are riding south on Highway 1A, cruising along the coast.

This has to be the richest stretch of road we've encountered on the entire trip. Mansions perch on acres of intricately manicured lawns and gardens overlooking the magnificent ocean. I pay two dollars for a pint of chocolate milk, wowed, almost forgetting the South Chicagos, Gary Indianas, and Pine Ridges that we have traveled through to get across the country. Places like this have a seductive beauty, but I wonder about the current tax cut debates and who gets what benefits.

Glenn Johnson, an Agriculture Economics professor, and one of my elder mentors, used to tell me, "Every economist, even the most conservative, agrees that redistribution is essential to a successful society. The difficult question is how to do the redistribution." We pedal on, knowing only that more work is left to do on this issue of who gets what.

"Amy is headed your way to pick up Robert," Anne says on the phone. The two of them are taking a weekend trip alone to explore Maine. "And I'll come back and pick you up," Anne adds, "after we get settled at the campground. It's way far inland. This day turned rough."

Robert and I got to pop the cork at the beach. Our support team deserves the toast. Carl and Nelia and my mom have also pitched in to find the campsite, attend to the children, make dinner, and keep the day going.

Amy drives up in the Westphalia for their weekend trip. As Robert loads his bike he asks, "Can you do this alone?"

"Time to start practicing. I'll do my best, and you have a great weekend."

We've had an entire summer together. It's strange when they leave and drive north for Maine. Only a week remains before they head back to Whidbey Island. Originally, I had expected that Robert and I would be doing a lot of riding on our own, meeting up a couple of times a day. Instead, especially after the first month, he has been at my side the whole way. A person gets used to the company after almost five thousand miles. The next hour of riding feels strange and lonely.

Anne picks me up at Hampton Beach. She's worn out and lets me know how hard it's been. "I don't know how we'll get through New York City if traffic is this bad here."

"I don't know, either. We'll see."

Nelia has spaghetti waiting when we return. The kids are playing at the campground. RVs are stuffed together because many long-term folks camp here. A few sites down is a boy who rides a unicycle. When our kids first see him, their jaws drop in astonishment. Then off they go, pedaling together, the frustrations of their long day instantly forgotten. I expect we'll get to New York day by day, the same way we've gotten this far.

Massachusetts

On Saturday morning, Carl drives me back to yesterday's finish point, and we cycle together for ten miles. Beaches here are packed with high-priced houses, shops, and motels. Seabury Nuclear Reactor sits close to the middle of all this. No wonder it has received so much negative attention over the years. When we get to Massachusetts, the road bends inland. At Salisbury we stop at Pat's Diner.

Ms. Pat seats us. Our table has articles posted about the opening of her diner. She bought it at the age of seventy, and she plans to run it for five years, retire again, and then go traveling. The long lines at the diner are the result of great food and great hospitality. She seems to be everyone's best friend. Pat visits with us for a moment and listens to our adventure.

"I'm buying your breakfast this morning," she tells us. "Let me know how everything turns out."

After breakfast Carl heads back to pick up the car and drive home for another week of work. "We'll see you at the statue," he promises.

"Great. Just one more week." I ride south into Massachusetts, our twenty-second state.

Newbury, Rowley, Ipswich and Beverly, all of them trace roots back to the early part of the 1600s. Historical markers are thick here, Beverly was the seaport for Washington's Navy in 1775 and 1776 during the Revolutionary War. The first covered wagon left from Rowley to make a new settlement in Marietta, Ohio.

By 10 a.m., Route 1A is crowding up with weekend traffic. I'm in Salem by 11. A photographer is waiting at the bridge to take a picture for the newspaper. Yesterday, the reporter who interviewed me by phone asked if I ever worked circuses.

"No, just churches," I replied.

He laughs. "I'd better not print that."

Salem, famous for witch hunts, has a national park service visitor center. I've only got ten more miles to my destination in Lynn. The morning is going well, even riding alone. At noon the visitor center is showing *The Past is Present*, so I wait around to see it to learn more of the area's long history. First were the Native Americans, then sailing, and then textiles; Lynn was once the biggest shoe-manufacturing town in the nation. Massachusetts was once the second most industrialized region in the world after England. One in three workers died here before putting in ten years at the factories, a cause for early union organizations. After the movie I get a call from Anne. "The muffler fell off. It got sandwiched between the duals on the back and popped the outer tire. We're on I-95 and dead in the water."

While this is bad news, there is much to be thankful for. The second tire didn't go flat, so it was safe to slow down and get off the highway. No one got hurt. A highway patrol vehicle was right behind Anne and pulled over behind Harvey to help.

Still, Anne and my mom are stranded on the interstate in ninety-plus temperatures with four kids, sitting in a motor home with no air-conditioning. I am back and forth on the phone with Anne for the rest of the ride to Lynn. The first tow-truck driver knows little. He calls for a big rig that can tow semis. I listen on the phone as Anne talks to him.

"It'll be here in four hours. Stay with the vehicle or they won't tow it."

"How much will it cost?" Anne asks him.

"I don't know, but you have to have cash."

Thankfully a second tow driver stops unexpectedly. He takes a look at the problem and has Anne driving in five minutes. "We can just pull that muffler out from between the tires," he tells her. No problem. "You can drive it in on one tire."

I'm in Lynn by this time. Pastor Neal has shown up at First Lutheran Church and has offered me his car.

When Anne gets off the freeway, she calls again, "We're staying at the McDonald's on the corner, and we're not moving out of the air conditioning until you get here. The tire sounds horrible."

Arriving, I see the shredded tire still on the rim. With a kitchen knife I cut it off. Anne and Mom and the kids go to Lynn in the Honda and Neal's car. I drive the RV slowly with Katie and Luther napping the whole way. Just the faintest skunk smell lingers.

We are thankful that we're making a stop and presentation in Lynn. Neal really saves us today. He first heard about us at a pastors meeting and started e-mailing to ask if we could make a stop at his parish. I hope he's still glad he asked after being saddled with all our troubles.

This congregation in Lynn used to be entirely Swedish. Now on Sunday morning a whole mix of different cultures arrives for worship. Several families of refugee immigrants from Africa are part of this congregation. One family from Sudan has been at the church for four years, and a God-speed blessing is prayed for them as they prepare to move to Lancaster,

Pennsylvania, to begin new work and live with a community of other Sudanese. Another young woman is being prayed for as she heads to Argentina for service work. Along with everyone else, the founding Swedes are still worshipping here. It's a real mix of cultures, unusual for the Lutheran church which is historically so tied to its northern European roots.

After lunch at Neal and Martin's home, we head back to church. Robert and Amy return from Maine, and Robert chides us, "We leave, and look what happens to you."

"Yeah, we're hopeless. You'd better ride back with us to California."

Their weekend has been fun—no catastrophes for them. In Freeport, Maine, they helped to celebrate L.L. Bean's eightieth anniversary. It got them free kayaking and canoeing. Robert got another new hat.

"It was sure cool up there compared to here. And a lot less crowded," Amy tells us.

"This is not Montana," Robert says. "Too many people and too many roads here for me."

On Monday morning we get the tire repaired but not the muffler. No one in the area has a lift for the motor home. We decide to drive it without the muffler until we find a place to do the work. It's really loud. Anne says, "Okay…but this isn't the way I was hoping to finish our trip."

We pedal off by 10:30, thankful the tire repair has been quick. Anne and Amy roar out of Lynn soon after. They are planning to take the interstate, skirt Boston, and drive all the way to Rhode Island.

Boston. For a boy from Los Angeles who loved the Lakers, there's something almost foreign about unicycling through the home of the Celtics. Boston was unimaginably distant to me as a kid. It was also my destination when I bicycled across the country. This is now the third intersection between my unicycle trip and bicycle journey.

For the last leg of my 6,000-mile bicycle trip, I rode out onto Cape Cod and camped on the sand dunes. An old dune person also was there: naked chest, sun-browned, reminding me faintly of my Grandpa Frede who would come from Denmark and lie on the beach in southern California until he was beet red.

At the end of bicycling the cape, I took a small ferry back to Boston. I sat at the stern, near my bike, near another old man who appeared to live on his ancient bike. He had tied bags all over. After three months of life-building conversations with so many people on the open road, I wanted to talk with this man, too, but he wanted no part of me. Standing next to him as we disembarked with our bicycles, I spoke one last time, "Have a good ride. Have a good day."

He looked at me then, as he got on his bike, and just as he was ready to pedal he said loudly, "Snow. S-n-o-w. I hate snow!"

Other than checking onto the airplane the next morning, that was the last real conversation of my trip.

I came away from that journey with strong convictions about the power of human experience and the capacity for land and people to transform us. I came away believing in the power of kindness and mercy. It was enough. Still, as I think of that old man who shouted "Snow," who spoke the benediction word for my ride, I wonder if I stopped my journey of bicycling experiences too soon.

Now here I am again, after all these years. Robert and I take the subway under the harbor and pop up downtown at Government Center. A bank sign reads ninety-five degrees as we step out from the air-conditioned train.

A red-haired patrolman fills out my Guinness Record mileage slip, and we ask, "What's the best way to get out of town alive?"

"Don't worry; it's daytime; you're safe."

I laugh and then clarify, "I mean, which road is safest for us to ride on?"

We start out on Tremont, and after a block we stop to see the cemetery where Paul Revere and John Adams are buried. Then we move on again, riding past history faster than we can absorb it. Boston is good to me as I unicycle. The drivers make it easy for us to get through. We get lost a couple times. Where the roads Y, we often see no indication of which direction to take. Twice we get onto wrong routes, but the corrections are easy.

With our good treatment, I am surprised to learn how bad Boston's reputation is for bicyclists. It is so bad that masses of cyclists sometimes gather to pedal slowly down a boulevard and clog traffic to protest the poor biking conditions.

"I think it just makes the drivers even more angry at us," says the bicyclist who shares the story.

"It hasn't rubbed off on unicyclists," I tell him.

Often we have thirty miles finished before breakfast. At 2 we stop for a sub-sandwich lunch, having come only twenty-four miles. Late starts make it feel like our odometers are broken, but we are making progress. Our goal before the motor home repairs had been Providence, Rhode Island. Soon after lunch we get a call from Anne.

"We're at George Washington State Park. It's a nice campground here, and the lake is warm and good for swimming."

George Washington State Park is on the west side of Rhode Island, even farther than Providence.

"Okay. We'll keep pedaling and see how far we can get."

Rhode Island

South on 1A we get to Woonsocket just after 5. We're riding through rolling forested land, and the miles go well even in the heat. Since we're out over dinnertime, I've offered to buy for Robert as thanks for the tour. Robert has lemonade, and I have ice tea with dinner. The glasses are almost quart-size, and we each drink four of them besides filling empty water bottles.

Riding into the evening makes us reflective; I ask Robert, "If you could pick one day to ride over again, the most perfect day of the trip, which one would it be?"

Together we recall days and events. No day was "perfect." Every day had something special in it. As we finish riding over Pound Hill Road, Robert says, "That was about as nice a piece of road as we've traveled the whole trip."

Compared to the congestion of the Massachusetts coast, this part of Rhode Island, our twenty-third state, is a rural paradise. Here we feel far removed from the roads of even the past few hours. A thunderstorm is rumbling just north of us. The sun throws a brilliant fringe on the thundercloud's edge. We stay on the dry side of the storm, finally making camp just at dark.

"You should go swim in the lake," the kids tell us. "It's warm like a big bathtub."

We take their recommendation, enjoying a quick swim in the dark to soak the sweat off before we fall asleep.

Connecticut

August 6—we have four more days to the statue. We ride rural roads alongside corn fields again today, going a full thirty-five miles to find breakfast in Onesca, Connecticut. The states are going by quickly now, Connecticut is number twenty-four. We end up in Mystic, meeting our families at the aquarium. Whaling ships made this town famous. Old Mystic has a reconstructed seaport that celebrates its past. The whaling had effects as far as the Inupiat people of the arctic and the Makah people back at Neah Bay.

While Anne and Amy take the kids to the aquarium, Robert and I get another new tire for the RV, because the front right side has started shaking. The salesman tells us our old tire is from 1985.

"Your steel belt is separating. That tire did pretty good getting you this far," he tells us.

Across the street is an auto parts store. Robert suggests we try fixing the muffler ourselves.

"Anne will be thrilled," I answer.

We get the parts, and Robert has the motor home quieted down in an hour, bolting pipes and a new muffler in place.

"Awesome, Robert," I tell him. "I don't know what we're going to do next week without you and Amy."

August 7—three more days to the Statue. We've got our sights on Hammonasset Beach State Park in Connecticut. With two interstate bridges to cross today, Anne drives shuttle to ferry us across each one. The temperature has cooled off by ten degrees. It is indescribably more comfortable to ride in this weather.

The area becomes increasingly populated as we approach New York. Still, there's lots of countryside to be riding through as we make our way on Highways 184, 156, and then 1. Hammonasset has no camping, so we end up at nearby River Farm Campground. We've come to a couple of RV places like this where folks have permanent campers set up, summer homes with porches, steps, small gardens, and storage buildings. Before Robert and I arrived, the kids covered themselves to their eyeballs in dirt and then decorated themselves with charred sticks from an old campfire. We take them swimming in a small pond, which removes some of the grime. Showers make them recognizable once again.

August 8—two more days to the statue. Into New Haven we ride through countryside. From here on it's city or suburb driving, constant commerce, growing ever thicker as we approach NYC. Our route is dense with McDonald's and Dunkin Donuts. With the fine weather, we easily make forty-five miles by noon. Drivers continue to be considerate. Enthusiastic folks holler out windows or from their work. A group of men on a construction project yell down to us from their fourth-story work area.

In Westport we stop for lunch at a Thai restaurant. Prices seem high, but after thousands of miles of American cooking, Robert and I are set to enjoy this treat. Our waiter tells us the owner wants our picture when we finish eating. "Martha Stewart was here two days ago," he adds. "The restaurant is brand new, only one month old."

The spicy food is a feast for sight, smell, and taste.

"Stand here," the owner tells us after we've eaten every last noodle. Robert and I pose with him standing behind the unicycle. Then he points to the rickshaw in the corner.

"I brought this over from Thailand. Here, you sit on the front," he motions to me. To Robert he says, "you sit here with me in the back."

This is fun. Media will be great if it shows up in New York, but the really good stories, the real excitement keeps happening day-by-day.

Another few miles and we're rolling into Ken and Candace's driveway. Ken is a distant relative. We grew up together in Los Angeles. Anne and Amy show up a few minutes before my brother from San Diego arrives to join us for the ride's finish. After visiting until late in the evening, I scramble one more time to get all the updates done, along with the Guinness stuff and the logistics for the rest of the way. In a few more hours, we'll be pedaling our last full day of riding on this trip across the country. All of us are wondering what it's going to be like to ride through New York City.

August 9—one more day to the statue. We make it to New York City, into Manhattan and Central Park, fifty-five miles from our start in Connecticut. Through Queens and East Harlem and places we have never been before, we ride to the exclamations and encouragements of horns, voices, and waving hands.

How is it to pedal through New York City? For a unicycle and a bike traveling together? Awesome. Bumpy roads. Tons of traffic. Loads of people. More to look at than we can take in. Sensory overload. What an energy rush. Swept along by all of it, we reach Balto in Central Park at 1 p.m., three hours before we'd promised Anne to be there for our pickup.

August 10—The Statue of Liberty! My brother Karl drives us back to Central Park from the Wal-Mart parking lot where we camped Friday night. Anne and Amy are along with their bikes for the final lap to the statue. The four of us will finish the journey together.

From the Balto Statue to the Statue of Liberty, we have seven final miles. The weather is perfect, clear and warm. We ride almost the entire way on a bike trail along the Hudson River; this last leg that we have wondered so much about turns out to be easy. In the last mile we take a slow and wordless walk around the ruins of the World Trade Center. Only two more blocks remain down Broadway to Battery Park.

Friends! There are twenty-eight of us altogether, a crowd of purple "One Wheel – Many Spokes" tee-shirts. The National Park Service is waiting for us with free ferry tickets. Security is tight for everyone; a search dog even sniffs my unicycle pack bag.

AP News and a Lutheran Magazine photographer join us for the ride to the Statue. "You know," the AP reporter says to me, "I asked your former student friends what kind of a pastor you are. They answered with one word—different."

Yes, and what a different, surprising, wonderful gift of a summer it has been.

5,032 miles.

2,819,000 pedals.

24 states.

110 days.

What a day of celebration we share, savoring it as long as we can. Finally we step onto the Staten Island ferry, which takes us back to the cars. Chrisy Bright calls to tell us that our finish has just run across the CNN ticker tape. Back at the motor homes we do what we do every day: load bikes and unicycles, walk dogs, get everyone fed, and on this evening, drive to friends we're staying with in New Jersey. As Carl observed, "Today felt like a wedding. You plan and plan and plan, then the day comes, there are lots of pictures and excitement, and at the end of it you're putting wrapping paper away."

"You're right, Carl," I answer. "And weddings change your life—forever."

At long last we have finally crossed the USA, and we have added countless spokes of experience to the wheel of our living.

I began the trip in search of hospitality.

I began the trip feeling crazy from round-the-clock reports of terror and violence and carnage.

These have been rushing days of festivities and celebration. When the end of the day comes, I lie down to sleep, but sleep is a long time coming as I look back on our journey.

For four months now, the members of our traveling band of eight have opened themselves to the surprise and uncertainty of our country's open roads. On a single wheel, I have been vulnerable, not only to every passing car and truck, but to every place and person. By unicycle or bicycle, there is no quick escape from anyone or anyplace, only the slow progression of pedal after pedal. Constrained to this one-wheel pace, Anne and Amy and the kids have shared this space completely. Day after day we have managed to proceed in the face of our imperfections.

We have been immersed in America, and everything we experienced across the country is right here in Manhattan. The whole island was bought for fishhooks and glass beads worth sixty Dutch guilders, a precedent of the continental conquest to come. In the midst of all Manhattan's history is also a triumph of visionary foresight—Central Park. On the other end of the island is the Statue of Liberty, perhaps our most enduring symbol of national and global freedom. Two blocks from the Statue is horribly violent wreckage, now just a hole that once was the World Trade Center—gaping sign of a violent world from whose cup we also drink deeply.

I remember back to Tim at the Colville Indian Museum in Washington. The root, which is the soul of Mother Earth, is still in its necklace bag and has been part of our journey across the land.

"When you get to the other water's edge," he had said, "kneel down and say the prayers you have kept all during your ride."

My prayers this summer have been questions. We seem a people of contradictions, living together in Huckleberry Finn's soup of odds and ends. I need more time on the road, more time for the juices to swap around, to taste this soup, to search for what balances our land, and to feel the soul of Mother Earth. At this far water's edge, I pray my questions:

How can a nation of such hospitality be so violent?

How can a nation of such violence be so hospitable?

How, in the midst of it all, shall I and my family live?

PART THREE

25
New Challenge

Habit is habit and not to be flung out of the window by any man,
but coaxed downstairs a step at a time.

MARK TWAIN

oast to coast...to coast!

We have four days to plan our ride back to the Pacific. Immediately we begin poring over maps to sketch in a rough route. Coming back will be a different adventure; we anticipate it will be more challenging. We will be traveling alone. Compared to coming to the Statue of Liberty, we have done virtually no planning for the return trip. We'll be on the road when school starts, so homeschooling will have to be figured out.

Sunday afternoon, Robert and Amy, Caroline and Nathaniel pack up their Westphalia and start back for Whidbey Island. Their departure leaves a giant hole behind.

"It would have been a miserable business to have any unfriendliness on the raft," Huckleberry once commented after the Duke and the King settled an argument. "For what you want, above all things, is for everybody to be satisfied, and feel right and kind towards the others."

That seems the perfect commentary to our four months of riding and living together. We had hooked up on a whim, hardly knowing each other at the beginning of this ride. We had no guarantees we would mesh together and thrive in one another's company. We part as family, feeling "right and kind" towards one another.

For the first day, the Martins will follow Carl and Nelia to their home in Pennsylvania. Carl and Nelia have our dogs with them and will keep them until we finish the trip. The coming months will likely be too hot, too busy, too unpredictable for Katie and Luther. Who knows how many skunks they might find!

Starting and ending adventures almost always spike my apprehension. That I got on the road in Tillamook four months ago without these jitters now surprises me. The hesitation is back. We are changing from a summer's adventure to a commitment of more than half a year. We have few contacts on the return trip to the Pacific. That old desire for predictability has crept back in—exploiting my uncertainties.

Tempering our doubts is the continuing celebration of our being here, of really making the ride across the country, of all the miles adding together with successful result. The *CBS Early Show* interviews me in Manhattan on Wednesday. *CNN* calls us to make arrangements for an interview when we reach Washington, D.C. We're staying these four days with Judy, Anne's childhood friend. Her family provides good balance to our flurry of activity and emotion.

Each of our four days of planning sees the temperature rising from the perfect weather of our finish at the Statue of Liberty. By the time we are ready to start out, the temperature is well into the nineties.

Along with the planning, we also have filled a fat three-ring binder with Guinness World Record documentation: maps for each state, detailed route descriptions with dates and times and mileages, and the signatures of over three hundred witnesses. We airmail the bulky records to England and begin waiting for word on the twenty-four-hour distance ride in South Dakota, and the ride across the country. We have included our plans for the ride back to the West Coast and our hopes to keep adding to the total mileage.

Late Wednesday night, we fire up Harvey and leave our friends to drive back to the Statue of Liberty. Harvey gets us as close as the Newark airport; the tangle of bridges and expressways convince us that we are close enough. At 2 a.m. we find a place to park which is as much figurative as literal; we are stopped next to a cemetery. The Ride East is over. The Ride West begins, and the first 1,500 miles will be southerly.

26
Underway

Supposing is good, but finding out is better.

MARK TWAIN

New Jersey

M e.

Just me now.

No Robert. It's going to be different.

I am on the road at 5:30 a.m. the morning of August 15, starting back across the country on three hours of sleep. The first Guinness signature is from the Hilton hotel around the corner. A circle of folks are waiting for the shuttle to the airport. They each take a business card for "One Wheel – Many Spokes" and wish me well. Newark is crowded, even at dawn. This whole eastern coast seems crowded—a sea of people next to the ocean. Anne phones an hour later.

"It's too hot to sleep. Where are you? I'll catch up for breakfast." She's feeling alone, too, now that she is without Amy, Nathaniel, and Caroline.

Highway 1. Highway 29. After New Brunswick, I head west on 518 toward the Delaware River. Anne and the kids are visiting the park where George Washington crossed the Delaware. She calls again on the phone. "There's a great campsite we found, twelve miles up the river. We'll meet you in Lambertville for lunch." All of us want time together as we adjust to being just the four of us.

Arriving, I am thankful to sit down. Breathing has been hard today. I take light breaths; the deep ones hurt. This is the first day I'm reacting to smog and heat. I remember these symptoms from when I was growing up in Los Angeles. I haven't felt this way since high school cross-country practices.

After pizza in Lambertville, I ride the last seven miles to the campground at Bull's Island State Park, crossing the old canal that was once used for hauling goods alongside the Delaware River to Trenton. We spend the last part of the afternoon swimming in the river. Folks let us borrow their inner tubes to ride the rapids; over and over the kids ask for one more ride.

The sun goes down. The first day ends. We're headed back.

"I will be there at 10," I told people at Philadelphia Lutheran Seminary when they invited us to stop by on Friday. This morning there are thirty-two miles to travel. I get a 6 o'clock start and arrive at the seminary at 9:57. Some days I am as dependable as a train. Anne drives up ten minutes later with the kids. Mark, the publicity director, has called the news stations about the ride. No media show up. One day we're on *The Early Show*, the next day nothing. You never know. After lunch and visiting I get ready to ride. Folks try to help with directions, advising, "There are some places in Philadelphia that are best not driven through."

"Heat index is a hundred and two today," I hear from a woman walking the sidewalk. It is a poor day to unicycle through Philadelphia. Tempers are high; patience is low. In one traffic jam, I weave between shoulder and sidewalk, passing jammed cars for miles. I leave Philadelphia on Highway 1, then cut south to Chester.

Chester is one of those places that makes the warning list. I roll through in the late afternoon. Families are on porches. Folks are walking the streets. Car windows are down. Kids and parents and grandparents, everyone here is African-American. After a long and careful day of looking in my rear view mirror and working my way through Philadelphia traffic, the greetings, looks, smiles, squeals and hollers refill me with energy. If I weren't trying to meet Anne in Delaware, I'd ask someone here for porch space to spend the night.

"Time is money," we are told—it seems the more that people believe it, the fewer the greetings I experience. In places like Chester, where more time won't make more money, people have time to spill on curiosity and hospitality. Maybe this is my connection with Chester. If time really were money, I wouldn't have set out on this ride across America.

Delaware

Ninth Street has no sign marking the border of Delaware. I find out I've entered our twenty-sixth state a few miles later when I check the map for directions to Wilmington. Anne meets me there. Just before she picks me up, a man blares his horn and hollers at me for walking across a six-lane boulevard. "Get out of my way, you damn idiot," he bellows out his window, racing just inches in front of me as he turns. I'm in the crosswalk, and there's a green walk sign lit. A half-mile more and I step gratefully into the refuge and family of Harvey.

Maryland

Saturday morning brings a new surprise. Corn again. After plugging through massive congestions of people since Connecticut, I end up hungry and thirsty in the rural farmland of Maryland. Towns are tiny and sparse, spaced far apart. What a surprise. After many dry miles, I come upon an old-time grocery where I get a half-gallon of orange juice. A block later I see a pizza place and stop there, too. The only bank thermometer I've seen read ninety-four degrees—and that was early, before it got hot.

The corn is suffering more than I am. A gentleman tells me there's been no rain for two months. The breeze rustles through corn with the dry sound of Halloween. Dry leaves, tiny cobs, soybeans a foot or less high: Damage is everywhere. The road warning sign just south of Wilmington reads, "Drought Area. Conserve Water." The front page of the paper tells how drought is affecting some forty percent of the country. Another article reports that Wilmington is starting to use its water reserves. The drought we've seen over so much of the country is hanging on and deepening.

I finish the day at Queenstown. We're staying with Ruth and Arne, Anne's friends, who live across the inlet. Arne tells me, "I'll come and pick you up by boat; it's much faster than taking the road around."

Ruth and Arne have three children. One is named Lars, the only other Lars I've met on the trip. "He's funny," Kai and KariAnna tell me that night, reporting on their adventures with the kids and a dead frog at Chesapeake Bay.

Sunday morning I'm in the Honda, driving towards CNN in downtown Washington, D.C. The unicycle is strapped on back. With me is Matt, a good friend from our Michigan State days. He's driven down from Philadelphia where he's attending Temple Medical School. I ask him how school is going.

"It's hard, really hard."

The strength of a faith, in my eyes, is whether or not it has capacity to deal with the dark side of the world, the "shit happens" part of the world. Matt has challenged me further in this direction than anyone else in my life. Certain people in this world seem to travel the knife-edge between hopeless despair and gritty survival; the journey often produces brilliant, compassionate genius. I haven't ever gone as far or deep as Matt. Somehow we became best friends, partners in the probing of life and faith. One day Matt came to me with a book from Douglas John Hall titled *Why Christian?* Handing me the book, he pointed to a line:

Our vocation is friendship, solidarity, and the stewardly care of others.

"I can wrap a life around this one," he told me. "This is where I'm looking to get."

Today we retrace our times past and enjoy being together again—joking, laughing, driving down the interstate, windows open to cool us on another broiling day.

At 11:30 a.m., Fredericka Whitfield in Atlanta interviews me in Washington D.C. I sit alone in a sound room staring at a black box that the CNN people assure me is a camera. I see nothing of the interview. Matt verifies that he saw it. The four-minute interview takes most of eight hours in travel time back and forth to Chesapeake Bay.

On Monday morning I continue the ride from the east side of the Chesapeake Bay Bridge. Annapolis, Maryland (home of the Unites States Naval Academy), forested land, small towns, and then increasing development mark my ride to the Capitol. I feel a thrill, after riding across America, to at last bear down on these symbols of our land, the Capitol Dome and Washington Monument, unicycling on Constitution and Pennsylvania Avenues. It is another "I can't believe I'm here" moment. Anne and the kids meet me downtown at the base of the Washington Monument.

This evening we're in Springfield to visit Mike, my high school buddy, and his family. We were also classmates at the Air Force Academy. Mike stayed in and has served the Air Force since graduating in 1983. A wall hanging with nine hearts dangling from it says, "Home is where the Air Force sends you…" Each heart has the name of a place they've been stationed. We don't see each other often; our children grow more than a foot at a time between visits.

Mike got all my e-mails from the winter before this ride, back when I was writing with ballistic vehemence against the notion that the war in Afghanistan was achieving our nation's goals of long-term safety and security. We talk until late in the night. He's more willing to believe that our anti-terror program is on the right track. Something inside of me remains deeply worried that the path our nation is on is going to have terrible consequences for the long term. And by now there's talk about going to war in Iraq.

✳

On Tuesday morning we load ourselves into a Hyundai rental and begin a one-week road trip nested within our larger journey. Our destination is Tyler, Minnesota, where we will give a presentation that was arranged long before our ride began. Driving seventy-miles-an-hour all day on the highway, while enjoying air-conditioning to keep us cool, and the chance to be all together makes the day a treat. KariAnna and Kai, without Nathaniel and Caroline since New York, have turned pretend play to a high art. Two small stuffed elephants, Ellie and Tweeker, careen with the kids through a daylong odyssey of fantasies. Anne and I keep the radio off and enjoy their show for hours at a time. By midnight we've gone over a thousand miles and reach Grandma in Decorah. After breakfast we drive to western Minnesota. An hour before we reach the Dannebod Danish Center in Tyler, we see smoke rising ahead.

Approaching, we find a barn fully engulfed in flames. Neighbors have arrived, but so far no fire department. We watch for a moment. The kids are transfixed, but we can do nothing to help. Driving on, we talk about what we've seen. KariAnna and Kai decide they will invite others to give gifts we can leave for the family on our return trip—another experience of their home-school education.

One of our presentations is standard—*Unicycling in America*. The other is specific to this Danish conference—*Growing Up Grundtvigian*.

My parents are first-generation immigrants from Denmark. Grundtvig of the 19th Century is the major figure who has influenced my maturing faith. I've grown to appreciate him more and more. In overly simplified terms, Grundtvig asserted that we are *Human First—Then Christian*.

In the 1800s, Grundtvig was the world's foremost Beowulf Scholar. He also learned ancient Norse mythology, where he found expressions of spirit that complement Christianity. He loved nature and found in it the hand of God. He loved culture, folk dancing, and singing. Grundtvig's theology prepared me to go to the Inupiat culture, appreciate what I found there, and learn.

Grundtvigians call themselves, "Happy Danes." It's wonderful to be part of this group. My only reservation is our lack of emphasis on dark-side stuff. I wouldn't care so much except that all of Grundtvig's joy for life comes after struggle. One of his biggest joys was falling in love with the mother of two students he was tutoring, but he fell into an agony of despair over the reality and the impossibility of this love. These Happy Danes sing and dance and laugh. I wonder what they do with the dark stuff of life?

I ask this question in my presentation, wondering what folks will say. Afterwards some thank me. The theology of "shit happens" is not morbid but realistic, and the scripture verse, "The truth will set you free" comes to mind. Reality, perhaps, deepens our happiness.

An elderly man comes up to me while I'm standing on the porch; he's a second-generation immigrant. "We need another Grundtvig, or another Luther, or another Jesus. We need something," he laments. "Our churches are dying. The creeds don't make sense anymore. I don't hear anyone talking about what matters anymore."

"I agree with you. I read that during the nineties the ELCA lost something like another 100,000 members." I tell him that Anne and I have been trying to figure out whether it's better for us to stay in the church or to work outside of it.

"What would you do outside the church?"

"I'm not sure. I know from being a campus pastor, though, there are lots of people with spiritual questions who will never go to a church. A lot of those people have good reasons."

As we head in for lunch and I sit down with our family, I know I will be thinking about this elder's remarks for a long time to come.

The kids have found a big sandbox and they're content.

"All the people are really nice here," KariAnna tells us, "and they have a *lot* of food."

Before we leave, people contribute over $300 to help the family whose barn burned.

On Saturday morning we leave for the 1,400 mile drive back to Washington. Two days to drive here. Two days at the conference. Two days to drive back. Nuts? Perhaps. To us it feels like a vacation.

27
Into the Appalachians

You see my kind of loyalty was loyalty to one's country, not to its institutions, or its office holders. The country is the real thing, the substantial thing, the eternal thing; it is the thing to watch over, and care for, and be loyal to; institutions are extraneous, they are its mere clothing, and clothing can wear out.

MARK TWAIN

Virginia

I resume the unicycle journey at the Washington Monument, in downtown Washington D.C., pedaling west for the Appalachians. The day is gray, the suburbs seem endless, and the Virginia roads are as poorly shouldered as any I've ridden on the whole trip. We have no more friends ahead of us until Atlanta, Georgia. Today feels like the real start of our trip back; the task feels suddenly huge.

I am not the only one feeling strangely. When Anne and the kids catch up, I hear that Kai begged to stay at Mike's house and keep playing with the Nintendo. Over lunch, KariAnna shares her fears of growing up; her primary concern is that she might forget about her elephants, Tweaker and Elly. Anne is keeping an even keel for the rest of us.

Back on the road, before I even get out of sight of the restaurant, I see flashing lights in my rearview mirror. They stay behind me. In disbelief I pedal off the road, dismount, and wait. The patrol car stops behind me, and the New Baltimore officer comes out of his car.

"I need to see your ID," the officer tells me.

Flustered, I hand it to him, and then flash anger.

"What do you need my ID for?"

"We had a complaint about your riding. Someone called and said you're riding all over the road, causing a hazard."

More anger. I keep silent. Earlier I had ridden by a gravel quarry and used all my experience to stay squeezed on the non-existent shoulder as gravel trucks and cars streamed by all through the late morning riding. My eye was constantly in the rearview mirror, checking for whenever I might need to jump off the road.

When the officer returns after checking my ID, he is friendly, asking questions. Where am I from? Where am I going?

But I am surly by this time, unable to lighten up even though I realize I ought to. Why, I wonder, don't you check out the person who made the complaint instead of me? Why don't your roads have better shoulders on them for safety? Why am I getting the blame?

Topping it off, a newspaper reporter has stopped on the road to photograph this moment. He's shooting from ahead with his long-distance camera. When I am freed from the officer, the photographer stops me and asks questions. I am short with him too, handling this whole encounter poorly.

On and on I ride, out of the suburbs at last and into something new— the states that confederated and fought on the southern side of the Civil War. I am entering the land that seceded on news of Abraham Lincoln's election in November of 1860. It was a war partly about slavery and the abolitionist movement, but as Abraham Lincoln replied to a *New York Times* article in August of 1862, it was about the survival of the United States.

> *If I could save the Union without freeing any slave, I would do it; and if I could save it by freeing all the slaves, I would do it; and if I could do it by freeing some and leaving others alone, I would also do that.*

Slavery and the fate of the Southern plantation was one issue; the 1850s census showed that half of all Southern wealth was going into just two out of every thousand families. Economic expansion for the North was another issue; worker strikes and rebellions had been growing in northern factories since the 1830s.

For untold miles ahead, I will be crossing battlefields. Of the thirty million people of the North and the South in 1861, 623,000 died and another 471,000 were wounded in all; over a million people, one of every thirty Americans fell in combat. Even after all the death, the racial and economic issues from that war remain.

The first battlefield I ride across is Manassas. The Confederates won both of the conflicts that took place here. The first one on July 21, 1861 caused 4,700 casualties. The second one in August of 1862 left over 22,000 soldiers either dead or injured.

In the afternoon, stopped with the motor home at the side of the road in Amissville, I see a car pulling up behind us. A man and woman get out and walk up.

"You must be on a quest," Mike says, looking like some cross between Don Quixote and Robin Williams. "I guess I'm on a kind of quest, too," he laughs. "First day of school, teaching high schoolers again."

We end up with an invitation to stay overnight at Mike's place. Southern hospitality is kicking in, and we thankfully accept. He is renting the old slave quarters on a large plantation. We park the motor home in the middle of a grassy field and spend the evening visiting. A dozen years ago Mike hiked twelve hundred miles of the Appalachian Trail. A girlfriend convinced him to come home that summer before he finished—he has been pecking away at the rest of it every summer. This summer he was up in Maine logging miles.

"I saved the best for last!"

At first I think that only chocolate milk and earthworms will be notable as I pedal towards the Blue Ridge of Shenandoah National Park. In Sperryville, at a tiny grocery, I discover locally produced chocolate milk. It is still sold in old-fashioned heavy glass quart containers. There's heft to this experience: the best chocolate milk of the whole summer. Hundreds of earthworms are on the road as I begin the climb into the park. The ones I run over stick to my tire and fly upwards with the wheel until they get caught on the forks of the unicycle, a gelatinous hanging gob. Later they dry out like pasta noodles.

But more than earthworms lie ahead of me today. On the ride up the mountain, a bear cub wanders to the shoulder of the road. When she sees me, she scurries back from the roadside and into the woods. I don't see mama anywhere nearby, but I watch carefully, feeling vulnerable as I pedal so slowly uphill. After the bear, the garbage trucks pass me, two full containers, chugging up the grade just barely faster than my unicycle, giving time for the full effect of their aroma to sink in.

"I saw you in Sperryville," the ranger says when I reach the entrance station at the crest of the grade. "I didn't think you'd make it this far."

As we visit, I tell her about "One Wheel – Many Spokes." When I reach for my wallet, she motions me to put it away.

"You can ride right on in," she tells me.

Then she puts an announcement on the park radio so the other rangers know we are here. When the family arrives in Harvey, she also lets them in for free. We climb to over 3,600 feet inside the park. The road is small, a two lane without shoulders, but the speed limit is only thirty-five mph. Since the only folks on the road are here to enjoy the park, the riding feels safe. The challenge is the mountains: I ride up and down continually.

Curves are constant. The views are hazy to start with and visibility degrades further as clouds move in. At the visitor center, I meet Anne and the kids.

"We've been expecting you," a ranger greets us. "Welcome."

The children enjoy a talk about forest fires in the park. Anne and I are fascinated to learn that Shenandoah National Park began as a conservation effort. The land in these steep mountains has always been difficult to wrestle a living from. As wild game was killed off and land erosion became severe, the resourceful people who lived here became more and more desperate. In 1935, the national government took over the land and created the park. Some who did not want to leave protested, but others were relieved that they finally had some money to help them move on. When the park started all the deer were gone, and there were few trees. Now, almost eighty years later, it's a lush place, teeming with wildlife. When fall comes, the narrow two-lane Shenandoah Parkway becomes a traffic jam of leaf-watchers.

The miles following the visitor's center still rise and dip, but the overall direction is once again toward lower elevation. At five o'clock Anne meets me on the road, "We've got a campsite up ahead at Loft Mountain. We're almost the only ones there tonight." I strap the unicycle on the back and climb into the car. The day has brought us to the Blue Ridge; we've reached the Appalachian Mountains, another milestone.

When we awake in the morning, Loft Mountain is fogged in. I try driving back to my starting point nine miles north, but can't see when I drive faster than ten miles an hour. I turn back. Together we pack up the motor home and then inch back to the park exit. We descend to Elkton where I can continue riding below the clouds. The road runs straight and level here in the Shenandoah Valley, a welcome break from the endless curves and climbs along the ridge.

Stonewall Jackson traversed back and forth through this Shenandoah Valley during the Civil War. He was at the Battle of Fredericksburg just before Christmas, 1862. Almost 18,000 were injured or died during this battle. Although Union casualties were double that of the Confederates, the overwhelming resources of the north were beginning to sway the outcome of the war. Even with this victory, General Lee was finding it hard to replace soldiers and supplies.

We are finding it increasingly difficult to keep up with our own supply needs. An hour after I leave Elkton, my phone rings, and Anne reports, "The whole front tire on the Honda is gone. This is a bad one." She has managed to drive the motor home off to the side of the road and drag the Honda with it. "I'll come pick you up in Harvey."

What looked like an easy day to Waynesboro turns into another vehicle challenge. No one we ask has answers. No one has heard of the wheels on a towed vehicle getting wrenched to the side and not straightening them-selves. We had the Honda checked out back in South Dakota, but they had no answers, either. Today it happens again and before Anne can get off the road, the right front tire has shredded off. It looks serious when I see it, but we're fortunate that the wheel and steering turn out to be okay after we replace the tire. Twenty-six miles is all I make today. The kids don't mind: more time for us all together. Anne and I are growing steadily more wor-ried about Harvey's prospects.

Thursday's ride is easier. Highway 11 is three or four lanes, with less traffic. The last nine miles to Ken and Delia's are rural roads, unmarked tar strips weaving through the foothills of the Alleghenies.

In this land once ravaged by war, Ken and Delia provide another exam-ple of southern hospitality for us. Back at the Statue of Liberty, a man on the ferry had asked a brief question of what we were doing with a unicycle on the boat. "Come and visit us in Virginia," he had offered. "We raise horses."

A note on our e-mail a few days later offered a formal invitation. At the time we didn't know if we would pass their way. When I called them to say we could come, Ken said that back at the ferry he'd had no idea what this ride was for. "I thought you were just some nut who looked like Jesus. Then, I checked out your web site. What you're doing as a family is great."

When we arrive in the early afternoon, Ken bows to each of us with his greeting, "Welcome to Virginia."

These are horse folks. But horses are no immunity from the cares of liv-ing. While Ken helps me jury-rig the awning on the motor home, he tells the story of their daughter getting cancer at five, of Delia getting cancer a few years later. Both are fine now. He tells of how neighbors paid their fam-ily's bills and left food on the porch, "I wouldn't ever wish this on anyone, but at the end of it, I did come out a better person."

Dinner is grilled pork chops, baked chicken, garden grown tomatoes, potatoes and homemade apple pie. Ken does his barbecuing on a "Benjamin Franklin Grill." Elliptically shaped, the grill is made of bricks, stacked seven layers high. The base is four feet long; each ellipse in the stack is smaller than the one below so the sides slope. The bricks are stacked with two- or three-inch spaces left for air to enter. The grill is placed across the top of it. Ken can cook with either wood or charcoal.

"Great draft. Great heat. And you can take it apart and move it whenever you want." They have plenty of room to move their grill—it's a big yard. Ken and Delia live on a knoll overlooking the Shenandoah Valley. Long ago a farm, it's now wooded-over except for the pastures and yard space that Ken cleared out.

"Watch out," I warn. "We might never leave this place."

After dinner we all brainstorm together, working on the endowment fund. We're still hoping something will come together and the fund will take off roaring.

"We'll do our best to help out," they assure us.

Ken offers a suggestion. "I think you could fill the endowment if you just disappeared for awhile and no one knew where you are."

The next morning they send us off with a great breakfast, a big gift for the endowment, and reassuring offers of help. "I know Virginia pretty well," Ken says. "If you need any help at all while you're in this state, just call."

"Thank you," I say. There's no adequate response to the depth of their hospitality.

Almost as soon as I leave Ken and Delia's, I enter mountains. The morning ride, following river grades along Route 39, is easy enough. It runs along the Maury River, which deserves every bit of the mapmaker's scenic route markings. With the drought, the river is only a trickle, but hardwood trees hang over the rocky river bottom all along this stretch.

From 39 I take 42 south to its end, stopping at an Exxon with a café. The cheeseburgers here are big, and as I put one down, the station attendant talks with me.

"How do you get through these mountains?"

"You pedal harder," I reply. "Are these the Alleghanies?"

"Yep, you're right in the middle of them." She takes the invitation to tell me more. "They're older than the Andes. Amazing really. All this was once covered by ocean. That's why the mountains are mostly all rounded off. Archeologists have found fish fossils around here. What's hardest to figure, though, is wondering how folks got through this land before roads."

"That's exactly what I've been thinking about," I answer. "Heat and cold, brush and trees, bugs, mountain slopes, I can't understand how folks used to travel through these lands."

"It must have been tough," the attendant continues. "One of my great, great—I don't know how many great's back—grandfathers fought in the Civil War. He was one of the people who survived the battle of Gettysburg, but then he was captured and held until the end of the war. It took him four years to walk home from Pennsylvania. Four years. Can you imagine?"

The afternoon riding makes it even harder to imagine traveling through these mountains without a road. When I make it to Clifton Forge, all the easy grades are finished. From here to New Castle is forty miles of tar strip country roads. After Lowmoor I climb and descend at grades of eight percent and more for at least twenty-five of the forty miles. It's beautiful, but tiring. After fifty miles for the day, my legs are telling me this is a big day.

After seventy-five I am wishing the outskirts of New Castle are the center, I am so looking forward to being done.

When at last I struggle into town, a police officer is standing across the street and motions me to cross over. "I want to talk with you," he says.

Trouble again? Thankfully not. He has seen our story in the newspaper from when we were at the Statue of Liberty. "It's getting dark soon, and we don't have any hotels here in town. If you need, I can give you a ride to Roanoke."

Five other officers are standing by, listening.

"Actually, my wife should be here in town for me soon. Maybe you've seen her?" I describe Harvey.

"It's right around the corner. You can park overnight in the sheriff's parking lot if you'd like," he says, offering hospitality again. After he signs the Guinness slip, he asks, "Would you mind riding on that street right over there? We're having a car show and folks would surely like to see you ride by."

I ride by the cars and some people sitting in their lawn chairs, then find Anne. She has been searching for me, worried when I wasn't here by the time she arrived. We have been out of cell phone range all afternoon, and the steep grades slowed me down. At the parking lot we cook up a quick dinner before going to bed. All of us are tired.

"I read a brochure at lunch," I tell Anne and the kids. "Alleghany is an Indian word for endless."

Endless is exactly how these mountains feel. The final day of August starts out cloudy in New Castle. Within a few miles, a steep climb has brought me up into the cumulus, into the fog, reminding me of Scottish Highland scenes. Farms are carved into steep slopes; with the mist, I can't tell if I'm riding on a ridge top or through a valley. Halfway to Newport I cross the Eastern Divide: 2,700 feet. From here the Stinking River flows to the New River, which is possibly America's oldest river. The water continues from here to the Ohio, the Mississippi, and finally to the Gulf of Mexico.

If we make it through these mountains, we will meet this water again at the Gulf.

28
Endless

The quality of independence was almost wholly left out of the human race.
The scattering exceptions to the rule only emphasize it, light it up, make it glare.

MARK TWAIN

48TH TRIP CROSS-COUNTRY
FOR MULTIPLE SCLEROSIS
STOP ME AND CONTRIBUTE

The big black-lettered sign is attached to the trailer of a touring bicycle. I see it when I arrive in Newport. Thomas Beasley is sitting by his bike at the only gas station and convenience store in town.

"Eleven years and eight months," he answers when I ask how long he has been on the road.

"Wow! How far have you ridden?" I ask.

"One hundred and sixty-thousand miles."

I'm stunned. "That's amazing."

"How about you?" he asks.

"I'm getting close to 5,600 miles." The number feels puny now, as if hardly worth mentioning.

"On that?" he asks.

I tell him what I'm doing.

"How much money have you raised?" Thomas asks.

"The endowment is at about $250,000. I thought it would be a lot more by now."

"Two hundred and fifty-thousand? You're doing great. I've only got $74,000 after almost twelve years. My goal is $80,000 before I finish. I've probably got another year of riding left." While we talk people come up and hand him dollar bills.

"Twelve years is a long time. How did you get started on this?"

"I was training for the Tour de France. My mentor died of MS, so I changed my plans from the tour to a cross-country benefit ride for MS research. I've been riding ever since. I love doing something I excel at that also helps others."

"Which way are you headed now?" I ask.

"I'm actually hoping to get a ride up to West Virginia. The Louisiana, Virginia Tech Football game is on Sunday, so there's not a room to be had within in a hundred miles. And it's supposed to rain."

We talk while eating peaches and bananas. Thomas always sleeps in a motel, except for once or twice a year when he gets stuck without a place within reach. He counts a cross-country trip as anything over two thousand miles. If he needs a ride from a pickup, he takes it. Outback Restaurant and others are sponsors of his ride, so he eats well, too.

"See this guy?" Thomas says to me. A man with a Louisiana Booster shirt has come back to continue talking to Thomas. "He drove 931 miles to come to this game."

Thomas says this with amazement, as if there is something unexplainably odd about this man's endeavor. And there, for a brief moment, I have a picture of the three of us, each doing what we have come to claim as normal, each seeing in the other some inexplicable oddness. Each to our own strangeness.

The visit ends too soon and I'm back to pedaling. Anne calls to announce a good campsite in Narrows, twenty miles ahead.

"You won't believe who I just met," I tell her.

When I explain Thomas's ride she responds, "Don't start getting ideas. Not if you want to stay married."

"I do want to stay married, Anne."

"Me, too. The owner of the campsite is giving all the kids rides on his four-wheeler trailer. And they're putting on a pig roast tonight for Labor Day. Everyone's invited."

"I'll be there as soon as I can."

Sunday. It's good to be resting after these last six days of riding. More mountains lie ahead. Waking up late, we make bacon and eggs and pancakes for breakfast. Then it is kids' choice for the day,

"Let's carve Ivory Soap bars."

They made their first carvings yesterday, and we make some more now. Everything turns out to have an Alaskan theme. We end up with a village scene on the hood of the Honda. No matter where we go or what we see, when we ask the kids where they want to live, the response is always the same: "Alaska."

When the kids head off exploring on their bikes, Anne and I get a chance to start catching up on logistics again. The campers in the next site have been sitting in their lounge chairs for the past two days.

"We don't do that very often," I mention to Anne.

"No," she agrees, "we really don't." And we don't drive a thousand miles to a football game, or go on twelve-year cycle tours. Each to our own strangeness...

West Virginia

Labor Day. Labor is a good description for these Appalachians. On Monday morning I am quickly into West Virginia. Getting here makes our twenty-ninth state. I don't know much about West Virginia, but Highway 460 has a twelve-foot wide shoulder, all the way into Bluefield. Folks have warned us over and over about the West Virginia mountains. We decide against testing the mountains any more than we have to. The taste we get includes road names like Possum Hollow Road and Greasy Ridge Road. Then we're in Virginia again, and the shoulder disappears instantly. Don't choose biking in Virginia if shoulders are important. We are heading west to Claypool Breaks before we swing up north to catch Kentucky.

Surprisingly, as we enter Virginia, the road levels out for the first time since the Shenandoah Valley. Things are looking good. I'm cruising along. Then Anne calls, "The left muffler fell off. We've slit another tire." She is almost matter-of-fact in her report, but in her voice I hear the sound of being overwhelmed. How much more? How many more times?

"We're on the side of the road. I'll unhitch the Honda and go into Richland to find a campground."

Another call a few minutes later: "No campgrounds, but there's a Wal-Mart back in Claypool Hills where we can park. I'll take it slow and drive Harvey back there."

We agree to meet in the parking lot. Oh, yes. The blinkers had quit working earlier in the day. A fuse was blown but changing it when we met for lunch still didn't get the turn signal working. Anne's fuse is also set to blow when we catch up with each other at the Wal-Mart parking lot.

A man walks over as we're inspecting damages, "I thawt y'all might be having some troubles." He's from Grundy, where we're headed, and after we tell our story, he offers directions. I pull out the map but he doesn't look at it; apparently one of the many non-readers that we've met. With all the Guinness Record slips I've asked to have filled out, it's been surprising to find how many people have politely deferred to have someone else do the writing.

"You wanna get to Grundy?…strahte through." Accents here are so thick that Anne and I find ourselves concentrating hard and still missing words. "You wanna tahr shop? Wahl-Mart raht here can do your tahrs."

Kai and I walk over to check, and sure enough, they've got a tire for our RV. Folks in the lube and tire shop give us sidewise smirks as we make our unmuffled roaring approach. What we look and sound like to onlookers I can only imagine. In a moment, though, Aaron and Lance are asking questions and helping us. They're young and energetic. First they want to see Anne's recumbent bicycle. Then they want to see me ride my unicycle, and then they want a demo ride from the kids. All day long they've been busy and now, during dinnertime, we're the only ones here, so they take their time with us.

"This jack won't lift the RV," Aaron calls out to Lance. He pulls out a second and they jack the rear end in tandem.

Many folks ask what the most beautiful state is that we've traveled in. While Lance is balancing the tire, he asks, "Whas the mos' rednehk place y'all been? Is it raht here?"

"Could be," I answer. "I think you might rank pretty high on the list. There were some spots in Montana, too."

By now Rex has joined the project. Lance has agreed to use his air wrench to pull the rusty muffler nuts off. For some reason the muffler has fallen off at the intake manifold connection. The bolts are still in place.

"No good," Lance calls out from underneath. "We'd just break off the studs. Rex, grab me a coat hanger."

He wires the muffler back in place and comes out.

"Ah do believe that mah't hold you awl the way back to Washington. Y'all could get it wail'ded, though."

Lance is checking air pressure on all the tires. I've told him about the updates I send out on e-mail. "So, are you gonna' wraht about us?"

"I could write about you," I reply. "You guys are great."

Another customer arrives just as they are finishing up with our work. We've had all three of them to visit and help for the last half hour, and we feel better after they get the tire and muffler fixed. The motor starts quietly, and we drive two hundred feet to the side of the parking lot where we can park and sleep overnight. That's our Labor Day.

Muzak wafts all night from Wal-Mart's Garden Center. I'm out the door at 6:30, heading "strahte" north on 460 to Grundy. Fog surrounds me. At first the road has a bit of a shoulder and some straight sections. After about eight miles the road leaves Richland, begins to climb more steeply, and narrows. I climb through one corner and suddenly, for the first time on the ride, I feel afraid. I jump immediately into the gravel by the roadside. Past town now, cars are going fifty to seventy miles an hour. Big trucks are roaring up the grade. It's a four-lane highway, but there's no center median, no shoulder and a rock cliff that's been carved out to make space for the road. A thick fog bank waits ahead by the next curve, ready to cut my safety even further. I walk a hundred yards, but the fear stays. On the other side of the highway is a driveway where I can get back from the road. Chewing sunflower seeds and drinking my water, I sit and try to figure out what to do. On the map I locate another route I can try. I'll have to ride back to Richland, then over to Honaker and north on 80. Attending to my fear, I turn back downhill.

I can't call Anne because we didn't have a place to charge our phones last night. But just after I start back down the hill a young man yells, "How do you rah'd that thang?"

He's shouting from a combination grave monument-ambulance cleaning-general services storefront. When I stop, they are happy to lend me a phone. I give a message to the muffler place Anne is planning to visit, and I leave a message on her phone. When I turn off Highway 460 onto 80, the little winding road feels like a bike trail, and I feel safe once more.

Today we are headed to Breaks Interstate Park so that we can ride into Kentucky. States are lined up close together here: West Virginia, Kentucky, Tennessee, North and South Carolina. As close as they are, though, these states are not easy pickings. The Appalachians ensure that.

"You've got a big climb coming up," I'm told while eating biscuits and gravy in Honaker. "A Mountain" is steep enough that I fall on the inside of a climbing curve. I have to hike fifty yards before the road gentles enough to remount. I stop one more time after an old man in a Dodge pickup stops for my picture. "I've got to have a picture for my son," he tells me. "He used to unicycle when he was a kid."

He shows me an old faded picture from his wallet. A teenager is riding a 20-inch unicycle, and on his shoulders rides his younger brother. "That's my youngest son on top," he says. "He died in a car accident when he was a young man."

He tells me about his son for a few minutes, lingering on the words as he wraps them around his memories. "Thanks for the picture," he finishes. "My son will like seeing this."

The descent on the other side is even steeper, with switchbacks stacked on top of one another. Then into Haysi the ride descends along gentle river grade. A thermometer at the lone bank in town declares the day to be ninety-four degrees. The recent temperate weather is gone. I'm warned about the coal trucks ahead. One of the grades is so steep that trucks are chugging hardly above walking speed. I'm heading downhill, which is great, except that I will have to turn around and climb it tomorrow to get out of Kentucky and head towards Tennessee. I will switch to the five-inch cranks tonight, but still I'm worried I won't be able to ride out of here. These mountains are living up to their name: "endless."

Finally I get to Interstate Park, where Anne and KariAnna and Kai have already gotten a campsite. They ride up on bikes soon after I get there.

"We learned how to use our gears!" the kids tell me.

Fifty-eight miles today—gears would have been nice. Anne's drive has been even harder than mine. She didn't get my message so headed up 460 to Grundy. A sign pointed to Breaks and she took it.

"That's the toughest road of the whole trip," she says, not proudly, but with exhaustion. She continues, "I miss Amy and Robert being along. There wasn't even a center stripe today, and coal trucks were all over that tiny road. It was so steep that I was in first gear almost the whole time, both uphill and downhill."

These have been some challenging days. This area is claimed as the wildest, most remote part of the Appalachian Mountains. After the kids fall asleep, Anne is crying quietly, "I don't know how we're going to do this."

I lie beside her. I don't know either.

29
Breaks

Blasphemy? No, it is not blasphemy.
If God is as vast as that, he is above blasphemy;
if He is as little as that, He is beneath it.

MARK TWAIN

The most famous feud in our nation's history happened right here in the area of Breaks. It was between the Hatfields and the McCoys, lasting from the Civil War all the way to 1921. Breaks Interstate Park was created in the 1950s to highlight these wild Appalachian Mountains. From the park we peer from overlooks down a thousand feet into the "Grand Canyon of the East." We're too tired to do more than note that back at Letchworth State Park in New York another sign also announced, "The Grand Canyon of the East."

Breaks Interstate Park is jointly administered by the states of Virginia and Kentucky. The only problem is not knowing which state you are in. Yesterday, with a mixture of hope and desperation, I had asked the campground host, "Are we in Kentucky?"

"No," he answered. "Everything in the park so far has been developed on the Virginia side of the border. You've got a few more miles on Route 80 before you get to Kentucky."

Close, but not close enough. Our thirtieth state is staying hard to get.

Kentucky

At sunrise I head out for Kentucky. The border is just three miles farther down the road, but all of it is downhill, and half the distance is steep. My only thought riding down is having to turn around and ride back up. When at last I reach the border, I take a picture of the plain green sign that reads, "Kentucky State Line." A dozen yards into the state I see another thousand trees, another steeply descending road, and not a single Kentuckian. I turn around and start back—it will have to be enough.

By the time I get back to Haysi, I've already ridden fifteen hard miles. Good fortune, though, has come for the day. Highways 83 and 63 both follow river grade until almost the very summit of the ridge near Trammel. I share the shoulder-less road with coal trucks and logging rigs all day long. They slow for me when they have to, and honk thanks when I can wave them around to keep their speed up.

Some road sections are cut into rock cliffs and don't allow for shoulders. Other sections easily have space to asphalt a riding shoulder. Strangely, I get a chance to share this thought when a man asks if he can take my picture. I slow and he tells me he's in, "sort of a photo contest. It's called *Transportation on the Move*, and this just may be the winner. My buddies at work won't believe it."

"Where do you work?" I've gotten off my unicycle to introduce myself.

"Vee-Dot."

"Vee-Dot?"

"Virginia Department of Transportation. V.D.O.T."

I share with him my vision of the perfect road shoulder; he takes a couple more pictures, and we part.

Big mansions still stick out when I'm riding roads. Simple housing and worn circumstances have become commonplace. They seem comfortable, full of interesting people with interesting lives. I count on kindness and am rarely disappointed. But here, deep in Appalachia, I can't help but notice the coal company housing, the paint that is sometimes multi-color on one house, and the yards filled with ancient rusting vehicles.

The town of Trammel looks desperate. Lined along the highway are a few dozen homes, mostly of the same pattern, more than half of them deteriorating badly. Fire has destroyed two of the homes; the burned-out shells are still standing.

Just beyond town the road turns to a modern three-lane with a wide shoulder. The river has run out, and now there's a grade to the summit. I stop at the base for water. Anne pulls up just then, and there's space for her to stop right where I am. Things are going better today.

"This road is a joy to drive on," she tells me.

We have our lunch together and talk some more about the challenges.

"This is the last of the worst, I think. But we'll have to figure out if we want to keep going on."

"I guess we'll see. Today's okay."

"If we decide it's too much," I add, "I'd like to make it to Cherokee before we drive home. It's one of the highlights I've been looking forward to."

After lunch I start up the grade. Harvey passes me soon after, going only twenty miles an hour. I'm doing four miles an hour for the mile and a half climb. At the top Anne has the video camera out. A fountain of sweat, I'm surprised at how hard the climb is even with five-inch cranks. My first thought is always that I'm somehow weak on days when riding is hard.

"Look," Anne says, pointing to a sign that reads "Ten Percent Grade." "That made a good shot."

It's the only grade sign we've seen in weeks. But there have been many climbs steeper than this one.

"I think St. Paul is as far as we're going to get today," I tell Anne. "Let's meet there and figure things out."

Hot weather has returned, and at St. Paul I find the family inside the Food City supermarket. With no campsites nearby, we have another parking lot night. We head for the library and get there ten minutes before the 5 p.m. closing.

"No, there's no mall to sit at in St. Paul," the librarian tells us.

We end up in Hardee's, sipping soda, doing homework, and catching up on the writing.

Pre-dawn the next morning is so foggy and with such poor visibility that I go back inside the motor home and nap for another half an hour, hoping the day will brighten up soon. Still, when I get on the road I've got my eye in the rearview mirror for the first hour, making sure that every car sees me and gives enough space. The red flasher light that I carry seems to work. At nineteen miles I'm in Nickelsville. Anne is waiting there, the sun is shining now, and we have breakfast together in the RV. Mr. Mustard, former vice mayor of Nickelsville, knocks on our door to give us an official welcome to this tiny town. The land has gentled; it's still hilly, but we see farms with cattle and corn and tobacco. Our tension eases a bit more.

A notch in the mountains gave Gate City its name; it makes for easy passage through this ridge of the Appalachians. Arriving before noon, we start searching for a mechanic to get our RV back in shape. At Sam's Automotive a man says he won't get under the RV to do the wired-up muffler, but when I ask a few more questions he says he'll take a look if we drive it over.

"What's your name?" I ask.

"Sam," he smiles.

"Now for the part I really love," Sam says. He has accepted the challenge of Harvey. "Welding on the ground. This is why I try to keep away from these jobs."

He puts a new flange on the muffler pipe. It turns out it had worn itself down over the years until it could finally slip off. After he's finished he puts some heavy-duty hangers on each side of the pipes.

"It's not going anywhere now."

Sam has also taken a look at our generator and lets me know there's something amiss with the carburetor on it. I check the muffler off the repair list and replace it with the carburetor.

It's after three o'clock before Harvey is ready. There are forty miles to Greeneville, Tennessee, and we need to get as close to there as possible to make the base of the Smokies tomorrow.

"I'll start pedaling as fast as I can. Today is going to be a late one."

"Call when you want us to come and pick you up."

Tennessee

A few miles south we're in our thirty-first state, Tennessee. I keep riding, skirting Kingsport, and passing the huge Eastman Chemical Plant with its array of smells. The road here has a shoulder. At mile forty-seven I get past all the busyness and back in the country. No shoulder again, but quieter. Much of the land is valley country with climbs and descents that takes me from one open area to the next. It's a gift after constant mountains.

Anne and the kids have made it to Greeneville, the birthplace of Andrew Johnson, who became president after the death of Lincoln. Anne sets up Harvey at another Wal-Mart parking lot and waits for my pick-up call. I make it to the city limits before it's too dark to ride. The stars are shining in the sky when the Honda pulls up. This will be the third night in a row without a shower.

While we're cooking up spaghetti, David Twedt telephones, "Hey, it's really you," he starts out.

For the last week, we've been playing phone tag, trying to coordinate when he'll come and ride a few days with us. David and I went to seminary together in Berkeley, and he's assured me he's going to catch up with us somewhere and ride. Now we're getting farther and farther from his Wheeling, West Virginia home.

"We've had too many meetings," he tells me. "I'm thinking of just getting in the car and coming down after church council meeting tonight."

It turns out to be a seven-and-a-half-hour drive that he starts at eleven. But David is there in the morning, with a full twenty minutes of sleep during the night. Still, I will be riding with the right guy. A few months ago he organized a ride around his West Virginia synod. He bicycled eight hundred miles in seven days to sixty-five churches in his synod, raising funds for bicycles for people in their companion synod in Madagascar. They had a goal of nine thousand dollars and raised thirty thousand. And this was West Virginia—lots and lots of mountains. He should be fine with twenty minutes of sleep today.

We get bacon and eggs from the store, and I fry the bacon up crispy the way Kai likes it. The kids have been hearing about this Dave and are glad to meet him. He has them laughing quickly. Kai has been asking why people ride Harleys. We are seeing lots of them as we travel. I point at Dave whose first purchase after seminary was a Harley, the better to work out the theological bugs from long years of study.

"Some things, if they have to be explained, can't be understood," David tells Kai.

"That's what I say about this ride sometimes. But I'm dreading the day Kai starts using that explanation on Anne and me."

We get a 9 a.m. start; today I plan just to relax and enjoy riding with Dave. I have ridden alone since August 10, and I have plenty of my own theological bugs to discuss after a summer of riding and thinking along the side of the road. Like so many others, Dave is curious about what's next for us, after the ride. "Are you going back into parish ministry?"

"I don't know. When I was in the parish, I was angry a lot. I haven't been angry on this trip. I'm starting to think I belong here on the shoulder of the road."

"But the church needs people working on changing it."

"I know. I just wish it wasn't so frustrating to me. It's an old saying but it feels true for me: Jesus came to comfort the afflicted and to afflict the comfortable. Church seems to be a lot of the opposite, keeping the comfortable comfortable."

We pedal on. Few cars interrupt our travel this morning. The temperature is just right. The land rolls through farm country without any steep grades. Towns are spaced well for food and drink along the way.

"That's why the 'Shit Happens' bumper sticker means so much to me. In seminary we called it the theology of the cross, but more people have heard of the bumper sticker. It turns church upside-down."

"What do you mean?"

"My favorite verses in the Bible are the ones in the Gospel of Mark when Jesus is baptized. The heavens open up, a dove comes and lands on Jesus' shoulder, and God shouts down, 'You are my Son, the beloved; with you I am well pleased.'"

"Why those verses?" Dave asks.

"Well, actually the next one is my favorite. Everybody would expect that with a blessing like Jesus just received, more good things should happen. Most people I know expect good things to follow after doing something well. But the very next verse is: 'The Spirit immediately drove him out into the wilderness.'"

"The bumper sticker?"

"Exactly. So many times in church I hear that if we love Jesus enough, or if we're good enough, then everything will go well. It doesn't even happen for Jesus."

"Like the endowment you're working on?"

"Yeah, I don't like to admit it, but it seems like all our good planning, and all our expectations aren't going to get that fund filled by the end of the ride."

"I don't know about the fund, Lars, but your ride is going to have influence beyond what you will ever know."

"I hope you're right, but I can't help remembering there are five million Lutherans in the church. That's only a buck a Lutheran for this ministry that's totally unique and has so much to offer the rest of the church. I thought this ride would generate all the momentum that fund needed."

"You may end up being surprised."

"Maybe, but whatever happens, situations like these are why I like that bumper sticker and those verses. They're real, at least the way I experience life. And what I like most is the choice that Jesus makes after the wilderness. He could have given up on God, or cursed God, or blamed himself for making a blunder at his baptism, or tried to get rich enough to build a buffer against the unpredictabilities of life. He didn't do any of those. Instead he chose to follow compassion and care for others, to care for everybody; I think it was the only choice that kept him from going crazy."

"Crazy?"

"Yeah, I think compassion kept him from going crazy. We've all got to find some way to face what's unexpected, or unfair, or unjust. According to the life of Jesus, living with that kind of care is the only choice that makes sense. I think that's the strength of the Christian faith and where it meets many other faiths, too."

"You get a lot of time to think when you ride, don't you?"

"Yep, and this is what I think about. What's the next step for our family? Where is the bumper sticker going to pop up next? How is this half-year on the shoulder of the road going to shape our decisions?"

The miles fly by with a good friend to talk to again. After Mexican food for lunch, we get into heavy traffic rushing towards Gatlinburg. Most folks are still gracious. Some, though, buzz past us without slowing or watching for opposing traffic. One calls the police, reporting me as being "all over the road on my unicycle." The policeman pulls me over in Cosby to pass on the driver's assessment of my riding. This time I don't get sullen: I'm learning. After he checks me out he wishes us well.

"I'll see you again when the next driver calls," I offer.

"Don't worry, I won't stop you," says the officer as he signs my Guinness slip.

We're in Gatlinburg by 6:30. Anne picks us up and drives us to Pigeon Forge where she has found a campsite. We've been talking by phone during the day.

"There's a classic car show here. You won't believe it. People have lawn chairs on the sidewalks, and folks are cruising all up and down the town."

"Did you get a campsite?"

"In an overflow section. When I told the attendant what we're doing, she was surprised. She said, 'No one around here is Lutheran.' And she gave us the site for free."

Later in the afternoon, Anne calls from Dollywood. "The kids are having a blast, but it's really expensive."

KariAnna takes the phone for a bit to describe the rides to me. "Daddy, we went on the water-slide! I got all wet!"

After dinner in the motor home, David and I get ready for the drive back to Greeneville so he can pick up his car and drive home. Logistics, logistics. We seem to have developed as much of a system for this ride as the church has developed for its own necessary operation.

We leave at 10 p.m., and I pull our little "One Wheel-Many Spokes" Honda into the cruising traffic. It takes over half-an-hour just to get out of town. Lots of rich exhaust fills the air, shiny chrome and layers of wax flash on the street, car lovers with video cameras film their favorites. Anne said earlier that I should have been cruising with the unicycle.

I don't get back until 2 a.m. Anne stirs when I walk in. We decide to take our Sunday off on this side of the Smokies instead of the Carolina side. The kids are sleeping soundly, and we don't disturb them when we make love. Lying there, holding each other, we stay awake talking.

Dave's visit has accentuated our isolation on this second half of our journey. With each passing day through these Appalachians, our embraces grow longer, the kids wait more longingly for me to finish my daily miles, our goals feel farther distant. Sitting together at the dinner table in the motor home has become such a highlight of the day that it gets harder and harder to imagine having bicycled all alone fifteen years earlier.

"How are you?" I ask, as we lie in each other's arms. "We'll be in Cheyenne the day after tomorrow."

"I'm doing better. The kids had a great day at Dollywood. That was fun. Next time we do a trip, though, I want it to be on a tandem bike again, wherever we go."

"We talked about ending in Cheyenne if this ride feels too hard," I remind her.

"The days are too hot. The trip feels too long. Kai is starting to miss being with other kids. But I want you to finish your ride. I want us to finish this trip together."

30
Deepening South

Whenever you find yourself on the side of the majority,
it is time to reform (or pause and reflect).

MARK TWAIN

"I figured out why Lars is still riding on this trip." Dave had been talking with his wife, Connie, on the phone after our riding together. "All day long people leaned out their car windows to cheer and wave and holler." The ride across Great Smoky Mountain National Park would have done nothing to change Dave's opinion.

The most visited park in the nation is being crowded even more by a classic car convention on the north side in Pigeon Forge, Tennessee and a Harley gathering on the south side in Cherokee, North Carolina. With just a thirty-five-mile ride across the park, I stick around and help load the RV in the morning. We fry up more bacon for breakfast and then drive back to my starting point in Gatlinburg, where I ride into the park. More species of trees exist in this one national park than in all of Europe. Its peaks rise above 6,000 feet, some of the highest in the Appalachians. The Appalachian Trail runs right through the center of the park. The single road across the park is two-lane, no shoulders; there's fifteen miles up on the Tennessee side and then twenty miles down on the North Carolina side. Near Cherokee the park connects with the Blue Ridge Parkway, which snakes all the way up to northern Virginia where we were two weeks ago. Cherokee is where the name says it is, right on the Cherokee Indian Reservation.

Smoky Mountain National Park today is a rolling car show. Except for a single rude and dangerous driver, traffic is so slow that the lack of shoulders is no problem. Cars hum. Harleys roar. No one goes faster than twenty miles an hour, often slower. The climb is steady uphill for fifteen miles with no descents. A canopy of trees covers the road, holding in the suffocating exhaust. The fumes today feel like the reason for naming these mountains "The Smokies."

Halfway to the summit, two Winnebagos overtake me, and I stop to wait while the line of cars passes. But the line keeps on and on. After a couple of minutes, Anne drives by in Harvey. Then I decide to start timing the length of the line while I wait. Then I give up waiting and pull out as a long line of motorcycles give me room to merge back onto the road. Before the last car in the line gets by, nineteen full minutes elapse. There is a break of a few hundred yards, and then more cars start passing again; the traffic feels like Manhattan.

North Carolina

The south side of the park has fewer vehicles but still plenty. In addition to the exhaust fumes I breathe in the stench of overheated brake pads. Cherokee is a welcome sight when it comes into view. We have arrived in North Carolina, our thirty-second state. The Dairy Queen tempts me in for a large Heath Bar Blizzard. Anne calls and drives over to meet me. They have a campsite in town and have spent the afternoon at the Cherokee Museum.

"If you go to the Cherokee Indian School," KariAnna reports, "you have to learn the Cherokee language. No one graduates without learning it."

"They almost lost their language," Kai adds to the report.

The guide told Anne that most of the good river bottom farming land stretching to Kentucky, West Virginia, Virginia, Tennessee, North Carolina, South Carolina, Georgia, and even Alabama, was first cleared and farmed by Cherokee. The present reservation is a dot in the middle of the original lands. And this speck was not granted to the Cherokees by treaty. They had to buy it, this land which was theirs to start with.

The Cherokee that live here are the descendants of those who fled to the mountains and avoided the Trail of Tears that forced most Cherokee to Oklahoma. The Cherokee are the most well-known, but only one of the many, many tribes who were "removed" from their lands to empty western locations like Oklahoma and Kansas. The Cherokee had even tried to assimilate and please those who were coming into their land. Chief Sequoyah developed an alphabet and written language, a local press was set up, missionaries were welcomed and a "western" style government was established.

Despite treaties promising land and rights for "as long as the grass grows and the water runs," President Andrew Johnson and the State of Georgia kept relentless pressure on the Cherokees. It became illegal for Cherokees to testify in court against any white. A law was passed prohibiting them from digging for the gold that had been recently discovered on their land. Cherokees who advised others not to join the migration were put in prison. So much pressure was applied that eventually five hundred of the seventeen thousand Cherokees agreed to migrate. That was enough for the government to go ahead with the removal of all seventeen thousand people, beginning on October 1, 1838. Of the Cherokees removed, some four thousand died on the trail. In December of that year, President Van Buren reported:

> *It affords sincere pleasure to apprise the Congress of the entire removal of the Cherokee Nation of Indians to their new homes west of the Mississippi. The measures authorized by Congress at its last session have had the happiest effect.*

People sometimes wonder if genocide like Hitler's Nazi regime could ever happen in this country. It did.

Today a person can ride right through Cherokee without ever knowing what happened. Ramada Inn and Harrah's Casino and all sorts of commerce make for a place that can easily host a Harley gathering and serve as a gateway to the park. A billboard as you leave town is painted completely black with three yellow words, lettered large, "Know Cherokee History." We hope our children get a flavor of the history, the artwork, the dances, the trials, and the hopes.

Since our time in Nome, I have often wondered what difference it would make if Native American history and loss and suffering were as much a part of our national consciousness as the Declaration of Independence and the Bill of Rights. Perhaps we would attend to things more humbly.

At our campsite in the evening a Harley pulls up with two riders, Danny and Kim. Kim's jacket reads "Property of Danny."

"What's this all about?" Danny points to the "One Wheel – Many Spokes" lettering on Harvey.

A good long conversation later, Danny tells me this is the most interesting thing he's heard about for a long time. He gives us the big bills from his wallet, and an invitation to their home if ever we're on the eastern side of North Carolina. Harley folks have been universally great on this trip. This day they were "no-hands" riding past me, and punching encouraging fists into the air. I stopped once to get a picture with a couple dozen bikes that were gathered at an overlook. They ribbed me for having no motor and just one wheel, and then gave me best wishes for good traveling.

On Monday morning I am quickly off the reservation and riding on Highway 107 toward South Carolina. There's very little traffic, the river winds just beside the road, and the mountains seem softer than back at the Kentucky border. At mile forty I reach the 6,000 mile point at another summit of the Eastern Divide. I am once again at the parting of water between the Atlantic and the Gulf of Mexico. The elevation is over 3,800 feet.

South Carolina

Occonee State Campground comes up at 5 p.m. We are in South Carolina. Everything has been downhill since the pass. With school back in session, summer's crowds are gone. A couple from Germany is camping nearby; otherwise, the place is ours. After dinner we walk to the dock and watch the lake absorb the sun and close another day. Back in Harvey we have time to pull out the maps and sketch a rough tentative schedule to Los Angeles. After two hours of plotting, we guess we might arrive on November 10.

Fifty states? A week ago it was taking everything we had to make it hour by hour through the Appalachians. I grew to understand for the first time what people have been talking about when they perceive our trip in terms of persistence. Last week California seemed too distant to imagine. Tonight it feels much more possible. South Carolina is our thirty-third state. Seventeen more to go.

There is lots of road still ahead, a lot of curves, and probably more of what we've come to count on: surprises. We'll keep taking them one at a time.

Georgia

Just a few miles beyond Occonee campground I finish with the Appalachian mountains as they shrink to foothills and the earth turns bright red. It was just a few years ago, on my first drive through Georgia, that I experienced the red hills which Martin Luther King, Jr. referred to in his "I Have a Dream" speech. Separating me from Georgia today is the Savannah River. No bicyclists are allowed on Interstate 85, which is the only bridge within miles. I end up hitching for a ride and three folks with a lawn and garden service soon stop with their truck. They pump me for info during the few miles across the Savannah, dropping me off at the first exit in the thirty-fourth state of our journey. Dad's Restaurant is at the off-ramp.

"Y'all eat at Dad's," it advertises. "It'll make you look good." The waitress serves me up a double portion of chops for lunch and I feel beautiful.

Four miles later Anne calls. At first I think she's joking: "We lost another muffler."

Like the other two, this muffler falls off and slits a rear tire (the inside left one this time) as it gets caught between the duals. She tells the details, "This time the muffler ripped off the handles on the sewer tanks. While I was pulling over we sprayed the road with a long brown streak."

"No way," I respond. "That's the third muffler on this trip."

"It's really crappy this time," Anne says on the phone. By the time she drives the Honda over and picks me up in Lavonia, I've bought a hacksaw and some muffler strapping to make repairs.

Attitude is everything. In these gentle red hills we are all in better spirits: less taxed, less stressed. We know the routine. Use the big kitchen knife to cut the slit tire off the rim, drive slowly to the nearest city, find some kind folks at a tire place. Rusty and Tony get us fixed up in Lavonia. We celebrate our survival with outstanding pizza, then drive to Tugaloo State Campground. Kai finds firewood and we pop Jiffy Pop popcorn on the campfire. Neighboring campers warn us to watch out for skunks after dark. KariAnna sees one and for the rest of the evening, she and Kai stay close, pointing their flashlights to search the dark.

It is September 10. Tomorrow is the eleventh, the one-year anniversary of the terrorist attacks on the Pentagon, the World Trade Center, and the plane which crashed in Pennsylvania. Three thousand died last year. I think of the children and the other surviving family members. I relish each day with our two kids and can't imagine us all living without each other. I keep seeing the big hole in the ground that we walked by during our time in Manhattan, and the pictures from last year.

Still, as I ride along and think of these things day after day, I am afraid that our nation's reactions are moving us into isolation from the rest of the world, and further from long-term global harmony. Compared to the three thousand who died at the World Trade center amidst such attention and grief, thirty thousand children die every single day from starvation, lack of water, and lack of medical care. Year after year, these deaths go largely unnoticed. And now whole communities are perishing and will perish in Africa from the AIDS epidemic.

As I pedal into the morning of September 11, the Atlanta paper deepens my reflection. The front page is filled with the names of every single victim. They are printed one by one. Somehow the children, the victims, all of us: We are neighbors.

Besides the grief of the page full of deaths, something is physically wrong inside of me this morning. The temperature hits ninety-four or ninety-eight degrees depending on the bank thermometer you choose. I've grown used to this, but today it seems hotter than ever. I ride five miles and feel as if I'm starting to vaporize from the inside out. I rest in shade and continue on five miles at a time until I meet the family at Dairy Queen in Winder. Food doesn't taste right, either, and I start getting chills. After an hour I only feel worse, so we have to call it quits. We've come fifty of the ninety miles that we planned to Decatur. Thankfully, on this night, we are headed to the home of friends.

As soon as we arrive I go to bed. Anne and the kids stay up, doing their best on the dinner that Becky and Michelle have prepared: five pounds of fresh mashed potatoes along with barbecued chicken, both regular and jerk style. Michelle has pulled out her childhood Hot Wheels cars, and the kids are having a ball. Anne is catching up with these good friends from Michigan State University. Campus Ministry comes through again for us.

I have officiated at a lot of weddings, but Becky and Michelle are the only two women who have ever asked me to officiate for them. That was three years ago, here in Atlanta, as we celebrated these two people and their ceremony to commit their lives to one another. They wore white dresses, and their attendants shone like angels around them in the little church where they were married. Michelle's boss was so taken with their wedding that he's ordered her to stay home with us as long as we are in town.

I wish this were enough description, just as for women and men who choose to marry one another, but in our society's polarization around human sexuality there is too much judgment. I've been a part of these conversations in the Lutheran church for a dozen years now. What continues to surprise and sadden me is how often our churches focus on dividing the world into right and wrong. This seems the exact opposite of what Jesus was all about. He constantly broke down barriers: including the excluded; loving the unlovable; and sharing the news that this unpredictable and mysterious world is best navigated with the compass of compassion.

Becky and Michelle are quite simply beautiful people. We are the richer for their friendship. If KariAnna and Kai can grow up to walk in the footsteps of their kindness, their caring, and their competence, we will be proud parents indeed.

In the morning I feel better, well enough to visit the "unicycle.com" store in nearby Marietta. I think it may be the biggest unicycle shop in the country, certainly the biggest Internet supplier of unicycles. John and Amy Drummond have invited us to visit when we come to Atlanta. They started the company three years ago with a dream and $700.

Walking in the front door we're greeted by John and Amy and a couple dozen different unicycles. Wheel sizes range from twelve to forty-three inches tall, and from one to three inches wide. The array includes mountain unicycles, road unicycles, giraffes, and penny-farthing spin-offs.

"This is the showroom and these are our offices," John points as he begins our tour. And then he opens the door to the warehouse. Wow!

A couple thousand feet of floor space are stacked to the ceiling with boxes and boxes of unicycles. There are hundreds of rims hanging from racks, and bins filled with unicycle parts. It's a feast just to look at.

"Roll your unicycle back here," John tells me. We put my rusting Coker on the work stand in the shop. The shiny new look is long gone.

"I want to do something for your ride," John says, beginning to inspect my unicycle. "It's an incredible journey you're on. How many miles so far?"

"Six thousand, one hundred and one," I answer.

He is amazed at my ride. I am amazed at how he and Amy got started. John tells me, "I worked for IBM for twenty-three years. They used to have a service helping customers set up web sites, and they got us going with ours. The whole time we were putting this together, I kept saying to Amy that I can't believe someone smarter hasn't already done this. Every day, I'm doing what I love."

John and Amy's three boys all unicycle. John's been riding since he was a kid. A corner of the warehouse is stacked with all kinds of wheeled things for KariAnna and Kai to try out when they return from breakfast. There are bicycles with three-inch wheels, scooters and hybrid uni-bikes. John and Amy seem to have perfected the combination of work and play.

We started out to just replace my bearings and true the wheel. By the time we're done visiting and tinkering, I have an all new super strong aluminum wheel instead of the original steel one, new black cranks that look sharp, and some standout yellow pedals that hold my feet in place well (I wish I'd had them in the Appalachians). When we spin out of there, I'm styling like I never have before on a unicycle.

"We're Christian people," John explains to me. "We teach kids at church and we're involved in an evangelism program there, too. Lots of unicyclists are Christians and we like to be supportive. We're really impressed with your ride."

Again and again I tell John thanks. In return he thanks us for taking time to visit them. If it's true that service matters as much as people say, "unicycle.com" will keep growing quickly.

After the unicycle excitement, we turn our attention to Harvey. We find a place to get the generator running, a new toilet installed, and the waste valves fixed after the most recent muffler trauma. I keep reminding myself that our whole RV investment in Harvey is less than the first year's depreciation on a new motor home. While it's still true, the repair bills are starting to add up. When we pick up the motor home, the mechanic tells us everything is fine again.

"That's a good generator you have. Those last forever."

On Friday morning Anne drives me back to Winder where I'd quit two days earlier. Becky and Michelle both have the day off and join me for the next forty miles. It's good to be on the road with friends, but this is not a road for visiting. We make our way from two lane to four lane, and finally to six lane congestion on our approach to Atlanta. Anne calls in the morning as we're riding, "Congratulations! Guinness World Records wrote us. Your records are now official!"

Certificates will arrive in eight weeks or so. Everything has been verified. They've been busy, Guinness apologized in the e-mail. Their delayed response had been a worry. Had they gotten our submission? Was it lost somewhere?

Hearing the news today is perfect in another way. Al and Rosemary Lieffring and their kids, Nick and Richard, were with us the day that we broke the record just east of Toledo, Ohio. They were on vacation from Athens, Georgia. This evening we're scheduled to drive to Athens and give a presentation at their church. The Lieffrings seem to be good luck for us.

"There was another note in the e-mail," Anne tells me on the phone. Walter Wangerin, the Lutheran pastor who was bicycling in support of The Lutheran Hour radio show, has fallen. His pannier came loose and caught in his wheel, sending him crashing to the ground and breaking his hip. "You be careful," Anne tells me, "I love you."

We finish the pedaling in rain, and get ready to drive to Athens. KariAnna doesn't want to come along; she's having too much fun at Becky and Michelle's house. She brightens after we arrive. Out back the kids are fascinated by an antique one cylinder "hit-and-miss" engine that is powering an ice cream maker. We get to eat all we want, but I stop far short of the half-gallon shakes the Lieffrings had bought for Robert and me back in Ohio.

Al has also brought his whole collection of unicycles to church. There are big wheels and small, even one with a handlebar, but no seat. And there's a short giraffe. KariAnna asks, "Can I try that one, Daddy?"

She's up on it quickly, and after walking her around for a while, she's riding on her own inside the church hall. Pretty soon she's doing circles. It turns out to be a wonderful night, for her and for all of us.

On the drive back there's heavy rain. The weather channel says it's a tropical storm moving through. Rain is expected for the next few days.

31
Gulf of Mexico

For all the talk you hear about knowledge being such a wonderful thing,
instinct is worth forty of it for real unerringness.

Mark Twain

Becky and Michelle's home in Atlanta is our last planned stop with friends before we get back to Los Angeles. This realization makes the Pacific Coast seem very distant. It rains hard in the morning, further dampening our spirits for departing. By the time we get everything set, it's after lunch. We are reluctant to start into this next long unknown. Instead of leaving, we decide I'll ride forty miles and they'll pick me up for one more night here. While I ride south towards Fayetteville, they will all go to the Martin Luther King, Jr. Interpretive Center.

The center is located in the neighborhood where King grew up. His boyhood home and Ebenezer Baptist church are there. KariAnna and Kai are getting more glimpses of the history of the civil war and civil rights, pieces of our past that still loom large today.

I turn to Martin Luther King, Jr. for faith, in the same way that I turn to Desmond Tutu, in the same way that I turn to Jesus. More and more I see certain people embodying the same spirit and the same power of compassion that I see in Christ. I open up King's speeches the same way I open up scripture.

With the increasing talk of war in Iraq these days, I recall King's courage in speaking against the Vietnam War. He did it even when many of his advisors cautioned him to focus on civil rights and leave the war to others. In a crowded Riverside Church in New York City on April 4, 1967, he described how speaking out could be a "vocation of agony," but it must be done. He noted too how the human spirit does not move "without great difficulty against all the apathy of conformist thought within one's own bosom and in the surrounding world."

After a last night with Becky and Michelle, I wake early and drive the Honda back south of Fayetteville to continue pedaling. John Drummond has said he'll meet me, and he does, at 7 a.m. in dripping rain. We shuttle his truck twenty miles down the road at the Blue Horse Café in the town of Gay, then drive the Honda back and get riding on two big Cokers.

"I ride about ten miles a day," John says. "Take it easy on me."

I'm privileged to be riding with John. A year ago I didn't even know that Coker unicycles existed. I was just learning that people do mountain unicycling. I never imagined that prices for unicycles range from seventy dollars to fifteen hundred. John is keeping notes on the history of "unicycle.com" for a book, and I am looking forward to the full story.

Accents are getting richer as we ride farther south from Atlanta. John is not native to the south, so when I tell him about our delight with the language, he asks if I have seen the book *How to Speak Southern*. I haven't.

"Fizu," he tells me. "That's one of my favorites."

"What does it mean?" I ask.

"If I was you."

We spin on down the road. I see my first armadillos. Not live ones but lots of road kill, their plated armor scattered across the road after lost battles with steel belted tires. After some miles John's knees start bugging him. By taking enough breaks, we keep going in the soggy rain. It's a reminder to me once again of how physically fortunate I've been on this trip.

We finish our ride at the Blue Horse Café where folks have gathered for after-church lunch. When we're ready to leave, the café empties out and everyone watches us take off. John and I each get a few pictures and say our goodbyes. I expect we'll meet again. A visiting Baptist preacher gives me twenty dollars for the ride. The rain has stopped.

Twenty more miles and I'm in Manchester. Anne calls and says the RV won't start.

"I'll wait here. Come and pick me up."

We are now so used to Harvey's temperamental disposition that we have few surprises. But there are two this time. First, Anne simply left Harvey in drive gear rather than park, so it wouldn't start. Second, this ride is doing me good. When, after checking circuits for twenty minutes I finally see the gear shift lever in the wrong place, I just smile. No frustration at the missed pedaling from forty miles of back and forth driving, just a growing appreciation that we're making it, even in the midst of all the mechanical and human imperfections. Together we drive the RV back to Manchester, stop for a treat at the Dairy Queen, and park overnight at the Piggly Wiggly supermarket. We're on the road again.

Monday morning answers our questions about how humid it can get in the South. The windows of the Piggly Wiggly look like an iced tea glass dripping with condensation. Even later in the morning when I stop at Coopers' market in Waverly Hall, the windows still look the same.

Alabama

At Columbus, we cross over to Alabama. In Phenix City, in the early afternoon, the bank thermometer reads ninety-five degrees. Stopping to tank up on liquids before leaving Phenix City, the cashier tells me, "You're just like Forrest Gump."

I hear this comment more and more frequently. Folks are incredibly friendly on the highway. Our story has just been in the *National Examiner*. Lots of honks and waves. People stop and take pictures often. More and more folks seem to recognize me.

Anne and I have decided to try to make Eufaula for the night. It's a stretch, but we have had so many delays that we're hoping to make up some miles. The Chattahoochee Indian Heritage Museum is right alongside Highway 165, but I stop just long enough to read a few signs. The Methodists started a school in 1822. It was closed in 1830 when the Creek were removed to parts west, eight years before the Cherokee Trail of Tears. General Andrew Jackson was again in charge, fighting the battles, coercing the treaties, and forcing the removal. It was against these same Creek people he had become a national hero in 1814; in the Battle of Horseshoe Bend, he led the killing of eight hundred of the thousand battling Creeks.

Oswichee is tiny, but I stop for a turkey sandwich at Fay J's Café, where I drink down three quarts of iced tea. I'm racing the dark, now only four hours away. Outside I walk into an encounter with the Alabama police who do their slow-talking best to stop me from riding on this road. Shotgun's benediction stays with me, "I prefer my preachers in the pulpit, not in the grave. You be careful."

These two officers are not unkind. Still, they want me off the highway. I remember our ride through Kalamazoo and having no space on the road. Whether the issue is cycling or native land claims, the ones with the most horsepower or firepower always seem to get the middle of the highway.

Tuesday is a simple day of simple riding. Good road shoulders. No police. Hot, humid Alabama countryside. I'm back on four-inch cranks. The land is leveling out. I can ride at ten or eleven miles an hour now instead of nine or ten as I've been doing on the four-and-a-half-inch cranks.

Chicken haulers pass me all day long, wafting the smell of dirty feathers as they pass. Fields contain rows of chicken houses, four or six together, each a hundred yards or more long—part of the six billion chickens that are raised in the United States each year. In Daleville, the police offer us overnight parking for Harvey.

On Wednesday the land changes from chicken barns to peanut fields, as we make our way to the Florida Panhandle. Farmers are harvesting now; their diggers plow the whole plant out of the ground, shake it and leave it lying upside down in the field, dull brown peanuts exposed for drying, an artistic contrast against the bright red earth.

In an effort to beat the heat, Anne has decided to get up and start driving as soon as I head out the door. Every morning I pray that the air conditioner in the motor home will continue working. She's set up at Grayton State Recreation Area by 9 a.m. and calls to give me a road report, "Once you get into Florida, there's a better shoulder to ride on." We have become connoisseurs and experts on America's roads.

Geneva comes up soon after Anne's call. A man on the street says I've passed the only café when I ask for breakfast suggestions. Figuring I'll ride to the next town, I see instead the City Café and Oyster Bar, just around the corner.

"We just bought this two weeks ago," says Sylvia after she seats me and brings a pitcher of water. The AC is humming loudly, dripping water on the brown naugahyde chair by the window. Everything here, from the concrete floor to the weathered sign on the front, looks like it's been here a long time. The breakfast menu is a laminated quarter sheet. The omelet comes with grits. Everything comes with grits.

"We can get you some biscuits and gravy, too, if you want. A dollar and a quarter for a half-order."

Sylvia brings them right out. I've ordered a few biscuits and gravy on this trip, and seen many more. They're a favorite of Robert's and he ordered them often. I wish he were here for these. A culinary writer could do much better at description, but the biscuits are the lightest, airiest creations I've ever had, and the gravy is mouth-watering. As soon as I'm finished with these, the omelet arrives. The onions and green peppers are both freshly sautéed. This isn't just home-style cooking; this *is* home cooking. Only two weeks into this adventure, they're still cooking as if everyone is family.

"This is the best breakfast I've had on the whole trip," I tell Sylvia. "You should do great here with food like this."

Dave and Sylvia let me into the kitchen to take their picture. They hold the biscuit pan. "This is Dave's recipe. He's a chef."

He sure is.

Half an hour later, I cross the Florida state line and enter the panhandle of this most southern of the continental states. It's another landmark day for our trip. Scorching miles. Heat index is over one hundred, even though it's cooler than the day before. Our thirty-fifth state. Eighty-four miles today. I cycle south to Defuniak Springs, then south to cross I-10, "alligator alley," recently famous for an interstate shutdown in search of terrorists. Then at last I'm on Florida's Emerald Coast. The kids and Anne are at the beach. Another family with children is here, and they've been playing and studying all afternoon. The kids have been learning about tides and jellyfish and this beautiful pure white sand that squeaks under their feet when they run. We snap some pictures, and then I jump into the eighty-five-degree water.

We've made it to the Gulf of Mexico!

In the evening, looking at the map, I'm surprised to find that we're also straight south of Indiana. Our southward journey has brought us a good ways West already. Our mileage total is 6,463. We are also back in the Central Time Zone again. Back in Columbus, two days ago, we crossed the line, but none of us noticed until today.

Our route since the Statue of Liberty has been like riding down the shank of a giant fishhook. From here we will ride through the bottom of the hook and then start heading north for the tip of the barb: the intersection of Arkansas, Oklahoma, and Missouri. If we get that far in good shape, the rest of the ride is a straight shot west.

When I head out in the morning, at least half the rush hour vehicles are pickups with trailers, hauling construction equipment. The man who signs my Guinness slip in the morning is a pipe fitter. "They haven't cut all the trees around here down yet," he tells me. "But they're figuring the construction will be going on another five or six years like this before it tapers off." High-rises and houses and shopping centers are going in left and right. Empty land parcels have "For Sale" signs as thick as election posters. This Emerald Coast is currently the Developer's Coast.

In Fort Walton Beach a news reporter flags me down for a picture and ends up talking to me while I eat lunch at Joe's Cajun Place on Highway 98.

"It's changed a lot in the ten years I've been here. This all used to be a pretty sleepy area," he tells me. "Where you stayed last night in Grayton, they used to close the stores when the waves were good for surfing. Now it's high-rises."

More heat. Today there's a tailwind exactly matching my forward speed. I slow-cook on the highway. Stagnant air envelopes me while radiant heat from pavement and sky bakes me from all sides.

At Navarre Beach a man comes to visit while I try downing the two ice cream bars that I bought across the street. He's interested in telling me about "The Great Race" that he's driven the past number of years. It's a classic car ride all the way across the country. There's an awning shading us, but between his talking and the temperature, I'm too slow. The second bar melts off the stick and falls into the sand. He points to the high-rises a hundred yards away. "See those? They're all new. Hurricane Opal destroyed the buildings that used to be there."

"Can people who build right on the beach still get insurance?" I ask.

"It's amazing, but yes they can."

Out of Navarre Beach, I enter Gulf Island National Seashore. It's a fifteen-mile ride along Santa Rosa Barrier Island. Anne and the kids are at the state park at the far end of the island. A bike trail here parallels the roadway. I meet a loader scraping sand off the trail; this is just like winter snow removal up north. More marveling. More sweating. Pure white sand, no trees, stifling tailwind—this feels like my limit for tolerating heat. Maybe past my limit.

I see high-rises miles before Pensacola Beach. Anne and the kids come out to meet me. The kids have brought bicycles for the last miles into town.

"Anne, why don't you go get a Daiquiri and wait for us some place cool in town?"

"Sounds too good," she answers, taking off immediately before another task arises.

As we ride, the kids tell me what they've been learning at Fort Pickens State Park. The old fort is now the visitor's center. They've learned about wildlife and sea life, and also about the arches used in the fort's architecture. When we find Anne, she adds that Chief Geronimo was imprisoned here after he surrendered to U.S. troops way over in Arizona.

At the campsite we change to swimsuits and walk out through the dunes to the beach. The nearest person on this beach is a hundred yards away. Back at the beginning of this ride, we had bald eagles circling overhead. This evening while Anne and KariAnna build a castle in the sand, Kai and I are splashing in the waves when suddenly we're visited by five dolphins. They're in close, in the waves, splashing, rolling, and even jumping within a dozen yards of us. We watch them while the sun sets red over the ocean, the water and their freedom making us peaceful, even as clouds gather in the distant sunset.

A tropical storm is working its way towards the gulf. People are starting to talk about it, wondering how strong it will get, and where it will eventually reach land. We walk back for showers, dinner, and a good night's sleep.

When I wake on Friday morning, I begin riding up the fishhook toward Oklahoma. The tropical storm became Hurricane Isidore overnight. It's the first one of the season, but it's still outside the Gulf of Mexico. The front page of the newspaper explains the factors that determine strength and path. No one knows yet where this one will go or what it will do. Currently it's moving at eight miles per hour. I can do ten, but it gains on us at night. We plan to keep pedaling and see what the next days bring.

Through Pensacola and headed for Mobile, I stop in Elsanor for something to eat. The café eight miles before in Seminole was closed, so I am hungry. The two gas stations here feature everything that can be cooked in a deep fryer. I get chicken and sit down to eat. A fifty-year-old man comes in, "You ride that thing?"

After he gets his chicken potpies he comes to sit down across from me. First, we talk about the hurricane. "This humidity is what really builds them up," he tells me.

He asks me questions about my ride, and then I learn he's a horse trainer. "I'm calling everyone who has horses on my place to come and get them in case the hurricane hits here. You can insure your buildings but not the livestock underneath them."

Before he arrived, I was wondering how the old woman who served me could count a chicken wing as a whole piece of chicken and then be so bold as to charge the premium price for all white meat. I forget the chicken and listen to this man who doesn't tell me his name. He grew up farming.

"I always loved horses," he told me. "Now that's all I do."

He trains them for rodeo and team riding and things I know little about. I learn that buffalo are great for training horses. "A cow will eventually go sour and just stand still after enough roping practice. But buffalo are wild. They never stop moving. They'll always keep trying to get back to their partner. Two buffalo are worth a hundred head of cattle for training."

I have found yet another person who loves what he does and can tell a good story. I take my time with the little fat-fried chicken wing. I'm tempted to call Anne and see if we can go out for a visit to his place, but she's already in Mobile, at the state park.

When I arrive at Meaher State Park on Mobile Bay, the family has driven into town to shop for dinner: hamburgers and chicken for the grill tonight.

There's a bayou feel to this place. The ranger has told us where we can take a nature walk this evening and maybe see alligators. He's also provided a can of insecticide, telling Anne to spray around the tires or risk an infestation of big red ants.

Folks are already out fishing on the bay when I cross the causeway into Mobile on Saturday morning. Bicycles are not allowed through the tunnel leading into downtown, but the driver of the first pickup stops to offer a ride. He lets me off at the old French Quarter. The flags of four countries have flown over this city: France, Spain, England, and the USA.

At 9:30 a.m. a bank sign tells that the temperature is already eighty-nine degrees. I am beginning to worry that the effects of heat are cumulative. My mood is being taxed, and Isidore is raising questions from its center still far in the gulf. I read headlines whenever I stop for something to drink. The weather channel is on when I stop for a half-pound burger.

Mississippi

Highway 89 from Mobile into Mississippi is a four-lane road with a wide median. It's the most Forrest Gumpy stretch of road I've encountered. Folks are out with family and friends, on Saturday drives. People stop and wait in the left turn lanes to watch me ride by and to have their children wave at me. One black SUV passes me three times in a row with cameras out the window. On the last pass it pulls over. One of the four young men gets out. "Keep going. I want to run with you." He's a baseball player it turns out, from the Mississippi coast. "You go fast on that thing," he says. "What are you doing?"

I explain "One Wheel – Many Spokes" during the quarter mile he runs alongside.

Later a ghost-like man is standing by the side of this big highway. He's holding a large cup. "Can you stop for a glass of cold water?" As I jump off he continues, "I saw you when I was driving home. What are you doing?"

I answer and ask the same question of him.

"Painting," he answers. White ghost paint.

And so the day goes, a mixture of heat and hospitality as I ride into Mississippi. At intervals big blue signs announce this is a hurricane evacuation route. The woman who serves me a pizza at Carolyn's Gas Station tells me that after 9-11 she had wanted to walk across the country, "There were a lot of people after 9-11 that suffered but didn't get any help. I thought I could walk and collect money for them. My mom told me that would take a lot of stamina. I think I could do it."

When I go back outside, it starts to rain, then pour. Isidore has thrown clouds up north which finally gather and dump. Like baptismal waters the rain comes down, giving some hope for weather's change. For the first time since Georgia, there's brief relief from the heat.

In Beaumont, Anne and the kids pick me up. "The electricity isn't working on the RV," Anne tells me. "Both the AC and the DC are dead."

They've found a place at Paul Johnson State Park. "Our site is right on the lake. It's a good place for Sunday break."

First, though, there's Saturday night to get through. Without electricity we have no air conditioning. The heat comes back, and the RV is cooking hot. Except for the night with the skunk, this is the most miserable one of the trip. The kids have conked out but neither Anne nor I can get to sleep. At midnight I step outside and sit in the lawn chair. It's a degree or two cooler, and there's a faint breeze. A full moon is shimmering on the lake. I sit there for a while. The Danish words "gammel lort" are going through my mind as I think of renaming Harvey. Translated, it means "old junk." Then I remember the literature on West Nile Virus that the Park Ranger handed us with our registration. After a few more mosquito bites, I head back into the motor home. Somewhere around four in the morning, the temperature drops enough that we finally get to sleep.

Sunday is better, a trifle cooler. We spend hours swimming in the lake and climbing on the playground. In the late afternoon we pack up and head for The Three Little Pigs Smoke House. This is the land where barbecue is famous. The owner sits and talks with us while we eat.

"Oh, yeah. Air conditioning is the big deal around here," he tells us when we start talking about the temperatures.

And when we ask about Isidore, he tells us, "I'll be the first to know. Highway 49 here is an evacuation route. If anything happens, folks'll head right by. No news so far."

Tonight we're camping at the Wal-Mart in Hattiesburg. It's a lot closer to Beaumont than the forty-five-minute drive from the state park. A few minutes after we park, a mini-van pulls up next to us on this Sunday evening. An elderly man with white hair puts his head out the window, "I used to sell these. I just had to see who could keep one of them running for all these years."

"Barely running, you mean."

Bob is soon inside our RV, helping us with the electricity problems. "Sometimes its just the breaker," he tells me. I had already checked it for continuity, so I figured it was working. He checks it again and readjusts the connections.

"Okay, you can go and turn on the generator now. But first, we're going to pray." He places his hand on the breaker box. "Jesus, this breaker is now ready to carry current. We pray that it will provide power for this motor home and for the travels ahead." He turns to me again, "Okay, go ahead."

It works.

32
Storms

Every time you stop a school, you will have to build a jail.
What you gain at one end you lose at the other.
It's like feeding a dog on his own tail. It won't fatten the dog.

MARK TWAIN

Perfect days don't come every day. On Monday morning I glide twenty-five miles from Beaumont up to Hattiesburg. The weather is cool today, in the seventies. Not to sweat like a water pump all day long is sufficient to make for a great day. But when I turn from Highway 98 to 49, a twelve-foot wide shoulder awaits me, another huge gift. I can ride straight and let my mind wander on this shoulder. I haven't seen one so good in thousands of miles. The University of Southern Mississippi is in Hattiesburg, and I have a salsa-filled Mexican lunch right across the street from campus. It brings back thoughts again of Michigan State. Two students start talking to me: one's a senior; the other, a sophomore.

"So do you have your life all figured out?" I ask the senior.

"Just about," she replies.

Her friend laughs, "Sure she does. One day she's going to be a teacher, the next she's going to go to pharmacy school. What else is it that you're thinking of? I can't keep up with you."

That was a favorite part of my college experience. I always had eight or a dozen dreams going at once, all of them possible until I had to finally make a choice.

Anne has gotten battery power working after a stop at the RV place north of town. But when she starts down the road, it soon quits again. She drives back to pick me up and together we return to visit Scooter. He gets it this time, working on old Harvey the RV right in the midst of the new motor homes for sale.

"Look, Anne." I point to the price tag on the nearest mega motor home: $247,749. "That makes repairing Harvey easier to bear."

Scooter tells me, "We don't do much work on old motor homes. It's the new ones we see all the time. They have so much stuff on them that we're always fixing something."

It's an encouraging word for Anne and me. Our total investment in Harvey, both purchase and repairs, is still less than $7,749: a $240,000 savings over the new one parked in the lot. We're soon fixed. Scooter apologizes for the need to return. Anne gets me back to Hattiesburg, where I resume pedaling. More gliding. The word now is that the hurricane is headed for New Orleans by the end of the week.

Tuesday stays cool; this weather is a precious gift. Up 49 again, we put more miles between us and New Orleans. In tiny Florence I stop for another Mexican lunch at Ariel's new restaurant. After he serves me, Ariel sits to visit while I eat. Born in Mexico, he has traveled all over the United States.

"Except for around New York, Mississippi is the nicest place I've found to live."

This is Ariel's second restaurant. The other is over in Byram, where I'll be riding later. We talk about billboards and business and having a restaurant.

"Right now the other place has about three times as much business as here. It takes time."

The Mississippi highways are as friendly as any I've found on this trip. On the road and in the stores there's an equal mixture of people black and white. I don't know how communities are divided up off the road, but the newspaper's front-page article today reports that twenty-seven percent of Mississippi children are raised in poverty. Poverty is evident in Edwards, where we finish riding for the day. We find a campground just outside of town.

The wind rises during the night, but the rain hasn't come by the time we fall asleep. Isidore is supposed to hit New Orleans on Thursday now, not Friday. For a while it had slowed down to moving five miles an hour, but it is back up to eight.

Unicycling in front of a hurricane is lonely business. It's raining when I wake up, and it rains all day. With a steadily increasing east wind, I ride the fifteen miles to Vicksburg. In town I pass a huge park commemorating the Civil War battle fought in 1863. The siege lasted from May 18 to the Fourth of July. How did the soldiers do it: all the marching over rugged terrain, all the big terrain, all the bugs, the heat, the cold, the poor supplies? How did they watch their partners die in battle after battle—almost thirty-six thousand here in Vicksburg alone? I come in from the wet and fill my plate twice at the Shoney's breakfast buffet. When I go to pay, another customer has already covered it.

Louisiana

Then I'm caught in Vicksburg for two hours trying to get across the bridge to Louisiana. The Chamber of Commerce sends me to the State Welcome Center who send me to the Bridge Authority. Finally they throw my unicycle in the back of a blue Ford pickup and drive me across to our thirty-eighth state.

Frogs are squashed into hundreds of garish poses on the shoulder of the road. Thankful for the rain, they had come out of the cotton fields to dance. Not one of them is a match for passing cars. East on 80 I arrive at Tallulah, which calls itself "The City on the Move." Turning north here, onto Highway 65, I find more rain, more cotton, and more frogs. A few miles north a long, long line of bucket trucks passes, convoying their way to New Orleans. Preparing in advance for the storm's fury, they are a sobering sight.

When I stop at a convenience store folks warn me to avoid Lake Providence.

"We're camping there," I reply.

"Oh," they respond.

Transylvania is first, though, one of our favorite town names on the trip. I slosh my way inside the convenience store and get a big ice cream cookie for the last dozen miles of riding. A cotton farmer, a trucker and the store-owner talk with me while I eat and drip a big puddle onto the floor. The cotton crop has been looking good. Everyone is watching the rain to see how much it will damage the harvest. The storeowner tells how once he'd been harvesting cotton and one rainstorm had wiped out half the crop. "That was when I decided I needed to get into something else."

Now he has his Transylvania store and a terrarium with a live tarantula. The water tower in town is painted with a big black vampire bat.

Back on the shoulder and in the raining weather, I finish the last dozen miles and reach the town about which I have been warned. Lake Providence is in disrepair, and once again the residents are mostly African American. Anne is at the only RV site in town, a run-down hotel that's "under new management and ownership." It works for us; we have a place to park and watch the wind and rain, wondering about Thursday, the day the hurricane is supposed to hit land.

I'm on the road by 7 Thursday morning. Anne passes me an hour later and pulls off the road.

"That's enough," I tell her. "Let's try again tomorrow."

Isidore is a giant swirling pancake of a storm. The wind is blowing over thirty miles an hour, right in my face. The clouds look as if they're scuffing treetops. Raindrops sting. With the wide shoulder, it's safe enough to be out riding, but there's no joy in it. It feels like a waste of energy. We drive north to Lake Chicot, the largest oxbow lake in the United States. Like Lake Providence, oxbow lakes are a product of the Mississippi's wanderings, from when the river changed its looping course and left long lakes behind, each one shaped like an eyelash moon. The state park campsite is huge but almost empty. Only three others are camping. Our site overlooks the lake and the cypress trees that grow in the water. Homework and games help pass the gray, lonely day inside Harvey. Harvey is mostly dry; there's an annoying leak from the center vent, but we've got a bucket underneath.

New Orleans gets fifteen inches of rain from the storm. Fifteen inches of snow would be a huge amount; as rain I find it unimaginable. Tennessee is supposed to get eight inches. We're supposed to get three to five here at the border of Louisiana and Arkansas.

Arkansas

Calm winds, blue skies, and perfect temperatures greet us on Friday after the hurricane. Isidore has let us off easy, and I'm soon in Arkansas, our thirty-ninth state.

In addition to the cotton I see many catfish farms. Eudora's water tank advertises the town as the "Catfish Capitol of the World." I order breakfast at a catfish restaurant that has no menus. The woman at the counter tells me she can make anything I want and scratches my order on a post-it note for the cook in back.

At lunch I take the ninety-nine-cent special at McDonald's in Lake Village. Leroy comes to talk about my unicycle. His job is setting poles for the power company. I learn that it requires anywhere from one to five gallons of expanding foam to set a pole.

"Foam has pro's and con's," he tells me. "It really holds the pole. It's flammable, though. Farmers don't like it much when they burn the straw in their field and a pole catches fire, especially when they get the bill for a new pole."

"Catfish," Leroy tells me, "that's the number one priority for the power company. Doesn't matter if your house or the town is out of power. If the catfish don't have power, that's where we go first…If power goes out to the aerators, you've got about two hours to get them working before the fish start floating."

In the afternoon, stopped south of McGeehee, a trucker asks me where I'm going.

"California," I reply.

"Have you been to New York, too?"

"Yeah, I was there a month and a half ago."

"Paul Harvey was talking about you on the radio today," he tells me.

This is encouraging news. I keep hoping that some newsperson will figure out that the real story is not the ride but the endowment. I keep hoping it will catch on and fill up. But I sure haven't figured out how.

After lunch I ride by more ponds; now I notice all the tractors with aerators attached, ready for emergencies. This is the most unique farming I've seen on this trip.

In Dumas, my family meets me at a catfish restaurant at the north end of town. It's Friday night, and the dinner buffet also includes shrimp. The owner pours them onto the buffet line by the five-gallon bucket. And now, except for Kai, we're fans of catfish, too. Once a boy who liked anything and everything, his tastes are going through a stage of being particular. He's still a big fan of mac'n'cheese.

Little Rock is eighty-four miles ahead when I get started on Saturday morning. The distance will make up for the day off from the hurricane. Dumping the sewer and refilling with water delays my start until 8. For the first twenty miles, I make the mistake of concentrating on how far I have to go today. This achieves only two things. First, it makes the miles go very slowly. Second, it takes all the enjoyment from them.

When I finally get my head back into the ride, I stop to watch a cotton picker harvesting a field.

"A hundred acres a day those pickers can harvest." A man had answered my questions the day before. I asked how long the cotton gins would be working.

"They'll be going 24-7 until the middle of December. There are hundreds of thousands of acres of cotton in this area."

Next, near Grady, I see the Cummins prison off the right side of the road, its shiny barbed wire a sparkling crown around the maze of chain link fence, which surrounds the complex. Ever since Desmond Tutu's daughter Naomi came to Michigan State University with her keynote message of peace, I can't pass a prison without remembering her words. "I want to thank you in America," she had said in a joking manner: "If it wasn't for you, we in South Africa would have had the highest incarceration rate in the world."

At the beginning of the new millennium, in the year 2000, the U.S. prison population reached two million, twenty-five percent of all the prisoners in the world. This for a country that has only five percent of the world's population, to say nothing of our laying claim to holding the highest standards of civilization.

A few miles later I stop to read an historical sign at the Moscow, Arkansas, post office. The sign is titled, *Quapaw Treaty*. On November 15, 1824, at the nearby home of Bartley Harrington, the Quapaw Treaty was signed. The Quapaw Indians ceded all rights to their lands, resulting in the removal of all Quapaw from the Arkansas territory. An immigration wave followed the signing of the treaty, the largest single factor in the settlement of southeast Arkansas.

I almost missed that sign.

Like a family secret, these signs are easy to overlook. The prison appears as an isolated unit rather than as part of a nationwide complex of incarceration. The road-sign marker appears alone on a country road. The pattern is often elusive. With my slow rate of pedaled travel, I am becoming aware, as never before, of the domination, subjugation, and extermination that underlie the claiming and the holding of this American land. It's so easy for me to miss. For days I ride along, admiring cotton fields and country towns, lakes and forests. Then a little sign like this reminds me of the process preceding this present arrangement of land and people.

If our history and our prisons resemble a family secret, then the effects will be unspoken but ever-present. Like a family with an addict in the household, life is spent behind the veneer that everything is normal, everything is fine. Behind the cover is the long-suffering quiet or violent chaos that shapes the family patterns. The only escape lies in exposing the secret, discovering its effects, realizing its toll, and learning better ways and better patterns.

As I ride, I see more and more of our secrets. Still, like so many others, I know too little of our history. Perhaps we are averse to the dark side of our experiment in freedom and democracy. Just forty years after the Quapaw Treaty, the United States was fighting the Civil War, and those effects are still present today. Even as I ride, new evocations of freedom and democracy are being hawked in our push against Iraq and terrorism: signs, it seems, that this land has yet to make peace with the harsh, dark side of our national secrets.

Up the road I reach Pine Bluff, switching from 65 to 365, riding through small towns on the way to Little Rock. In Refield, at the Mammoth Orange, I buy a hot dog and ice. Two kids are eating inside with their dad, having finished a football game against a neighboring town. "You'd better get through the next couple of towns before dark," Dad advises. More warnings. His kids absorb them with each hearing, the lessons passing on to unfolding generations. Ahead I find black towns, poor towns generous to a passing unicyclist.

Darkness stops my ride within four miles of Little Rock. Anne picks me up in Sweet Home. She and the kids have found a campsite at Lake Catherine State Park. It's a bit of a drive, over near Hot Springs.

"Shall we go and see Little Rock Central High School while we're here?" I suggest. It's a national historic site now, the place where nine young men and women started the integration of our public schools. It still operates as a high school. While we are eating a hamburger, we ask an Emergency Medical Technician for directions.

"Let me get my good map out of the ambulance. Just a minute." When she comes back, she tells us how to get there. "Watch out," she says, with a now-familiar warning. "That's a real rough neighborhood. Anything south of the freeway is bad."

The *Arkansas Democrat* had an article today about a weeklong conference on race, which was organized by Little Rock's Racial and Cultural Diversity Commission.

> *The crowd – at a weeklong conference billed as a dialogue on race – was almost void of white men. That, organizers and attendees say, illustrates the daunting task of dealing with race issues: getting different people to talk about them can be as difficult as agreeing on them.*

Race, culture, land, weather, people—home school is going well for our kids. It's hard to get as many math and reading lessons as we'd like; our weariness is showing. But as for exposure to this land and its people, the kids are getting the experience of a lifetime. School is in full session for them, for Anne and me, too, as we continue on this ride. The kids fall asleep as we make the hour-long drive to Lake Catherine, where we will take Sunday off.

In the morning Kai attains a long awaited goal: paddleboating. He's been begging for this since before New York, but either the lakes haven't had paddleboats or the boats have been locked up for the season. He finds paddleboats here and beams for the hour that he's on the lake. After his ride we keep walking back to the boats, inspecting them, comparing the fine points of red paddlers versus green ones.

Our friend Nathan Thomas drives up from Shreveport, where he is a drama professor. We spend Sunday evening making s'mores on the campfire and visiting. "What's the biggest surprise of the trip for you?" he asks.

Thinking about his question, I come up with three big surprises.

One is how little money this ride has generated for the Seward Peninsula Lutheran Endowment. I have plenty of time to think about this while I pedal, but I don't have answers.

Another big surprise has been the accumulating impact of the Native American losses, removals, and suffering that have been such a major part of our American history, but that remain largely an untold and unknown story.

The third surprise is Harvey. We bought him, needing his services for ten thousand miles, back and forth across the country. That's not far for a vehicle to travel, only fifty miles a day on country roads. We had expected fewer problems. Tonight, though, everything is fine as we visit around the campfire until late at night.

Arkansas will remain a favorite state despite yet another muffler mishap. On the interstate, in the early Monday morning darkness, I am driving back to Sweet Home. The rest of the family sleeps until a loud explosion startles us all, signaling a popped rear tire. I pull over only to find, for the fourth time on the trip, another muffler pipe has fallen off.

This time, along with exploding the right inner tire, the outside tire also has a slow leak, so we're stuck. We call AAA and they send out a tow truck, beginning a five-hour odyssey of mishaps. After the first half-hour, it is clear I have come to know more about this problem than they do. Hours later a tire service professional finally pulls up in his truck to ask if we need help.

"Yes," I answer before the AAA man can say a word, "we absolutely need help."

In ten minutes he has the tire plugged. Using the big compressor on the back of his truck, he quickly fills our tire with air, just what I'd been asking for all morning long. I drive to a tire shop for another new tire. After four of these episodes it's clear that the previous owner's conversion from a single muffler to dual mufflers has been poorly done. The exhaust pipes are located too close to the rear tires; somehow they are getting caught and torn off. I finally get unicycling at one o'clock—seven hours later than planned.

While I get the tire fixed, Anne and the kids take the Honda to downtown Little Rock to spend the afternoon at the Discovery Museum. I meet them for ice cream at Little Rock's River Market Café, a collection of small shops, many of which have pictures of their owner posing next to Bill and Hillary Clinton. While we drink down shakes, I explain the repairs and tell Anne where to pick up the motor home.

"I'm glad you were with us for this muffler breakdown," Anne says.

"Maybe we're supposed to be learning something from Harvey on this trip?" I say.

"What would that be?" Anne asks.

"I don't know yet; we still have a month to go."

Highway 365 takes me north; I pedal as quickly as I can, and we end the day at dusk in a grocery store parking lot in Conrad.

Tuesday goes more smoothly. It is the first day of October. Anne catches up with me in time for breakfast in Morrilton. The owner of the café treats us to breakfast. As we eat, the kids tell us they want to bike after breakfast. Road shoulders have been wonderful in Arkansas, so we pull out bikes and the four of us cycle together for some miles. A newspaper reporter takes our picture and interviews us. When the kids begin to droop, Anne pedals back for Harvey and returns to get KariAnna and Kai.

In Russellville I find a pizza place for lunch. It's 2 p.m. by the time I get here, and I'm almost the only one in the restaurant. I take a seat by the TV, watching it for the first time in a month.

CNN shows President Bush speaking. I am surprised to see his finger stabbing the screen, his words coming across harsh, talking about the villain in Iraq. It's strange to watch my president speak and find the scene resembling a battle of the bullies. 9-11, Afghanistan, now Iraq—the splitting between good and evil that became dominant with 9-11 seems to be continuing with full force. I ride for the rest of the day, deeply disturbed by the images.

This harsh division between good and evil is one of the biggest differences between fundamentalism and more embracing, inclusive views of the world. There is a simplicity to separating good and evil so broadly; the villain is easily identified, as someone other than myself. A wider view understands that there's always some villain in my own heart as well as outside myself, some complicity in the ambiguity and imperfections of existence. In my Lutheran tradition, one of Martin Luther's great insights is that we are always simultaneously both saint and sinner, that good and evil mix strangely together. It's Huckleberry's simple observation that the soup made from the barrel of odds and ends is better than the "civilized" dinner that the Widow Douglas prayed over, food that was "cooked all by itself." If we were to attend to Luther's and Huck's insights, we would at least publicly acknowledge that we might have had some role in creating the crisis, and in providing weapons to the very same Saddam Hussein we are now vilifying.

After all I've seen on this trip—Native American history, slave history, immigrant history, and the West—it's clear that we need a more embracing worldview if we are to honor our world's barrel of odds and ends, and to achieve justice. People in our own nation's history have been enslaved, suffered and died for simplistic versions of good and evil. As Keith Cash had said back in Schenectady when we were watching the news together, "I like to think we're the good guys, but when you watch this all the time you start to wonder."

Ironically, this afternoon I am riding past road signs marking the path of the Cherokee Trail of Tears. Back then, President Andrew Jackson and most people thought it was simply good policy to remove Indians from their tribal lands. Today, for those who know the stories, the actions taken are some of the most regrettable ones our nation ever enacted. Perhaps a hundred years from now we will look back with terrible regret on our actions in these present days.

Having protested the War in Afghanistan, I appreciate Twain's 1905 essay on war: "The half dozen rash spirits that ventured to disapprove of the war and cast a doubt upon its righteousness straightaway got such a stern and angry warning that for their personal safety's sake they quickly shrank out of sight and offended no more in that way." In the first months after 9-11, it felt almost traitorous to critique our government.

The hospitality we are experiencing on our unicycle journey is a complete contrast to the fear, violence and hostility that dominate public discussion. Our family is living into this hospitality state by state, person by person, and the cumulative effect is powerful. I am convinced that this hospitality can make a difference in our world. I find myself wishing our roads could be filled with cyclists, out gaining this view of life's compassionate side. By evening I have pedaled to Clarksville. Our campsite, in nearby Spadra, overlooks the Arkansas River and gives a peaceful ending to our day.

Wednesday is a long ride; I cover eighty-two miles through the Ozark Mountains. Other than one steep mountain to cross, everything is graded gently. The Ozarks feel like hobby mountains compared to the Appalachians and the Rockies. We end the day in Fayetteville. As I approach, a big historical sign marks the first place Bill and Hillary Clinton practiced law in Arkansas. Our campground is a concrete slab, packed next to a hundred other similar slabs, no restrooms, no showers—twenty-five dollars. To get away, we take the kids bowling.

From Fayetteville north, we ride through thirty miles of strip malls, chain stores, and restaurants. At the north end of all this development is Bentonville, where I pass the home office of Wal-Mart.

Anne finds Harvey again having troubles with the electrical system and with the generator, this generator, which would "last forever." We end up with a new AC power cord and a diagnosis for our generator. The mechanic tells Anne, "It's bad. The main bearing is worn out. That's where your oil is leaking from."

Anne asks how long it will take to fix.

"Three days. One to get it apart, the next to order parts, and the third to put it together again."

When Anne calls me on the phone, we agree to make the rest of the trip without the generator. The temperatures aren't going any higher than the eighties these days. If it doesn't turn to scorching again, we'll be okay.

Missouri

Soon after Bentonville I cross into Missouri, our fortieth state. A sign on Highway 71 announces this road as the most deadly in the state. Trucks roar and cars zoom by me. The shoulder is weathered with age, cracking up, adding to the challenge. Joplin is our goal for the day, but with the lousy road, I call Anne from Anderson and tell her I'm heading west on 76, towards Oklahoma. Hills are surprisingly steep. Anne catches up at Patterson Heights, a single church at the crossroads of Highway 76 and 43. We get permission to park for the night.

"Sure," the pastor offers. "Plug your power in. Make yourselves at home. You're welcome to water, too, if you don't mind the sulfur taste."

I plug our brand new power cable into the outlet in front of the church. KariAnna and Kai gladly help me get a cold shower, spraying me with the hose while I shampoo and soap down. There's a swing and a big lawn to play on as the sun sets on our only night in Missouri.

With the kids asleep, Anne and I pull out our maps, take stock, and assess damages.

"This motor home is a real beast." I say.

"It's really tiring, not knowing what's going to happen next," Anne agrees. "Every time I get comfortable with Harvey, something new goes wrong."

We've reached the top of the fishhook, having traveled all the way down the Appalachians to the Gulf of Mexico and now working our way up this corner of Arkansas, Missouri, and Oklahoma. From here our route is almost due west. The unicycling, at least, continues to go well. I made it across the Ozarks on four-inch cranks. I feel strong enough to expect I can ride through whatever challenges lie ahead.

The weather has tempered a bit, and we are all thankful for that. Harvey, though, is sucking our energy out as he limps along. The kids feel it, too. KariAnna still loves being on the road, but Kai needs more time around other people. When Harvey intrudes with a problem, Kai gets that much less attention.

We had been looking forward to a great celebration here in Mark Twain's home state. Instead, Anne and I settle for toasting each other with a glass of chocolate milk. We go to bed wondering what lies ahead for the last month, the last major section of our journey.

33
Oklahoma Wisdom

We are called the nation of inventors. And we are.
We could still claim that title and wear its loftiest honors
if we had stopped with the first thing we ever invented,
which was human liberty.

MARK TWAIN

Oklahoma

From Patterson Heights I am quickly into Ottawa County and our forty-first state, Oklahoma. We are catching this corner of the state only because we changed course yesterday. The vegetation has been getting more and more arid these last days of riding west. The sky is clear, the air has finally dried out, and at long last, it is cooler.

The first hint this morning of the nature of the day comes when I get to Highway 10 in Oklahoma. There at the junction is the Seneca-Cayuga Tobacco Plant. Months ago, way back in New York, we'd ridden over the Seneca and Cayuga Lakes, two of the Finger Lakes. We'd camped at Cayuga Lake State Park. I remember that Robert and I arrived there late for the waiting campground feast that Amy had prepared for us. The next morning we had pedaled by signs protesting the Cayuga Land Claim. We are a long way from Upstate New York.

A few miles later I ride by the "Wyandotte Nation" sign, which announces the tribal center. We crossed their land way back in Ohio, at Sandusky, the day I broke the Guinness World Record. I pedal a few feet past the driveway before deciding to jump off and walk back. Sherri greets me when I walk in the door. She's the community liaison specialist. She signs my Guinness form before we start talking.

"Wyandottes come originally from near Toronto, Canada," she tells me. "There are nine tribes here in this county. All of them come from somewhere else. Wyandotte's have been in Canada; Mackinac Island, Michigan; Sandusky, Ohio; Kansas City, Kansas; and here." After talking some more she asks me, "Do you want to meet the chief?"

I tell her I would like to.

"Chief Bearskin is eighty-one," she informs me, giving me background as we walk over to his office. "He's been the chief here for twenty years. He used to be an Air Force Officer, a bomber pilot in World War Two."

Sherri sees the chief ahead of us and points to him. He is walking into the tribal center from the parking lot. Tall, with close-cropped white hair, he is wearing a green and white golf shirt with khaki pants. He walks quickly, looking as though he could play a good eighteen holes.

At Chief Bearskin's office, Sherri introduces me. He offers a kind welcome, and I ask if he has time to visit.

"Have a seat," he offers, pointing across his desk. A small bearskin hangs on the wall behind him. On his desk is a model of the bomber he piloted in WWII and his flight log. Official commendations from other agencies and other states are displayed on the walls of his office.

I tell the chief about riding through the Southeastern states and finding so many places where Indian removals have taken place. "How many people know the story of the removals?" I ask him.

"Not many," he answers, "and even if people knew it they wouldn't believe that our country did those things. Our people have a saying here, though. You can't march forward by marching backwards. The United States is still the greatest country in the world."

"I've spent a lot of time on the road this summer," I continue. "I've been wondering how our unknown Indian history affects our actions as a country today. I've been thinking about how we reacted to 9-11, and now the talk of war with Iraq."

"We're policing the world," he answers simply. "We should be making friends in the world. I could talk about this on and on." And he does, from his experience as an Air Force Squadron Commander, consultant to Washington D.C., and leader of his people. I sit here soaking in the wisdom of this eighty-one year old man.

In one breath he tells me, "Your vote doesn't matter. I go to Washington D.C. often, and I see how things work, how votes are traded and people don't even read bills. If people knew what goes on in Washington, there would be a rebellion."

In the next breath he tells me, "We're still the greatest country in the world, but we should have a hundred-year plan for our country. Every person elected to serve our government should agree to work for that plan. If they don't agree with it, then they should get out so we can elect someone who will work for the long-term good of our people and our country."

"With everything you're telling me, why do you still say this is the greatest country?"

"People have more freedom here. We've gone a long way down the road of abusing that freedom. Sometimes I'm glad I'm eighty-one and won't be around much longer, but we're still the best."

I tell him about taking this year off for Anne and me to look at what we want to make of our future.

"Follow your heart," he advises, "and care about people. Care about *everybody*. It doesn't matter who they are or where they come from or anything. Care about *everybody*—that's what I'd say."

When at last I get ready to leave, he asks, "Do you need anything for your ride? Food, money, anything? We've got a cafeteria right here."

"Thanks," I say, "just prayers for the RV. We're doing fine. I'm really thankful to meet you."

Chief Bearskin and Sherri walk me out to my unicycle. We take a couple pictures, say our goodbyes, and they watch me ride off.

Chief Bearskin's capacity to hold realism and hope together is something I strive for myself but often fail at. Elders in Nome have been some of the best examples I've seen of this ability to see things truthfully and yet not give up. Riding on, I feel uplifted.

One time back in Nome, after my first year, I was struggling with whether to finish out my interim position or accept the invitation to stay on as the called pastor. I went to visit an elder.

"Come in," Robert had shouted to the door from his couch. I walked in to my accustomed chair facing the familiar CNN program on the TV.

In Inupiat culture, talking is not required. It is permissible to have a wordless visit. When words do exchange, they are slow, reflective, holding a pace far different from my Los Angeles upbringing.

Over the space of two hours, I explained my predicament to this elder of the church. Actually, mostly we watched CNN. My telling did not take long. Should I stay here as pastor or not? The congregation wanted me to. The official church-wide rules said that interim pastors can't stay on in a permanent capacity.

Robert hadn't said much, perhaps this problem mattered not to him; after all, he'd grown up in a sod hut, hunted on the Bering Sea in a sealskin kayak, seen things I could never dream of.

After two hours my white-man's patience was about used up. I thanked Robert for tea and prepared to leave. He stood, looking straight at me.

"Sometimes," Robert said, "life is like being in a small boat on a stormy sea."

I walked out the door, my load immeasurably lighter. Sometimes the only gift needed is to be heard.

Riding further into Ottawa County, I come next to the Shawnee tribe. Anne calls me while I am eating a hot dog at the convenience store.

"We're still in Miami," she tells me.

I had been planning to ride another five miles farther north to Quapaw to see the settlement of these people whose lands I'd ridden through last week in Southeastern Arkansas.

"There are a lot of tribal offices here," Anne tells me, so I change course and ride to Miami, Oklahoma, and that is as far as we get. The rest of the afternoon we spend visiting with tribal groups. Everyone seems glad and willing to spend time. Perhaps not many other people come asking questions.

At the Inter-Tribal Council, a woman named Helen spends time telling stories of her family. Her father had fought in World War II and met her German mother in Europe, bringing her back when he returned to Oklahoma.

"When I grew up, the Indian School was right next door. I didn't attend, but when I was nineteen I had a teaching internship there. I grew up thinking that school was great. What I found out is that they were brainwashing those kids, taking away their language and assimilating them. That's when I started learning about my history. We know about the German Holocaust, but things happened in our own country that were as bad: giving blankets to Indians that had been used in hospitals and purposely infected with smallpox; removing Indians to promised reservation lands that didn't exist; giving land allotments to Indian families who ended up losing the land. We have plenty of our own holocausts in this country."

The Miami people are here. They come from Ohio. In their tribal center, the person running the gift shop tells me that she is Cherokee.

"I'm third cousin to Will Rogers," she says. "Check out the library; you'll find more people there to talk with."

The Shawnee are here. They were relocated twice before ending up here, the most recent move being from Kansas. Since 1860 they've been recognized as part of the Cherokee tribe. Just two years ago they received their own federal tribal recognition after decades of legal work. Two workers are in temporary offices at the Inter-Tribal Council.

"You've heard of the Cherokee Trail of Tears," one of them tells me. "There were many trails of tears, some of them worse than the Cherokees.

What's amazing is that some people have survived this and still have hope."

We came through Ottawa County today simply to avoid the potholed Highway 71 in Missouri. We ended up with one of the biggest highlights of our trip, receiving more of the story of our nation, and more hope from people we met.

The next morning, just a few miles north of Miami, there's a definite feel of the west in the air. The sandy land supports scattered brush and cottonwoods. Everything feels drier. Its cool enough to feel chilled for the first time in months. On this Saturday morning, folks at the Country Girl Café in Picher give me the same directions three different times.

"A mile north is the Kansas border. Two miles farther is Four Corners. There you go west on 169…"

Kansas

Kansas, Oklahoma, and Nebraska: They have reputations as states to be endured on the way from one place to the other. At ten miles an hour, Kansas, our forty-second state, is beautiful. This southwest corner is mostly ranches with trees. Before lunch I cause five stampedes of cattle, just as we did in Montana when I was riding with Robert. The shoulder on the road is decent, but strewn with a larger than normal assortment of rotting armadillos, raccoons, and opossums.

Entertainment for the day comes after lunch in the tiny town of Edna when I stop at the Conoco gas and convenience store. A display of Styrofoam cups above the soda machine shows their prices. Ninety-nine cents for the forty-four-ouncer is a better than average deal. I look for the Styrofoam cup to match the one on display, but the dispenser has only plastic cups in it. Taking one, I fill it with lemonade. When I turn around I finally see the forty-four-ounce Styrofoam cups. They're in a corner, behind me as I face the pop machine. The attendant at the front asks me for $1.59.

"It says ninety-nine cents on the display."

"That's for the other cups, not for this one."

"You've got to be kidding."

She just looks at me.

Three different times I try telling her this is not fair, not right, and not possible. "You can't really charge me sixty cents extra for this cup."

Each time she looks at me and replies, "I don't have a choice."

I could have been quicker, left the cup with her and gone back for a ninety-nine cents Styrofoam cup. But I wasn't. I paid the price, read the newspaper while I drank each one of the ounces down and wished the attendant a good day as I left. If it hadn't been for her, I might not have remembered Edna so well, or where they keep the Styrofoam cups.

At Caney, Anne and the kids come back in the Honda to pick me up. Together we drive to Hulah Lake at Wah-Sha-She State Park, where they've set up camp and have been playing all afternoon. Our site is on the lake's edge, and as soon as we arrive, the kids plead, "Daddy, come and see our houses." Huge table-flat boulders at the lake's edge have been great for climbing and for their pretend play. There's a fire red sunset and a cool breeze coming in the windows when we go to sleep.

We wake up late on Sunday, make a hot breakfast, and spend the morning rock-climbing along the lakeshore. After lunch we decide we'll go back to Caney. From there I can pedal back to the campsite, while the kids and Anne go to the safari. Caney is a small town, but we saw the sign yesterday for Safari Zoological Park.

"On the way back, we'll bring you a soda," Anne says when they drop me off to for the short twenty-five miles.

"Take your time. Have fun at the safari."

On my ride back to the campsite, crossing into Oklahoma on Highway 75, I pass a sign announcing this as Cherokee Nation. Somewhere along the way I switch to Osage Land, but there's no sign to indicate where. A huge cattle brand hangs near the road. It's the Cross-Bell Ranch. The woman at the convenience store back in Copan had told me, "People around here are still in the cowboy and Indian mode. I wouldn't ride on that ranch, if I were you."

Of Bartlesville, a few miles south, she'd advised, "That city will be changing soon. Phillips Petroleum got started there, and they just got bought out."

The grasshopper pumps on oil wells move rhythmically as I ride past the Cross-Bell Ranch. Indian history, ranchers, farmers, oil and minerals: Oklahoma at ten miles an hour is real adventure.

Anne and the kids pass me just a few miles before we get back to the campground, handing me an icy soda. When I get back, they talk about the Wild Animal Safari and Tom, the owner. A picture of him at the entrance shows a six-year old boy holding a monkey. Ever since then he's been hooked on helping endangered species. The kids have discovered another person following his heart and his dream. Tom has taken a picture of them holding a four-month-old tiger, something for them to remember when they grow up.

When we get back, there's another fire red sunset. The barbecued steaks are great. We finish the s'mors just before dark.

"Look at all the birds," KariAnna tells us.

Out on the lake, stretching all the way across its width, is a line of birds skimming along the surface. Only they're not birds, we decide. They're bats. Big bats. And then it's dark.

Pop, pop, pop. I hear a new sound in Oklahoma as I start out on Monday morning. One cylinder "hit-and-miss" engines are powering the oil pumps in the fields and the hills. We see more and more of them as we head west. The land here is cattle country, and the grass in this area really does grow as high as an elephant's eye. It hides the backs of the grazing cattle.

Pawhuska holds the Osage Indian Museum. I ask around for directions, but two people say they don't know where it is. The second person turns out to be standing around the corner, just a hundred feet from the entrance to it. There's another twist here to this story of removal. Somehow, when the reservation was turned into individual allotments, the Osage retained the mineral rights. When oil was discovered, a few of the Osage people joined the ranks of the richest people in the country.

By evening we're at Kaw Lake, named for the Kaw people. Tribes were stuffed into this land one after the other in the middle 1800s. Tomorrow morning we'll be going through Ponca City, named for the Ponca tribe.

In the middle of the afternoon, in the middle of nowhere, I see a live turtle on the road. I have seen dozens of dead ones, flattened road kill. After first passing it, I stop and come back. Figuring to set it back from the road, I pick up the five-inch little guy and then think to call Anne.

"What about a turtle for the kids?" I ask. "I just found one in the road and saved it from being road kill."

"Where would we keep it?" she asks.

"It's a box turtle. We could keep it in a box."

"Okay, we're at the museum right now. We'll catch up in awhile."

The turtle fits in the pocket of my riding shirt. This works for ten minutes or so until it comes back out of its shell and starts trying to claw its way out of my pocket. Fearing I might be the one to turn this turtle into road kill, I stop to pull it out of the pocket, but not before it pees on me, once in the pocket and once while I pull it out. I take my shirt off and put it on backwards so the pocket is in front and I can keep an eye on this turtle. I ride this way for half an hour. Along the way I pass two dead tarantulas and then a live one crawling on the shoulder. Given the choices, the turtle seems the better traveling pet.

The kids jump out the door as soon as Harvey passes me and parks by the side of the road.

"You have a turtle, Daddy?"

It pees on me a third time before I hand the prize over to them.

"I love him," Kai exclaims.

I suggest Okie or Twister for names. Kai chooses Shelly.

They're playing with Shelly at the campground when I arrive at Kaw Lake a couple hours later.

"I think he's a little bored with me," Kai has told Anne.

On the way to Ponca City the next morning I stop at a convenience store to stand in line for the bathroom. An older man begins asking about my ride.

"Are they Inuit people who live on the Seward Peninsula?" he asks me after I've explained the ride.

"You know about Inuit people?" I ask.

"I've read lots about Alaska. And I've seen lots of shows. That's a beautiful state."

"The people on the Seward Peninsula are Inupiat or Yupik or Siberian Yupik people. All of them are part of the Inuit people who circle the northern extremes of the globe."

"I hope they don't drill for oil in Alaska," he says.

"Really?" I ask. "I'm surprised. This is oil country here."

"There are lots of people here who don't want to drill in the Arctic National Wildlife Refuge. Money isn't everything."

He goes on to say he hopes we don't go to war now, either.

"What do people here think about that?" I ask.

"Older people, people who have served in wars, they don't want to go to war. Younger people I talk to don't seem to care. I can't figure that out. They've got the most at stake."

His turn for the bathroom comes and he goes inside.

When he comes out, I ask if he wants to have breakfast with me, hoping to hear some more from this gentleman.

"I already ate this morning. I just took my kid, my grandson, to school."

We say goodbye, and I ride on. Anne and the kids stop at the library in Ponca City to do turtle research.

"It looks like a diamond-back terrapin," they report when they catch up. "The only problem is they need brackish water, and this is hundreds of miles from the ocean. Maybe it's something different."

From ranch country the land changes to flat farms as I head west on 11. We have over two hundred miles ahead in this remote part of Oklahoma. Most remarkable today are the flooded fields in this dry land. The rain is from a week earlier; seven inches fell in places. The rivers are still flowing fast with red muddy water. Many sections of fields with newly planted winter wheat are washed out.

Late in the afternoon two young people drive past in their decrepit Datsun 240-Z. Harry and Jenna stop ahead of me. He takes a picture. She holds out a two-dollar bill.

"We talked to your family back in Medford. This is for your trip. Two-dollar bills are lucky."

He has painted black fingernails. Her hair is electric blue, different from all the ranchers and oil-workers I've seen this week. We talk a few minutes, and then they leave, waving until they are far ahead of me. I put the two-dollar bill in my wallet and resume riding.

Maybe encounters like this are the reason for my unicycle ride. All across the country people have been asking us why we're doing it. When I think of all the people I've met and the places we've seen, the experience itself seems sufficient answer. Spoke by spoke our one-wheeled journey is growing richer. But why are we getting to see so much?

"We're going slow," Anne will say, with her view of the road from our sputtering Harvey.

"And we're vulnerable," I add to her thoughts.

We need food and water. We need directions and advice. We have needed air-conditioned restaurants and stores for relief from the heat. And every day, without established connections, we ride into a new land, dependent on finding what we need. A unicycle doesn't allow for a quick get-away. We pass through a place just a pedal at a time. People have responded with hospitality beyond our imagining.

Harvey has made us vulnerable, too. At this point, every mile that he makes down the road is more gift than given. At every difficulty, though, people have been there to help—Robert, Sam, Neal, Scooter…

From the vantage of my unicycle, it seems particularly strange that our country admires rugged individualism. I suppose I even fit the image, riding day after day, alone on the shoulder of the road for two Guinness World Records. But that's not what this ride is about. It's not so much about individual achievement as the experience of community. It is our vulnerability that is giving us this window into our country and the overwhelming generosity of so many of its people.

Maybe that's why this talk of war now is jarring me so much, so much more than I want to admit. The strident language declaring that our country can do whatever it wants, on its own, independent of the rest of the world is a stark contrast to what our family is experiencing on this ride. Being vulnerable, we are very dependent. Accepting this, we experience not violence but hospitality.

By evening I arrive at Salt Plains Wildlife Refuge and State Park. Over three hundred species of birds make their winter home here. Our campsite is right along the river. Pelicans are so thick that the edge of the water appears crusted with spring snow. Some seasons, up to 600,000 pelicans winter in this area.

On Wednesday at noon, Anne and the kids catch me in Alva. I've ridden just thirty-three miles, but they convince me to take the rest of the day off and come to Little Sahara.

"We can ride a dune buggy there," the kids tell me. And so we do. It's a thirty-mile drive south from our route. Arriving, we get a site for Harvey in the sandy lineup of RV's, dune buggies and four-wheelers. The kids' eyes are large with fascination.

Formed ten thousand years ago from the Cimarron River, these sand dunes are now constantly busy with buggy traffic. There's a dune store that gives rides, and we all climb in the big seven-seater. The kids think this is the greatest thing. Our driver is a young guy who lost his front teeth and almost bit his tongue off two weeks ago in a dune race.

"If I'm not giving rides here at work, I'm out riding my own dune buggy all the time." He is a hero to our kids, and they babble with excitement as we walk back to our campsite.

Two campsites up from us is another old Sportscoach motor home. Since Harvey has taken on such epic qualities on our trip, we stop to compare notes.

"Never had a lick of trouble with this one," Jerry tells us. "I keep thinking of trading it in for a newer one, but I can't find one that sleeps as many people."

Remarkable news. Just two nights ago, I was repairing the water storage tank with Shoe-Goo. It was an easy fix, but why should a heavy-duty plastic tank spring a leak now, along with all our other problems? Jerry's is a 1973 model; ours is 1978. Maybe we bought too new?

"Fall break is starting at the schools tomorrow, so this place will be full in a few hours," Jerry warns us. "The dunes are open twenty-four hours a day. It will be noisy all night here."

We offer the kids an opportunity to go back and sleep in a parking lot in Alva so it will be quiet and so we won't have to get up for an early morning drive back to the start point. "Let's stay here!" they chorus, so we wait until the next morning to drive to Alva.

There are miles and miles of miles and miles here in western Oklahoma. We've come to the beginning of Red Country where mesas shape this cattle land. Then the terrain flattens out to farming again. I smell the first sage since our return to the west. In almost that same breath, a coyote lopes across the road ahead of me.

Camp Houston has just a single gas pump, and I'm thankful to see it. Expecting only soda and a candy bar, instead there's a table full of ranchers and oil-workers inside.

"You want lunch, too?" the cashier asks as I enter. "Ribs today. They're good."

I take a seat and answer questions about my unicycle ride, sitting beside an old man in his cowboy hat. Someone tells of watching a TV show about horse training, telling how a horse had put its head down and refused to cooperate no matter what the trainer did. Bernie is the old man sitting next to me, and he mutters under his breath, "Last week my horse put his head down, and I ended up on the ground."

"You know where Anaheim is?" Bernie asks me.

"Sure, Disneyland. I grew up an hour from there. Do you have relatives there?"

"No, but I'm leasing land from a friend who lives there now."

Bernie, it turns out, grew up here in Oklahoma. "I'm one of the only ones left that remembers the dust bowl. I'm eighty-two."

I wonder how he survived.

"Had to put sheets up over the windows to try and keep the dust out. Lots of people moved to California, but the rabbits stayed. We ate a lot of rabbits. Never went to the store."

By the forties the economy had still not recovered.

"I hitchhiked to California on old Route 66 and worked in San Diego and Richmond. Then I spent some years in the army before coming back here."

"Richmond, that's right next to Berkeley." I tell him that I graduated from Cal Berkeley.

"I used to live right by the football stadium," he tells me with excitement.

We keep visiting. He's talked the waitress out of a second piece of cake by now. When he stands to leave, I see that he is six-foot-four or -five tall and straight for all the horse riding he still does. When he leaves, the waitress tells me, "You have to keep your eye out when Bernie's around. One time he pulled a horsehair from the tail of his horse and brought it with him to the café in Freedom for breakfast. He ordered pancakes. When they came, he took the top one off and coiled that hair inside the stack. Then he called the waitress and pulled out that hair while she watched. She grabbed the plate and ran back to the kitchen. People say the cook gave a real loud scream."

Maybe the stories and the pranks and the jokes helped his family survive the dustbowl and eat all those rabbits. Today is October 10. If we stick to our schedule, we have exactly one month to go.

34
Harvey Crisis

The calamity that comes is never the one we had prepared ourselves for.

MARK TWAIN

"It feels like we're coming out from being in a sweat lodge these last two months," Anne says.

The weather has cooled. Perhaps the steep slopes of the Appalachians and the long hot humid days of riding in the south have primed us for whatever we'll experience in this final month on the road.

From the perfection of the previous day I hit a strong south wind on Friday. Early in the morning I pass the historical marker telling us we're in "No Man's Land." Back when the states were getting divided up, this section was unattached to any jurisdiction. For a decade it became the home of outlaws. Eventually it became part of Oklahoma and joined it in statehood in 1907.

Riding straight west, perpendicular to the wind, I still make the eighty-three miles to Hooker. Late in the day a three-mile jog to the south, directly into the wind, takes a full half hour. Anne and the kids drive out and follow me into town for the last six dusky miles.

KariAnna preps me, "We found a great campground."

She has decided to operate a campground when she grows up. Her imagination is becoming more and more elaborate each day. This particular campground qualifies as great, just because it exists. We'd expected to park at the side of some road in this tiny town. Instead Tommy Tucker has an RV campground in his backyard: "Tommy Tucker's Tuckered Out RV Park." "I like to travel by RV, too," he tells Anne. "I thought our town needed an RV Park."

Tommy has three pull-through sites, with power, water and sewer. We're on the corner of the street, just across from huge grain elevators. Elevators in every town are busy, dryers going full blast during fall harvest. We sleep to the sound of their constant whine. A great campsite. Just ask KariAnna.

Texas

On Saturday the strong south wind turns 180 degrees to push at my back. I'm riding southwest on Highway 54 today and for the next couple of days, alongside the Union Pacific Railroad. Reaching our forty-third state at Texhoma, the Texas landscape now widens further; trees and buildings become even more rare than in the panhandle of Oklahoma. With the tailwind, I make ninety-one miles, the longest since Upstate New York. XIT signs are everywhere as I pedal the last stretch into town. Back in the 1880s it was the largest ranch in the world. It covered ten Texas counties and was over three million acres, supporting 150,000 head of cattle. It got its start when the State of Texas gave this land to the Capital Syndicate of Chicago in exchange for building the state capital in Austin.

The RV site in Dalhart advertises level pull-through sites. When we arrive, we see that everything in Dalhart is level, in fact, pancake flat. The site owners have been here forty-two years. Next month they're turning it over to their grandson. The kids like the playhouse and a teeter-totter, and we pass a comfortable Sunday rest day, getting steaks and barbecuing our evening meal. The week before we'd celebrated getting to the top of the fishhook with a barbecue. The kids enjoyed it so much we've decided to make steak a Sunday tradition for the rest of the trip. Evening time comes too quickly.

Before dark we pull down the five-foot giraffe unicycle and put KariAnna up on it. Anne and I walk along on each side of her. Completely unexpectedly, she's riding on her own within fifteen minutes. Before she calls it quits, she has pedaled 110 independent pedals.

"Good job!" Kai tells her. "I want to try too!" A few more inches of growing and he'll be up also.

New Mexico

Forty-two desolate miles through Texas bring us to New Mexico, our forty-fourth state. Yucca cacti, more sage, two cattle feed lots, and a headwind; it's a long distance between any services. The Red-X gas station in Nara Visa has only a post office and an antique store for company. We make it to Logan and Ute State Park, which boasts the best walleye fishing in the state. The kids rate it high, another great campsite.

"They have really nice showers here," KariAnna announces.

Tucumcari, New Mexico, has long been one of my favorite towns, for the sake of its name alone. This is my first time here. Main Street is old Route 66, the legendary road that first connected Chicago to Los Angeles in the 1940s. We will be following it off and on from here to the end of the ride. Sitting outside a grocery store and eating breakfast, a man rolls up on his bicycle. He might be at the top end of his 50s.

"There you are! We passed you a few days ago on Highway 54."

While I eat my apple, I ask him if he's on a long trip or a short vacation.

"Twenty years," he answers. "My wife and I decided we'd give traveling a twenty-year chance and then decide if we like it or not."

"Seems like you'll make a pretty good decision by then. How long have you been on the road?"

"Three years. It's good and getting better."

They are headed from here to Arizona for the winter.

A mile out of town a car is stopped, and the driver shouts to me with a thick accent, asking permission to take a picture. I give him the thumbs up. He snaps a picture, and I stop to say hello.

It turns out that he is a young man from South Korea. A Route 66 baseball cap tops his head. Route 66 collectibles fill the back window of his small Nissan. He is driving from Chicago to Los Angeles.

I ask how his trip is going, remembering road trips from when I was single and alone. He tells me he had a motel room last night, but the three previous nights he slept in the car.

"Sometimes hard," he tells me. "Bread and milk in the car for meals some days. Other times are wonderful, like this pretty place here."

He tells me, "I am trying to overcome myself."

I'm sure there is something missing in his translation of his thoughts, but I like the words.

Interstate 40 here runs the same route as Highway 66 once did. In some places the old highway still exists; in others, it is covered over. The frontage road out of Tucumcari is a rough road and hard to ride on. Three miles later I come to an unexpected dead end. I-40 is a hundred yards and two barbed wire fences away. I carefully protect the tire of the unicycle as I cross the fences, but forgetting about the seat, the barbwire pops it. The police have said I can ride the interstate if there are no side roads. It's noisy with the traffic of trucks and motor homes, but the shoulder is wide. I pedal all day to Santa Rosa. On arrival, the odometer hits eight thousand miles for the trip.

The air is completely still when I wake up on Wednesday. I am on the road just as the sun comes up, and the wind begins almost immediately. It blows straight in my face, quickly growing strong enough to make cars stop early for gas.

A lone Chevron station is my first stop, thirty long miles west of Santa Rosa. I microwave a burrito and eat it slowly, talking with Rudy, the owner. "Elevation is six-thousand feet here," he tells me. I'm surprised. "And Cline's Corners is at seventy-two hundred." I had no idea we were so high. It's the western edge of the Plains and the land is open, wide, and mostly flat. Still, it's the highest point of our ride so far.

"Summers are really busy," Rudy continues when I ask him what life is like with nothing to interrupt his view to the horizons. "This time of year is what you call steady. This is snowbird traffic; all the motor homes are heading to Arizona."

I had planned to make Moriarty, but early on I call Anne, explain how tiring the wind is, and ask her to wait at Cline's Corners.

"The engine is running rough," she tells me, "Maybe it's the climbing and the altitude."

Five miles after the Chevron station there's a rest stop. Marx and Phyllis are visiting with me. "Marx," he says, "like Harpo."

Phyllis has just answered a passerby with, "I'm fine." Then she asks me, "Why do we all say we're fine, even when we're not?" Maybe we're trying to overcome ourselves.

On their way to Quartzite, Arizona, for the winter, their old Chrysler mini-van had broken down, and the parts took up all of their gas money. They're headed there to fix other people's RVs this winter.

"I do some computer work, too," Marx tells me. "Quartzite has 4,000 people in the summer. The winter population will be over 240,000. As soon as we get there, I'll be working all winter."

I let them use our cell phone to call their contact in Arizona, but the line is busy. I give them ten dollars for gas. They offer to stop and check out our RV and why it's running rough. After they leave, I call and tell Anne they may be stopping.

"Funny," she says. "I just filled the tank for a couple here. They're headed to Texas. Her father is having surgery. It makes me think of the Oklahoma dustbowl and the old migrations to California."

Marx and Phyllis do make it Cline's Corners, meet Anne, and check on Harvey. "Your spark plug wires have gone bad." Marx tells Anne, "That messes up the engine at these high altitudes."

Cline's Corners is at Exit 218. It has gas, a diner, a gift shop with south-western memorabilia, and an endless view. Signs have advertised this little place for the past two days of unicycling. The wind finally stops during the last two miles, but not before one of the hardest pedaling days of the trip. It has taken all day to make these sixty-two miles.

After Mexican dinner at the diner, we end the day under the motor home with a flashlight, replacing the bad sparkplug wires. During the day Anne and the kids drove over to Moriarty to get parts. I've also had my first flat of the trip today. The leak was so slow that I rode the last fifteen miles just pumping it up twice. There are goathead stickers everywhere, blown onto the road from the desert, and the interstate is full of steel wire from shred-ded tires. My old tire, with two-thousand miles on it, could probably make the final thousand. Instead, hoping to avoid any more flats, I replace it with the fifth new tire of the journey. Everyone is ready for sleep when we turn in. The moon is high and bright here, stars fill the sky, and the air is crisp and cold at the top of the high plains.

Thursday dawns still and calm. Dropping to 5,000 feet, I arrive in Albuquerque by 3 p.m. Tijeras Canyon is a highlight. An age-old route between the high plains and the Rio Grande Valley, it holds both Route 66 and Interstate 40 in a snaking descent to the city.

The kids and Anne have spent the day at the zoo. "We saw a Komodo dragon. They're the biggest lizards in the world," KariAnna reports.

"We saw polar bears, too." Kai adds.

At a population of 400,000, Albuquerque is the biggest city we've come to since Atlanta, and it's the biggest we'll see until the trip's end in Los Angeles. We decide to take a day off here for errands before heading into the country again.

Palisades RV park is at the edge of town. Long-term residents are stacked tightly together in dusty sites. Another person in cycling shorts shows up to share the congestion. Chrisy and her husband Mike are mountain bik-ing the Divide Trail from Canada to Mexico, taking a day off in Albuqueque. "Five flats today," Chrisy reports. Their riding has been even more rural than ours. For days at a time, they ride cross-country, sometimes getting water from windmills in cattle fields.

Anne had felt a new vibration in Harvey as she drove through Tijeras Canyon and into Albuquerque. I check the sparkplug wires again, and put new spark plugs in as well to see if that will help with the power. I change the oil and give Harvey a test drive. Everything seems normal. We're on schedule for an easy arrival by November 10.

Our friend Katherine Roach comes to visit us on Friday. "I wouldn't ride through Albuquerque," she warns. We decide to take the day off to wait until Saturday morning when there will be less traffic.

Pat, Katherine's husband, was a professor of mine in college, and he's out of town for the week. Katherine tells about their bicycling. Leading cycle tours has become one of their main endeavors since retirement. "We left Albuquerque ten years ago and moved south to get to places we could bicycle." Now, with a Wal-Mart and Home Depot being built in their town, they are moving again to a smaller town.

Pat was my professor, but mostly I remember him for a bicycle seat. In reaching Albuquerque, we've come on our journey to the fourth intersection with my bicycle ride of 1985. All the way to Albuquerque I had bicycled with a sore rear end. I held up fine until I reached sixty miles each day; every moment after that was painful. When I arrived in Albuquerque, it was a relief to stay overnight with Pat and Katherine. We relived memories of riding the Davis Double Century together. Pat recommended another seat to me. I paid twenty-eight dollars for it, a big chunk out of my sparse riding budget. From then on I rode in comfort every day for the rest of the journey.

Saturday morning I get out of Albuquerque without any traffic problems. A reporter from Channel 7 comes out, and as I ride north, he shoots an hour of video. He seems to like the angles from behind trees; I ride along trying to guess where he'll show up next. It makes the miles go quickly.

"Good luck. God bless." he says when he's finished. "I hope you're successful in your cause."

Out of town after Bernalillo, I'm finally back in the country. Elevation is rising again as we near the Continental Divide. Just past noon Anne calls with the familiar news, "Something is wrong with Harvey. A loud clicking noise just started in the engine. What should I do?"

Park the RV. Disconnect the Honda. Catch up with me at mile thirty-seven of my ride today. Deal with kids who show their anxiety by being cranky. Drive back to Albuquerque.

It's a really loud noise this time. All the RV places are on the other end of town, so we start Harvey and inch him carefully to the east side. We try three different shops, but no mechanics are working on Saturday afternoon. Finally we spot a man closing the garage door at an auto sales place.

"It might be a push rod. Those 454s bend a lot of push rods." He calls his friend Ricardo, who says he'll look at it. "It's a transmission shop, but he does all my work."

We get to MT Transmission and find out that Ricardo doesn't do this kind of work, but Moses, the owner walks us next door to Lance's shop. Lance and his partner listen to the motor. "We could do it all right, but an

RV place would know all the tricks for getting to it. And we're going racing tonight, so we couldn't get to it until Monday.

"Thanks." I tell them. It's at least some hope.

"If they give you an outrageous estimate, come back and we'll see what we can do."

There's a campground nearby, so we chug Harvey over to it Saturday evening. I'm planning to ride on Sunday to catch up, but after we settle in it's clear we're better off staying together until we see this latest twist through. The campground has a hot tub, which helps us soak some anxiety away. We go to church on Sunday morning at Faith Lutheran. Sunday evening we have our weekly steak barbecue.

The highlight of the day for the kids is bowling. The highlight of the day for Anne and me is our visit to the Pueblo Indian Cultural Center. This is the land that Coronado explored and the Spanish settled. Long before their arrival, people here were living in two- and three-story structures in highly developed communities. I easily could have spent four days at the center.

Instead, we are spending four days in Gerardo's world.

Monday morning early I try to find Lance and see which RV place he recommended. His place is locked, but Moses from the transmission shop is already at work. "Were you on the TV this weekend?"

He makes some calls. "I have a friend who is good with RVs. He's not answering his phone. Let me drive you there so you know where it is, and then you can talk to him when he comes in."

"Did I see you on the television?" Gerardo asks when I introduce myself. I tell him about our ride.

"It would be an honor to help you get back on your travels."

Monday morning: Gerardo's helper Gabriel pulls the valve cover off on the left side and we see nothing wrong. I start pulling off the other side while both of them are busy. A rocker arm is sitting askew when I get a look inside. This looks simple. The push rod is bent too. Gerardo comes to inspect. It looks easy to him too, at first, but something's not right. And then he tells me

"You have a stuck valve. See here."

These heads are only six thousand miles old. They were put on in South Dakota during our trip. What are the chances of this?

During the weekend we'd thought of whether to make this Harvey's last gasp, his final resting place. With three weeks of riding and just six states to go, all of us want to complete this ride. But how to do it? Have Anne and the kids drive the Honda home and let me finish alone? Get a pickup truck and a tent? Fix Harvey one more time?

Gerardo makes a call to the machine shop and they tell him they have heads in stock.

"My problem," he tells me, "is I am trying to catch up this week on the cars I have. But, if you can take it apart and put it back together again, then I can help you and we can do it."

I like mechanical work and every other option seems worse. Harvey's innards are all exposed, anyway, here in the middle of Gerardo's lot. I agree.

"We can get the new heads in the morning; you can be out tomorrow night."

The kids and Anne have taken the world's longest non-stop tram to the top of Sandia Peak today.

Tuesday morning: Gerardo's compound is a warehouse shop with a barbed wire enclosure around it, stuffed with a dozen and a half cars in all states of repair and disrepair. We have camped here overnight. A nearly new motor home is here, too, which he parks on the street all day and brings in when he goes home at night.

"The owner needs to come and pick it up," he explains.

With our two motor homes here, the lot is jammed full at night.

Gerardo goes in the morning for the heads and then returns.

"Bad news." It turns out the phone information was wrong. They don't have any in stock and ready to go. "If we get these heads out this morning they can machine them and have them ready for you tomorrow morning."

Okay…one more day.

We are very thankful to have met Gerardo. I don't feel as though I'm on a unicycle ride while we're here at his shop, but he's inspiring to be around. "I almost closed this shop down a month ago," he tells me. "That's why I'm so behind right now and trying to catch up."

A year ago Gerardo had a stroke. He recovered well, but the medication made him "fuzzy," and he couldn't do the work he used to. "I was all ready to close down, but I told my family I had to try one last time, so I quit taking the medication. Now I am feeling better. I can do the work again."

In the meantime he's accumulated a long backlog of cars awaiting his attention. "This week I am hoping to catch up. My nephews are coming in at night to help me."

With Gabriel, his assistant, they are taking cars apart, waiting for parts, and reassembling others all day long. The shop appears to be in disarray. An additional challenge was having to move out of the place he was renting in the middle of his recovery. Gerardo hasn't had time to set up again the way he would like. No task, though, is too big or too small for this two-man show. They pull engines and rebuild transmissions as often as they change brakes. I help with the simple tasks while I wait. I can tell Gerardo loves this work. Instead of cursing the surprises, he laughs when he encounters the unexpected. When he hits a setback, he calls it "a loss of momentum." Mechanics is a puzzle, and he is a master.

Anne and the kids return in the afternoon from another day at the zoo. "The Komodo dragon was eating today." KariAnna fills me in. "It's gross when he eats, so people can't watch." The polar bears weren't wrestling today as they had been on the previous visit, so the kids have spent a lot of time at the zoo playground. Anne has painted watercolors of the lions and the giraffes.

Wednesday morning: The heads are not ready. I spend the morning alternating between helping with brake changes and reading *Of Earth and Elders*. The book is by Serle Chapman and is filled with interviews of native leaders from around the country. It adds to our experience of riding through these places all across America.

We get the heads at 3 p.m. and bolt them in place, but we don't have enough time or momentum to put the motor back together. The unicycle has begun to feel like a distant unreality.

Anne and the kids took in a mall today.

Thursday morning: Gerardo is cruising today. I go with him to the parts store, and while we're buying new push rods, he scores two more repair jobs from salespeople at the store. I work steadily putting our engine back together. Gerardo sets the valves by mid-afternoon, and I hear him say, "Fantastic."

I figure he's finished with the task, but, no, he's just dropped the feeler gauges onto the ground. He jumps out of the motor home and crawls underneath to fetch his tool. His alternative to cursing is, "fantastic." I start thinking we'll be out of here by dinnertime. In the rush of other jobs, it turns into a late night. At 9 p.m. Gerardo is free to do the last work on our motor home. We're out the gate at 11:45. Puzzles, challenges, complications, success. Another day for Gerardo. A huge hurdle overcome for us. What could have been a disaster has become an inspiration.

Anne and the kids, burned out on Albuquerque by now, have spent the day reading books and watching children's videos. With the kids asleep, we drive thirty miles north under a full moon, parking the motor home near tomorrow's starting point.

We're back on the ride.

35
Painted Desert

*Independence … is loyalty to one's best self and principles,
and this is often disloyalty to the general idols and fetishes.*

MARK TWAIN

After a week of mechanics with Gerardo, the first few pedals on the unicycle feel strange. Soon it is all familiar again, except that my image of the trip this morning is a picture of nuts and bolts, puzzles and problems, persistence, and solutions. One could compare our ride to the rebuilding of a motor and not be too far off. We've learned a lot, and we're still moving forward.

With the week-long delay, it is now unlikely we can finish by our tentative date of November 10. Having replotted dates and distances, we're shooting for Tuesday, November 12. Today is the 25th of October. After all the Harvey issues, the end of the ride has become more tentative and more tantalizing. From here on we're taking a minimalist focus for our route, hoping to maximize our chances of a successful arrival. I've scratched rest days for the remainder of the ride. We plan to circle the Four Corners rather than venture deeper into Colorado or Utah. Instead of riding to the Grand Canyon, we can save thirty miles by going through Flagstaff.

The Santa Ana, Zia, Jemez, and Jicarillo Apache reservations are on the ride today as we head northwest on Highway 44 (recently renamed Highway 550). This is mesa country, filled with long views and abrupt skylines. The ride is almost all uphill. I reach Cuba, where Anne has found a campsite in the yard behind Theresa's Barber and Beauty Shop. There's a big puddle in the driveway, which the kids are splashing around in; the weather feels too cold for water.

After resting, I head on, reaching the Continental Divide in ten more miles. There's no dramatic pass, just the top of a long, gentle incline. Still, at 7380 feet, this is the highest point of our ride. A sign from a biking club is spray-painted on the road, "Yeah, Baby, It's all downhill from here!!!"

Robert must have said the same thing to me a hundred times during the summer.

Anne and the kids pick me up at dark and drive me back to Cuba; we make burritos for dinner and are soon asleep.

A historical marker for Cuba announces that this town was first settled after a grant from the Spanish governor but was then abandoned after attacks by "Frontier Tribes." Many years later it was resettled.

It really does matter who gets to write the signs. It was frontier to the newcomers. To the "Frontier Tribes," it had been home for thousands of years.

Back at Tucumcari a road sign made an impression on me. A line from it continues to pop up in my mind, "This area was troubled by Comanches and Comancheros, the people who traded illegally with the Indians."

Clearly it wasn't the Comanche people who wrote that sign or made the rules about trading.

In *Of Earth and Elders,* one writer relates that the population of Native Americans in America was once thirty-three million. Another estimates it was fifty million. Both note that by 1900 the native population in the United States was only 250,000.

A former student from Michigan State e-mailed back after hearing about our visit with Chief Bearskin. Erin is now living in Ontario, Canada, where the Wyandottes once were. She student-teaches in nearby Amherstburg,

> *The public high school in town is called General Amherst High School. Both are named after General Jeffrey Amherst, who is believed to be the first military officer to sanction the use of biological weapons. He ordered his soldiers to distribute to the Native population blankets that contained scabs and pus from men infected with smallpox. On my drive into town, I pass by a small, old cemetery on the Detroit River. The sign says, "Wyandotte Indian Cemetery." I have to wonder how many people buried there died of smallpox. I stopped there once after school on a nice day. It was hard to imagine when the Wyandottes lived on the river, with forests as far as the eye can see, and no one trying to take their land and kill them, which was done all too effectively. It's hard to imagine those not killed being removed to a reservation in Oklahoma, a completely different environment...I'm still struggling a lot with religion and values...*

Like Erin, I too am still struggling a lot with religion and values. I can't get the population figures out of my mind. This is our history. This is the sign that we have written. Today the Native American population is up to two million.

I encounter more wide-open mesa country on Saturday. Heavy thunderstorms and cold weather have me shivering in the afternoon. From the

Apache reservation to Navajo country, much of the ride is near seven thousand feet. The road is a good four-lane with big shoulders, but there are no towns marked on my map. I didn't know if I'd find food along this route. Every ten or fifteen miles, though, I come upon a gas station and convenience store, or a trading post that serves the area.

Late in the afternoon, Anne decides to drive out and see how I'm doing. She sees my unicycle at one of the rare convenience stores along the way. She bounces up to me wearing a court jester's hat, the one she's gotten for me for Halloween. And around the corner is Harry Potter. Hair dyed black and wearing a cape and shirt, Kai is a ringer for the little wizard. He runs up and thwacks me with his wand.

We visit together amongst the traffic of this busy little store. All of us are taking refuge from a severe thunderstorm that soaked me before I arrived. Some of the many Navajo customers ask questions about my unicycle. Harry is particularly interested: "I used to run marathons," he tells us, "on the reservation, in Albuquerque, all over." He's hurt his knee, though, so he can't run anymore. He comes back to us again a bit later. "Here," he says, "I want to give you something for your trip," and he opens his wallet to hand over a ten dollar bill. "I used to ride rodeo, too," he says, perhaps feeling a connection with unicycling, "but a horse rolled over me and broke my arm."

Anne has found a campground with a hot tub, which provides motivation for the last thirteen cold and soggy miles. I make it to Bloomfield in another downpour. First settled by hunters and gatherers in the 1100s, Bloomfield's economy today is oil, gas, and coal.

Sunday morning I pedal towards Shiprock without sabbath rest, passing churches where cars are parked during worship. Later, after Farmington, I ride past the Four Corners power plant, a huge coal-powered generating facility that is surrounded with controversy for the amount of pollution it creates. Then I am into the Navajo Nation, the largest reservation in the United States.

After a hamburger at Shiprock, I pedal west on Highway 64 into some of the most open, desolate land of the entire trip. Vegetation is limited to scrub brush spaced widely to compete for scarce water. Although today is cold, the land has the look of perpetual baked heat. Naked mesas are colored from black to white, with reds and browns and beige as well. The highway fades into nothing as it crosses far valleys.

Arizona

Anne and the kids have driven north into Colorado for the day to see Mesa Verde National Park. We are out of phone contact much of the day. By late afternoon we still haven't crossed paths, and I wish we would. I am feeling sick. The queasy stomach, headache and weak legs only make this land feel even more desolate. I rest for half an hour, sitting on a rock, measuring the need to recuperate against the time to make Teec Nos Pos, Arizona, before dark. When I start riding again, I still feel weak, and it is too late to finish in daylight. At last a few lights from a convenience store appear; I pedal towards them as the sky goes black and the road becomes indistinct in front of me. A quarter mile before I arrive, the lights of Harvey show up, approaching from the north. We have made our forty-fifth state. The store clerk gives us permission to park across the road. Against the dark outside, we make dinner, play table games, and I hear about Mesa Verde. It is a strange combination; this land that feels desolate brims with life and history.

Riding across the Navajo Nation turns out to be the most challenging five-day stretch of the trip. All the way across the United States, and all the way back, we met the mileage goals that we set for whatever day we were riding. For five days in a row I miss our plan. It starts with a delay; the Four Corners is locked. Five miles north of Teec Nos Pos, I have arrived forty minutes before the gate opens to the monument. Anne drives up with the motor home and we wait, looking out across far distant skylines into Utah and Colorado. When the corners open, I pedal a dozen laps around the monument. In less than a minute we go from five states left to three: Nevada, California, and Hawaii. After getting signatures I start across Arizona, heading west on Highway 160. A wind comes up, and by the end of the day I fall short of Kayenta by twenty-six miles. Anne picks me up at Dinnehotso and drives me into Kayenta, where the motor home is parked at a shopping center with a movie theater. She and the kids have spent the afternoon at Monument Valley. After dinner we walk over to a showing of *Country Bears*.

In the morning it's blowing another strong headwind and there's a trace of snow on the ground. We wait for the sun to come out, and I end up starting at two o'clock, hoping to recover some energy with a morning of rest. With a headwind in my face all afternoon, I barely make the miles back to Kayenta.

On Wednesday the wind continues strong. A constant, cold, steady force, it takes the joy out of rest stops and makes this wide-open land feel endless.

I feel almost no sense of progress as I pedal hour after hour. Thoughts of finishing in Los Angeles are on hold. Whatever sense of achievement I've had on this long ride is gone. Now it's just pedaling in the midst of this wind and this land. Upthrusts and downthrusts of thousands of feet of rock have created a massive geography, an unending variety of texture, shape, and color; in the midst of which I am nothing. I am as strong as I have ever been in my life, and yet my progress depends on factors of weather and land over which I have no control. Sand blows in my face throughout the day. In the loneliness I remember my friend Grace and her patience.

I was Grace's pastor in Nome. I ended up being body parts for her.

Seventy-five years old, weathered and bent, Grace was more comfortable speaking the Inupiat language than English. She was always ready for a ride to choir practice at church. Well, almost always ready. One evening we arrived and after she struggled to get her uncooperative body to the choir loft, she began to laugh with quiet mirth, then gave a big-gummed smile, "I forgot my teeth. You go home and get my teeth. By the bed," she told me. I drove back and fished them from their cup of cleaning solution. When I brought them back to her, she fitted them in place and gave me yet another smile.

A few months later Grace told me, "You be my eyes."

The evening program of singing was about to begin. Two hundred Inupiat people were gathered from surrounding villages at the Teller Village School Gym. Two hours into the four-hour songfest, Grace's turn was called. I helped her to the front, following the slow pace of her cane. As a child Grace had been saved by the Lutheran Orphanage after her parents died from an epidemic. Now she was coming forward to sing her thanks, to make her testimony, to voice the deepest roots of her being. Her vision gone, my task was to sing the words so she could follow with her memory.

Someone took a picture of us that night, long ago. I still look at it, reminded how often we are eyes for one another.

Windbeaten by the end of the day, I step off the unicycle and into the old mercantile store at Red Mesa. Chainsaws and galvanized tubs hang from the ceiling. Soda pop waits for purchase in the coolers. Space blankets, lantern wicks, and bubble gum share space with a thousand other inventory items that cram every corner of this old stone building. The elder running the store tells me about lack of rain for the past twenty years. "Our sheep are having a hard time. Our people are having a hard time making it on the land."

I head back out into the wind, in this land that is harsh to everyone. Anne picks me up soon after. Again I miss my goal; this time I'm twenty miles short of Tuba City.

On Thursday I have only fifty miles to Cameron. Worn down by these days of cold biting wind, though, each mile feels long and labored. I get a flat before Tuba City, the second one here on the Navajo Nation. I'm down to my last patch. Fortunately, I find another repair kit in Tuba. West of Tuba, all previous sense of desolation is suddenly magnified. The land dries up even further, now devoid of any shred of vegetation.

A legend still circulates that NASA brought astronauts to train here back in the sixties because the land so closely resembles a moonscape. An elder and his son saw the strange apparitions and approached them. The elder couldn't understand English, so his son translated. When he found out they were going to the moon, he asked if he could send a message along. Excitedly, the astronauts grabbed a recorder and taped his message. No one would tell them what the message was until money was produced, at which point it was translated for them: "Watch out for these guys, they come to take your land!"

In Cameron I finally catch up with Anne and the kids. Today is October 31. They've gotten an RV site and are decorating Harvey for Halloween. They have been carving pumpkins. "What took you so long?" Anne asks.

"I really don't know," I answer. "This land is taking everything I have."

"Do you still have enough energy to go into Flagstaff to trick or treat?" she asks. The kids are excited. They've been excited about Halloween for the last six weeks. We bought costumes way back in Mississippi.

"Of course I'm coming," I answer. An hour later, we're driving off to another world from the one that has shaped our past week. We eat at The Olive Garden Restaurant, shop for black hairspray, and head to a wealthy suburb of carefully arranged homes with neatly manicured lawns. KariAnna spends the evening as a BumbleBee. Kai brings his unicycle and seems to glide from house to house, his Harry Potter Cape draping over the wheel of his unicycle. Before we started our rounds, Kai had explained to Anne and me the magic of Halloween, "Daddy, see this bag? You won't believe how full it's going to get tonight."

Surprisingly, the kids are moderate in their appetite for trick-or-treating. Content with a few pounds of candy each, we get back in the car and start for Cameron. I make my own Halloween stop before we leave Flagstaff, buying another two dozen energy bars for the road. With the long distances between towns, I've been carrying most of my own calories along on the unicycle.

Full health has still not returned. Whatever weakness struck me back in Shiprock has been pressured by the constant winds and challenges of the last days. Still, on the drive back from Flagstaff, I can't resist thinking about the Grand Canyon, even though riding to it will add thirty miles more than going through Flagstaff. Time feels even shorter now than when we left Albuquerque. The last week has pushed me hard, and yet we know that the wind could have been stronger, the snow could have been deep, rain could have been more chilling. We decide to decide in the morning. Whatever I do, Anne will drive the kids to the Grand Canyon, so at least they can see it. She'll find me at the end of the day, whether at the rim or in Flagstaff.

On Friday morning I sleep in after sunrise. Getting up, I dawdle over breakfast and then poke around getting the unicycle packed and checked for the day's ride. Anne is anxious to get going, but I am still vacillating on which route to ride. Finally I tell her it's the Grand Canyon. It's already 8 a.m. by the time I leave Harvey.

"I'll get a campsite at the rim," she tells me. "If you're not there by an hour before dark, we'll come and get you. I love you."

There's already a bit of vegetation in Cameron, and it increases as I head west on 64. Just three miles into the ride, I am passed by a motorcyclist who stops ahead of me. He points to his camera. "Okay?" he asks as I approach.

"Sure." I jump off after his picture and we communicate between his broken English and my broken Spanish. Francisco is from Barcelona, Spain, here for a six month journey that he hopes will get him to Central America. He's slept the previous night behind one of the two gas stations in Cameron. He has wild hair and a scruffy beard, and all his possessions look as weathered as he does. Even his motorcycle looks the part, a moderate Suzuki 600 with a plastic cover missing, exposing frame and fuel valves. Bags are strapped on the back. Campgrounds are too expensive for Francisco to afford each night, so I invite him to camp with us at the rim, describing Harvey and telling him to introduce himself to Anne when he gets there.

"Thank you, thank you," he says before he rides off. I wonder if I'll see him again.

After a few more miles, I realize the wind is gone. The constant, draining, sucking force is silent. After a week with the wind, I expect it to return any moment. The day stays calm, though, as I pedal along this road that rises steadily towards the park entrance.

At ten-mile intervals, I pass Navajo roadside vendors. Stan is the first one to motion me to a stop. From him I learn the land here is "frozen" pending litigation between the United States government, Peabody Coal, and other interests. No one can make any improvements or additions to dwellings until the suit is settled.

These plywood roadside stands are lined up in a row next to each other. Tables hold pottery, jewelry, sand paintings, and weavings that artisans have created for sale. Nelson is the next one to wave me over. I tell him what I'm doing. He tells me about driving through twenty states when he took his daughter to Maine to begin college. We've traveled similar places along our routes. I share how much the removals in the East have made an impression on me.

"The Navajos had their own removal," Nelson tells me. "We called it The Long Walk. They took us to Oklahoma. We stayed for four years. Then we walked back."

"Crazy," I remark. "How are things now?"

"Still pretty crazy."

He gives me his business card. On the back is printed the Navajo beauty prayer.

Beauty is before me, and
Beauty behind me,
Above me and below me
Hovers the beautiful
I am surrounded by it.
I am immersed in it.
In my youth I am aware of it,
And, in old age,
I shall walk quietly the beautiful trail.
In beauty it is begun.
In beauty it is ended.

If there is truth to the native understanding that life is circular, then I am seeing that truth. Again I remember Tim from early in the ride at the Colville Reservation. I remember him blessing me with the piece of root. "This is the soul of Mother Earth. And you are riding over Mother Earth this summer." Our one-wheeled journey continues to fill with spoke after spoke.

Two more hours brings me to the Grand Canyon and the Desert View overlook. I have been to the Grand Canyon many times: with my parents as a kid, hiking it with my dad and brother when I was in high school, hiking it for a week as a young adult, and later visiting with Anne. Like every other time I have been here, I am overwhelmed. Something in me simply can't hold the grandeur of this place. It is too vast, too far beyond my imagination. A mile deep, a dozen or more miles across, formed by the patient work of the Colorado River over hundreds of millions of years, I have never seen anything like it anywhere else. Arriving here is the completion of another circle, the fifth intersection with my bicycle journey of fifteen years earlier. From Tuba City to Los Angeles, the beginning of my bicycle ride across the country coincides almost exactly with the end of this unicycle journey.

Reaching the Grand Canyon by bicycle from my starting point in Los Angeles was one of the biggest milestones of that entire trip. I had survived my first week, pedaling through the Mojave Desert, coming to this grand, mythic, massive canyon in the earth. I had done it with nothing more than leg power. My trip was well begun, and I was beginning to believe I might actually make a far stretch across the country. I took two days here to soak in the majesty of it all.

A sermon on Sunday afternoon almost ruined the experience for me. Seated at the rim of the Grand Canyon those of us gathered heard whoever the pastor was tell us a story about a lighthouse. A lighthouse? It felt so out of place, so ludicrous! Here on the rim, in the middle of this magnificence, we were told a story about how Jesus is like a lighthouse. All the grandeur of this canyon, all this power, all this overwhelming matter surrounding us, and the story we heard was about an ocean shore, the nearest being hundreds of miles away. It felt like an affront, a disregarding of this place, a sacrilege in its own way.

This preacher disturbed me. His words kept coming back all the next day as I pedaled the East Rim out of the park. The question about lighthouses spun through my mind and quickly transformed to a question about Jesus. "What place does Jesus have in a place like this?"

Hundreds of millions of years old, the Grand Canyon makes Jesus look as if he hasn't arrived on the block yet. The animal species that have evolved to their particularity in this place, the Colorado River that has carved the canyon's intricacy, all these make Jesus seem a grain of sand sweeping along the river bottom. People talk about being one with Jesus. I had read Colin Fletcher's description of hiking the canyon, of his becoming one with this place. It fit much better than a lighthouse.

From the Grand Canyon and Jesus, I had bicycled east to Hotevilla in Hopi land and Window Rock on the Navajo Nation. Jesus was worded into that land too, but other stories were also there, older stories, stories that had grown from the dirt and sky of their particular place.

Today, as I unicycle along the East Rim of the Grand Canyon towards the village and campgrounds, these memories mingle with vistas of the canyon and riding on the road. Four British motorcyclists stop to visit in the afternoon. They have rented Harleys in Phoenix and are touring the Southwest. Compared to Francisco they are princes.

For myself, I sense a transition to the last section of this ride. A hopeful expectancy is returning after the past three weeks of testing and trials.

Francisco is with our family when I arrive. The kids have been hiking with Anne down the Bright Angel Trail. They are beaming with stories to tell me about their day. "We hiked so far! I like the Grand Canyon!"

Dinner is burritos, and we spend the evening struggling in both Spanish and English to talk with our traveling guest. Francisco has made lots of journeys like this one, working a couple years to afford a half-year of traveling by motorcycle or moped. From the North Cape of Norway to the Southern tip of Chile, Francisco has been there. India is next on his list. It turns out we were born within a month and ten days of each other; maybe he is my Spanish twin.

I am glad I didn't skip the Grand Canyon. After replacing Harvey's heads back in Albuquerque, we have no time to take off and savor this canyon, but just being here, riding the rim and camping overnight, brings past experiences and present joy to life.

36
Beyond the Canyon

You can find in a text whatever you bring, if you will
stand between it and the mirror of your imagination.

MARK TWAIN

Sunrise makes the Grand Canyon look even more spectacular than during the day. I am up early enough to be at the rim to watch the canyon brighten into all its shades of red. When I pedal away, the canyon is immediately out of sight, once again a memory.

Southwards to Williams, I ride through a changing land of juniper, sage, and pine. The highway was newly paved the summer before. Today is Saturday, and most of the traffic is on the other side of the road, going into the park. In the early afternoon, far ahead of me, I spot a truck stopped at the top of a grade. The driver stays in his cab, watching the entire time as I slowly crest the grade. I stop to talk. White-haired Roger turns out to be a retired volunteer at Grand Canyon Village and an avid cyclist.

"I'm thinking about doing a five-hundred mile race this summer," he tells me. "Gotta have goals."

"Must be great training around here," I suggest.

"It is. But there are hardly any other riders. Most of the workers back at the canyon think I'm nuts."

"I haven't met many other cyclists on this trip, either," I tell him. "I don't know if fewer people are biking or if I was just on different roads."

"It's mountain bikes, I think. Almost every bike sold now is a mountain bike, hardly any road bikes."

"Hardly any unicycles, either," I add. Roger wishes me well and promises to check the ride on the website.

Anne and the kids have stretched their time in the Grand Canyon as much as possible, hiking once again down the Bright Angel Trail. I arrive in Williams two hours before they do and wait for them so we can camp here. The date is November 2.

From this day, it will take almost four months for the main meaning of my ride to surface in my mind. It will happen on February 28, 2003. On that day, getting a ride back from a writing conference on Whidbey Island, I will answer another writer's question:

"Why did you go on this ride?"

I give her the long answer, the cascade of reasons that flows from KariAnna wanting to learn to unicycle all the way back to my bicycle ride across the country. Suddenly she laughs: "You're trying to recover your youth!"

For a moment I hear the words just as her own projection. Ever since conceiving of this ride, I have envisioned the experience in terms of the future: as help for Anne and me in living out the second half of our lives. But she is right. In another moment the whole ride cracks open anew. She has hit upon the essential insight of this journey.

My bicycle ride across the United States was the pivotal event in my life. Now this unicycle journey has prodded me to recover what I gained from that journey.

Fifteen years earlier, by the time I had reached Boston, the experiences of land and people from the ride had created a powerful cumulative impact. From it I made a conscious commitment to follow the inspiration of that experience. But how to put language around the shape that land and people had given to my life? How to interpret it? How to go forward? That was the reason I had entered seminary after the ride.

Seminary did concern itself with land and people, with my experience, but everything there happened in the context of God. It had to at seminary. At the time I was working so hard to learn the language of theology that I didn't realize I was running into problems with the conventional thinking about God. It was often like preaching about lighthouses in the Grand Canyon.

On my bike ride all my experience had been framed by land and people—directly—The Grand Canyon, the Midwest plains, Cape Cod. These were the core realities, core experiences, core insights. I realize now, after this half-year on the road again, that my time since seminary has been a struggle with the status quo surrounding God. Too often I have wandered away from human experience.

"Why don't you talk and write more about Jesus?" a few asked as I unicycled through state after state these past months.

Why? Because you can interpret Jesus and faith according to any convention you want. As soon as you say the word "Jesus," you have to start explaining what you do and what you don't mean about this historical, celestial Christ, Savior, Messiah, Rabbi, Teacher, Friend, Crucified and Risen, Almighty, Everlasting, Servant, King. The shoulder of the road is more direct: A "Shit Happens" bumper sticker in the wilderness becomes an invitation to consider that simple kindness makes sense in this world.

"But don't you love Jesus?" comes the next question; too often I hear the sucking sound of invitation into some new set of rules and answers.

I love that "Shit Happens" bumper sticker which Jesus ran into in the wilderness, and I love his answer to it—compassion without compromise. Wherever I find it, inside the faith or outside; in the examples of Mother Theresas, Martin Luther Kings, Gandhis, Desmond Tutus and the like; on the road, or off—compassion is convincing.

"You are still a Christian; right?"

Not the kind of Christian, I hope, who has through various points in history damned Jews, Moslems, Native Americans, scientists, women, slaves, and homosexuals for not fitting into the right categories.

I'd like to be Mark Twain's kind of Christian, although I don't come close to the example set by Huckleberry Finn. He found this tension between convention and compassion all along his way down the river; he called convention being "sivilized." On one occasion he landed amongst the Grangerfords, one of two families—Christian families—involved in a bitter blood feud. Every Sunday these two families gathered at the same church, guns stacked by the entrance, and heard the same sermon. As Huck described the preaching, it was

> *all about brotherly love, and such-like tiresomeness; but everybody said it was a good sermon, and they all talked it over going home, and had such a powerful lot to say about faith, and good works, and free grace, and preforeordestination, and I don't know what all, that it did seem to me to be one of the roughest Sundays I had run across yet.*

The next day the feud erupted, and these same churchgoers shot back and forth until they brought death to each other.

Huck never figured himself a worthy Christian. He never fit the "sivilized" mold but always thought he ought to. His conscience, shaped by the Christianity of his time, often plagued him. One time, resisting turning Jim back into slavery: "My conscience got to stirring me up hotter than ever until at last I says to it, 'Let up on me—it ain't too late yet...'"

At the end of the raft trip, Jim is captured and plans are made to sell him farther south, back into slavery. Huck finds himself in the biggest dilemma of his life. He knows, according to all the arrangements of church and society, that Jim should be back in slavery. Yet the idea of Jim being sold is too much for Huck. He decides to write a letter to Miss Watson, so she can send for his return. Then he remembers all the times that he and Jim had on the river, all the kindness shared. He sees the letter:

> *It was a close place. I took it up, and held it in my hand. I was a trem-*
> *bling, because I'd got to decide, forever, betwixt two things, and I knowed*
> *it. I studied a minute, sort of holding my breath, and then says to myself:*

> *'All right then, I'll go to hell'—and tore it up.*

Some say it's the greatest line in all of American literature. In that moment Huck went so far beyond convention that he thought he'd land in hell for sure. From that moment on Huck began planning Jim's escape. Any study of Jesus' life would show that same willingness to acting outside of social bounds. Like Jesus, Huck had found the thing that makes life on earth meaningful: Love your neighbor as yourself, and love your enemy too.

However dimly I have understood it, the lesson of my bicycle ride was empathy for others. And now I am hearing the same message from my unicycle ride. This wisdom may come with or without the language of God. It may or may not lead to any discernible good. But I know this—here at the middle of my life—it would be a bad thing to trade compassion away for the security of convention.

All of this revelation must be rumbling in my subconscious when I pedal into Williams. The reality of my life will not likely be as clear as the insight splitting convention and compassion. It is difficult to head in the direction of Huck's hell and Jesus' crucifixion. Martin Luther often repeated that we are at the same time both saint and sinner. Mark Twain, of course, found his own way to express it, "The human race is a race of cowards; and I am not only marching in that procession but carrying a banner."

Anne has phoned; they will be arriving in Williams in another two hours. As I wait, my unnamed thoughts do their best to manifest themselves. I feel a strong urge to move here, just an hour's drive south of the Grand Canyon's rim, to this place that has become a cornerstone of my life experience. I stop at the Chamber of Commerce for details about this town.

Williams, I find out, is 6,700 feet in elevation, covered with pine trees. They get one hundred inches of snow a year whenever they are not in a seven-year drought, as they presently are. The population is fewer than 2,500. There is good hiking to the south as well as the canyon to the north.

Interstate 40 bisects the town, giving the "Gateway to the Grand Canyon" easy access for traveling to visit parents.

"This could be a good place to live," I tell Anne when she shows up. The rest of the story is still deep inside me, waiting for time to percolate and be named.

37
50 States

All good things arrive unto them that wait—and don't die in the meantime.

MARK TWAIN

" G et your kicks on Route 66." Most of the remaining ride will be on this route, perhaps the most storied road in our nation. We make it to Seligman today, a tiny town that lives on memories of the famous road. Seligman was the first to apply for Historic Route status. Almost every other place with a bit of the original highway followed suit. This stretch here to Kingman is the longest unbroken section.

It's steak night again. The kids spend Sunday afternoon bicycling around the nearly deserted KOA campground. The bathroom is wallpapered with the whole Route 66, from Chicago to Los Angeles. Studying it I see that the highway ends at the Santa Monica Pier, the same place Keith Cash started his unicycle trip across the United States in 1971, the same place RAAM [Race Across America] starts each year. Anne and I have been trying to decide just where to end this ride. "What do you think?" I ask Anne when I return to Harvey and tell her about the map.

"With all the riding we're doing on Route 66, it sounds good. Let's finish at the pier."

Monday morning: a day and a week left. From Seligman to Kingman the route follows the railroad, climbing and descending gently for eighty-six miles. Just ten miles out of town, I come upon a cyclist ahead of me, different from any other I've ever seen. He is stopped by the roadside, watching a train move slowly up the grade. Crutches stick out from either side of his small blue twenty-inch Schwinn with an old-fashioned banana seat. He wears a small black backpack. I call out as I approach, hoping not to startle him in this otherwise deserted land. "Where are you riding to?" I ask when I stop beside him.

"Flagstaff to Needles. I'm going to spend the winter in Needles. No winter there." It's around two hundred miles from Flagstaff to Needles. His gear, not to mention the crutches, looks unlikely for the journey.

"I used to ride those," he points to the train. "Missed a jump once. That's why I have these," he says as he lifts a crutch. "The doctors had to amputate both feet right above the ankle. I made my own feet." He lifts his jeans to show me his creations, a pair of crudely carved wooden blocks.

"Cutter Bunch, that's my name," he tells me. "I might make Peach Springs tonight." Peach Springs is thirty miles ahead. "It will be fine wherever I get to. I've got the rest of my life to make it to Needles. No pressures. No worries."

With open space to spare here, I ride through the Hualapai Indian Reservation in the late morning and have lunch at Peach Springs: a "Hualapai Taco" with all the fixings on fresh fry-bread. In Hackberry there's a Route 66 Museum. A woman has a food stand there and gives me cinnamon rolls she's baked.

"A lot of people come through Hackberry," she lets me know. Her favorite is the round-the-world cyclist from the USA who kept running into the round-the-world backpacker from Japan. After three such meetings, they started e-mailing and ended up married. "That's the most romantic story I've ever heard," she finishes.

Upon leaving Hackberry I start a race with nightfall and lose, finishing in the dark in Kingman after eighty-six miles on Route 66.

One week to go. I can't imagine what it will be like to wake up and not be on this ride. First, though, before we deal with the end, we have the Mojave Desert.

Nevada

After Kingman distances are deceiving. I see Union Pass from across Golden Valley, and it looks nearby. For ten miles I ride downhill and then ten more uphill before I reach the pass at thirty-six hundred feet. After another eleven miles down a steep grade I am at the Colorado River, just 504 feet above sea level. On the descent are barrel cacti, ocotillos, chollas and the land that I remember from childhood trips to the desert. Across the river from Bullhead City is Nevada and the city of Laughlin, a casino town where I meet Anne and the kids for a $2.99 buffet lunch. From here to Needles is open desert. The weather service sometimes reports Needles as the hottest place in the nation; thankfully, we are here in November. The temperatures these days are cool. Twenty-six miles south brings me to where Anne has set up camp. California! We've traveled now in Alaska and the entire forty-eight continental United States. Only Hawaii remains.

California

Six days left. I ride into the heart of the Mojave on the shoulder of Interstate 40; there are no services for fifty miles. At that point I see a tiny gas station off the highway, and then another sign warns: "77 Miles to Next Services." As I head into this next desolation, Anne calls me. "Harvey is overheating again."

"You're kidding!"

"No."

"All right, come and pick me up." Less than one week to go, and once again we have trouble with Harvey. I ride on until Anne and the kids arrive in the Honda.

We refill with water, and then going up the fifteen-mile-long grade out of Needles, Harvey overheats again. We park and let Harvey cool, playing in the desert while we wait. Filling the radiator twice more gets us over the crest. We drive all the way to Newberry Springs together. "Just get Harvey there, and I'll drive you back to start riding again in the morning," Anne orders. "I don't want to drive it alone right now."

In the morning, driving the Honda, she takes me back out to restart in the desert. Five days left. I make Ludlow for lunch, just an off-ramp to the interstate. It has a Dairy Queen, however. People have seen me on the highway, and one truck driver gives me twenty dollars for the Seward Peninsula; she used to unicycle when she was a kid. Another man buys my lunch. At a table filled with highway workers, they tell of seeing me two days before in Laughlin, Nevada. An older man walks in, covered with protective gear, looking even odder than I do. He's just filled his dirt bike with gas.

"We're riding cross-country today," he tells me. "It's two hundred miles from Lake Arrowhead to State Line, Nevada. It's an annual birthday event," he says. "See that guy outside? He's seventy-two, and he keeps right up."

From Ludlow on, I can ride old Route 66 again. It's in lousy condition here, but twenty-six miles later I'm in Newberry Springs. Our camp spot has two catfish ponds. It turns out the Mojave River goes right by here—underground.

My mom has arrived earlier in the day, and right now they're visiting Calico ghost town. The kids have been so excited to have Grandma come and join us these last few days of traveling. When Kai gets back, he tells me, "I didn't know all this was California. I thought California was just Bedstefar's house and Grandma's house and Uncle Karl's house. California is big."

It's big all right, but now we have fewer than two hundred miles to go. We've been talking with friends who are arranging the finish of the ride on Tuesday at the Santa Monica Pier. Some of the local pastors will be coming out to see the finish and provide a reception at a nearby church.

Four days left. Our destination was Victorville. A strong headwind turned into a desert sandstorm by noon, and we quit early in Barstow. It can go years without rain in this desert. This morning we had a shower.

Three days left: 150 miles to go. The wind is stronger than yesterday, huge today. I pedal straight into it.

Gone is the focus on destination, replaced by a concentration to avoid getting blown off the unicycle. Gone is the thought of progress; when the strongest blasts come, there's just one leg press after the other to keep from toppling. Even then, I get knocked down three times. Headwinds usually tire me. Today this wind is a thrill—a forceful reminder that each day and every pedal of the trip has been a pure gift.

The desert howls into a dustbowl later in the morning. First the horizon turns brown and then, as the wind grows even louder, the sky goes gray with dust. Head down to avoid as much grit as possible, I look a few feet ahead at a time, pushing along in amazement. Four and a half hours after I start, Anne and the kids and my mom pull off ahead of me with lunch. I've covered just twenty miles.

Five more miles and we all meet again for pictures. We've hit the nine-thousand mile mark. The fury of the wind is finally beginning to let up. A sign advertises, "Vacation Where You Live." We take it as a Zen commentary on our last half-year. Gathering next to it for a picture, we remember the "Etcetera" sign way back when we hit the first thousand miles. A van pulls up and the driver asks if I'm the pastor riding across the country. He shakes my hand and hands us a huge canister of pistachios. Back on the road, the wind finally calms. But then it begins to rain for my last hour on the road—these were fifty hard miles.

Two days left. On Sunday, we travel again without a rest, riding across more desert. There's a breeze in my face, but nothing compared to yesterday. I ride through Pearblossom, and then through the San Gabriel Mountains to Soledad. Family friends who have known me since I was born drive out to meet us for dinner. We overnight in a supermarket parking lot.

One day left. I ride into the San Fernando Valley on the streets of my childhood. The smog haze that is typical of Los Angeles has been blown out by the windstorm. The air sparkles, and the views of the mountains across the valley are crystal clear. The temperature is Southern California balmy.

A man in a hardhat runs across the street to where I'm stopped at a red light. "Hey, did I see you in Barstow on Saturday?" He had been working on a drilling truck there. Today they are drilling at this gas station. We meet again after a hundred miles of desert amid the fifteen million people of the Los Angeles area. What are the chances? For a minute together we remember the Barstow wind.

An hour later I cross my home street of Saticoy ten miles east of where I grew up. During lunch at a Mexican restaurant I call Robert and leave a message. He calls back just as I pass the Hollywood Bowl.

"I wish you were here," I tell my riding partner. "This is fantastic, but this morning I felt nervous. I can't imagine not being on this ride anymore."

"Take your time," he advises. "And enjoy Hawaii. Transitioning out of the ride has been hard. I still don't feel settled. I still wish I were riding."

I tell Robert about the storm in Barstow. He would have liked that.

From the Hollywood Bowl to Hollywood Boulevard, I ride into the Los Angeles Basin and all the energy for which it is famous. At the Guinness World of Records Museum, the manager comes out to talk with me.

"We could put your unicycle in the museum after the ride," he offers. We arrange to talk after my return from Hawaii.

Anne has successfully navigated Harvey to our friend Lynn's home in West Hollywood. Another friend from campus ministry in Michigan, she lives just a block off Route 66. She has been helping to arrange our finish day.

Just a ten-mile ride to go. Tomorrow Lynn and my dad will bring the kids to the pier. Anne will pedal with me so we can finish together.

The last day is here. Arrival is scheduled for one o'clock at the pier, so we have until 10 before Anne and I start riding. There's a Starbucks around the corner from Lynn's, and our family walks to it for coffee and hot chocolate. Sitting at the outdoor table, we watch the traffic going by on Santa Monica Boulevard: Millions and millions of people are starting their daily routine. Watching the cars and the people, we feel the strangeness of reaching the last day of our own "One Wheel – Many Spokes" routine.

Back at Lynn's we check Anne's bike, then the two of us pedal off to finish the ride together as we did at the Statue of Liberty. With each pedal today the memories of the ride add together, Neah Bay and Manhattan, all the people and places in between. Six-and-a-half months we have been on the road—205 days. The entire winter before that was spent preparing for this ride. We are completing more than a year of work and dreams. As we ride, our sense of exhilaration builds.

A block before St. Paul's, we meet KariAnna and Kai. They have their unicycles out of the car, ready to parade into the pre-school at the church. After a couple of laps around the playground, KariAnna and Kai join the kids in the sand box. Pastor Jim Boline invites me to visit with the Bible Study group meeting inside the church. Jim introduces me and invites me to tell about the ride.

"Well, for the last half year, for 9,136 miles, we traveled through forty-nine states telling people about Seward Peninsula Lutheran Ministry. All we have left is Hawaii."

One more time, I tell the story.

"Reindeer. Orphanages. 108 years of ministry. What if you could find a place where traditions are one-hundred-percent renewable and recyclable, a place whose primary values for survival are sharing and avoiding conflict, a place where people have been perfecting these values in the harsh environment of the arctic for the last twelve thousand years?

"What would it mean to you to know that this culture is being supported so that its people can make their own best decisions for how to carry their values forward and thrive into the future?

"That's Seward Peninsula Lutheran Ministry, and that's what we've been riding for."

"Is the culture being threatened?" an elderly woman asks.

"Yes," I answer. "Almost anywhere that native cultures have been confronted by this culture that you and I are familiar with, there has been conflict and loss of native ways. I've been told that here in the Los Angeles area there are sacred native sites located every few miles. Most of them are covered over by developments."

"Did you unicycle through many reservations on your trip?" another elderly woman asks.

"As many as we could." I tell them about the Black Hills, Pine Ridge, Ottawa County, Oklahoma, and the smallpox blankets first distributed by General Amherst.

"You don't mean this happened in our country, do you?" a third woman asks.

"Yes, I do mean this happened in our country, our United States."

Jim asks how much has been collected for the endowment now.

"It's still under $300,000. It's still a long ways from the five-million-dollar goal, but we hope this ride has gathered momentum for the endowment."

It's time to go. I walk back outside to Anne and the kids. My brother Karl has arrived. He's been taking care of KariAnna's cat during our trip, and now he hands him over to KariAnna. She takes Taffy with a tight squeeze of pure reunion joy.

Then Anne and I are riding the last blocks to the pier, the end of Route 66, and the fulfillment of a dream. We ride up to the pier and a cheering group of friends and family. Balloons and a sign declare , "You Made It!"

We made it. Six dolphins are swimming in the ocean beyond the end of the pier. We made it!

Hawaii

Four days later we are over the Pacific Ocean, flying to Hawaii. My mom has been talking for years about making this trip.

"This would be a good year," I had suggested months ago, either as a celebration of unicycling all fifty states or as a consolation for having to quit somewhere along the road.

Karl, my brother, has taken care of all the arrangements. "We'll just try to show up in time for the flight," we promised.

At the luggage carousel in Hawaii, I unwrap the plastic bag covering my unicycle, and while Karl gets the rental car, I ride around the airport. I'll do some more riding in the next two weeks, but, at last, it's official: Fifty states!

A few days into the trip we tour the Polynesian Cultural Center. Among all the exotic and beautiful displays, we find no word about the cultural strife that has been a part of these many Polynesian cultures from Tonga to Hawaii since first contact with Captain Cook and other explorers. Yet, the story that we found in Alaska, the story that we found unicycling through the Continental United States, that story is here, too. Today in Hawaii less than ten percent of the population is Native Hawaiian.

After a week in Hawaii, Anne asks me, "Are your eyes going funny again? You're starting to look far away."

"Yeah, maybe a little. Robert warned us the transition away from the road might be hard."

"Relax! We just finished the biggest trip of our life. Every single car and truck passed you safely. We made it to every presentation we scheduled. We made it to every single state, and Harvey finished the ride, too. And we all still love each other. Relax. We'll figure the next part out, too."

A few days later, we call our friends on Whidbey Island: Karl, Deb, and Kaj Fredrik, the ones we'll be living with when we return. Five-year-old Kaj Fredrik is talking to our six-year-old Kai about when we'll be back together. In a talkative mood, Kaj Fredrik goes on at length about how we won't have to pack everything up every day and move every day and not know where we are going to sleep and not know if Harvey will start. Kaj

Fredrik has clearly been thinking a lot about the daily routine of KariAnna and Kai. Kai listens carefully until they go on to other topics.

Afterwards Kai tells me,"He's funny. But he doesn't understand. We just did this ride to have *fun*!"

Laughing, I take my unicycle out for a sixteen-mile loop along the coast and into the hills. I ride past the starting line of the Ironman Triathlon, which is held here every year. That afternoon we go to another of the white-sand palm-lined beaches of Kona. We spread out the towels, slap on sunscreen and look out across the waves.

KariAnna starts building an intricate sandcastle. Kai duckwalks over to me on the sand, almost tripping on his flippers, his blue goggles skew over his eyes.

"Come on, Daddy, let's go snorkel!"

Epilogue

there ain't nothing more to write about, and I am rotten glad of it,
because if I'd a knowed what a trouble it was to make a book I wouldn't
a tackled it and ain't agoing to no more. But I reckon I got to light out
for the Territory ahead of the rest, because Aunt Sally she's going to
adopt me and sivilize me and I can't stand it. I been there before.

MARK TWAIN
CONCLUSION TO THE ADVENTURES OF HUCKLEBERRY FINN

As I entered the water to go snorkeling with Kai on that day in Hawaii, I entered a different world—of sparkling salted waves, rainbow colored fishes, coral, and sea turtles. Likewise, my half-year unicycle tour was entrance into another world, the world of vulnerability and trust, hospitality and care. To see that world from the shoulder of the road is to have one's life changed forever. It is to know that the great sages of all time have been right: No power is stronger than compassion.

Within a few months of finishing this ride, our nation did go to war against Iraq. For a little while, during the final run-up, I had hopes that the global surge of passion for peace would prevail. And then after the war, for a little while, I had hopes that the passion for peace would be stronger than the hunger for violence. Instead, in the aftermath of military victory, there was euphoria in this country, and a new language—*preemption, hyperpower, empire*. Then, as I prepared to send *One Wheel – Many Spokes* to the printer, questions began arising about the basis for the war and the challenges of occupation.

I have been so poor at predicting our nation's actions that I no longer have a sense for how this will all turn out. Will the violence increase? Or will we one day wake and regret these years of fear and violence? Will we turn again to the insights of the sages, that if we are in some manner, in some language, the spitting image of God, part of the same DNA family, then we are all connected in a common human bond? Will we recognize that we live with good and evil strangely mixed together, and that we are made sane by recognizing honest compassion as the most powerful entrée into a true and living experience?

KariAnna and Kai keep riding their unicycles, and they keep talking about breaking my new Guinness World Record. I will do my best to hold them to their dream, not for the sake of the record, but for the love of the shoulder of the road. Anne and I will do our best to teach our children what can be learned by seeing life edge-wise. And when they grow up and set out on their own roads, I hope they'll find them as rich as these roads we have lived together on this journey. I wish everyone could pedal across the country, either alone, or on a honeymoon, or with a family, or with a partner like Robert. If everyone did, this would be a different world—civilized perhaps in a way that even Mark Twain would approve.

The Seward Peninsula Lutheran Endowment

T hank you for sharing in the story of *One Wheel – Many Spokes*. If you would like to join with others to reach the $5,000,000 goal of the Seward Peninsula Lutheran Endowment, we welcome your support. All gifts are tax-deductible.

To mail a check:
> ELCA Foundation
> 8765 West Higgins Road
> Chicago, Illinois 90931
> *Make checks payable to: Seward Peninsula Endowment*

To give on-line:
> ELCA Web Page: http://www.elca.org/do/splm.html

To call for further information, for the current endowment fund level, or for legal and estate planning services:
> ELCA Foundation: 1-800-638-3522 ext. 2970

Your gift helps ensure a hopeful future for Inupiat Eskimos with their 12,000 year tradition of living harmoniously in the arctic of Alaska.

On behalf of Seward Peninsula Lutheran Ministry,
Thank you.

Acknowledgements

T he one wheel turned 5,118,000 times on this journey, but there would have been no voyage without the many spokes that supported me and our family and our goals. Let me at least make acknowledgments in these three areas.

Reaping: Thanks to all who care deeply about Seward Peninsula Lutheran Ministry and are helping to support the goal of the endowment, especially the people of Seward Peninsula Lutheran Ministry and the Alaska Synod of the ELCA (They even had a treadmill at their annual gathering and were taking pledges for miles walked.). Thanks to Bishop Ron Martinson and to national church staff members Marlys Waldo and Dick Wendt. Thanks to Ross Hidy and Charlie Downs for untiring publicity efforts.

Riding: Unicycling across country is a team sport. From the convenience stores with the chocolate milk, to the mechanics who fixed Harvey, to John Hammond of unicycling.com, to the Martin family who accompanied our journey across the United States, there is no escaping the truth of Jesus's remark about the blessing of being offered a cup of cold water when you're in need. To all the people and congregations who hosted us, the media who shared the story, and the people who gave encouragement, thank you.

Writing: Like reaping and riding, writing on this scale is another new adventure. Thanks to Eunice Scarfe, and to Deb Lund and the Whidbey Island Writer's Conference for inspiration. Thanks to Alice Acheson, Darrel Berg, Bob Cochran, Michele DeFilippo, Gary Ferguson, Anne Jackets, Brian Kontio, DeeDee Pearce, Dan Poynter, Don Ranstrom, Wes Hanson, Mike Swenson, and Kate von Seeburg for help with the manuscript.

I give thanks, most of all, to Anne and to our children KariAnna and Kai. The joy of every day is a dozen times greater because it is shared with them.

About the Author

Lars Clausen balances multiple interests on his single wheel. His undergraduate education includes both the US Air Force Academy and UC Berkeley, to which he has added masters degrees in mechanical engineering and theology. His resume ranges from designing windmills in Denmark to preaching in Alaska with Inupiat Eskimos.

In the specialized, polarized, time-starved world of our modern day, Clausen is a wide-ranging explorer. "I never dreamed that my 1987 bicycle tour across the United States would one day lead to a fifty-state ride by unicycle." On June 5 and 6, 2002, he established the Guinness World Record for the farthest distance unicycled in 24 hours (202.78 miles.) On November 12, 2002, he achieved his second Guinness World Record, for long-distance unicycling (9136 miles in 205 days.)

Although he pedaled alone, his family followed by motor home. Anne Jacobsen Clausen is a watercolor artist, and their children KariAnna (born in 1994) and Kai (born two years later) are already unicyclists who dream of someday breaking Dad's records.

Clausen is an ordained pastor in the Evangelical Lutheran Church in America. He and his family live at Holden Village, an ecumenical retreat center deep in the heart of Washington's Cascade Mountains. Clausen is sought as a professional speaker; with his wide experiences of life, he shows how we can turn our uncertainties and challenges into new possibilities and fulfillment.

More information is available at *www.onewheel.org*